Giving Type Meaning

Giving Type Meaning

Context and Craft in Typography

Mia Cinelli

BLOOMSBURY VISUAL ARTS
LONDON · NEW YORK · OXFORD · NEW DELHI · SYDNEY

BLOOMSBURY VISUAL ARTS
Bloomsbury Publishing Plc
50 Bedford Square, London, WC1B 3DP, UK
1385 Broadway, New York, NY 10018, USA
29 Earlsfort Terrace, Dublin 2, Ireland

BLOOMSBURY, BLOOMSBURY VISUAL ARTS and the Diana logo are
trademarks of Bloomsbury Publishing Plc

First published in Great Britain 2024

Copyright © Mia Cinelli, 2024

Mia Cinelli has asserted her right under the Copyright,
Designs and Patents Act, 1988, to be identified as Author of this work.

For legal purposes the Acknowledgments on p. vii constitute an
extension of this copyright page.

Cover design by Louise Dugdale

All rights reserved. No part of this publication may be reproduced or transmitted in any
form or by any means, electronic or mechanical, including photocopying, recording, or any
information storage or retrieval system, without prior permission in writing from the publishers.

Bloomsbury Publishing Plc does not have any control over, or responsibility for, any third-party websites
referred to or in this book. All internet addresses given in this book were correct at the time of
going to press. The author and publisher regret any inconvenience caused if addresses have changed
or sites have ceased to exist, but can accept no responsibility for any such changes.

Every effort has been made to trace copyright holders of images and to obtain their permission for the use of
copyright material. The publisher apologizes for any errors or omissions in copyright acknowledgment and would
be grateful if notified of any corrections that should be incorporated in future reprints or editions of this book.

A catalogue record for this book is available from the British Library.

A catalog record for this book is available from the Library of Congress.

ISBN: HB: 978-1-3502-5641-5
PB: 978-1-3502-5583-8
ePDF: 978-1-3502-5585-2
eBook: 978-1-3502-5584-5

Typeset by Integra Software Services Pvt. Ltd.
Printed and bound in India

To find out more about our authors and books visit www.bloomsbury.com
and sign up for our newsletters.

This book is set in FF Milo (designed by Michael Abbink and Paul van der Laan), Univers LT
(originally designed by Adrian Frutiger in 1957), and Bembo, a typeface cut by Francesco Griffo
c. 1495, revived in 1929 by Stanley Morison for the Monotype Corporation.

CONTENTS

Acknowledgments vii
Introduction viii

CHAPTER 1
Social Context 1

Context + Meaning 1
   Visual Inflection 4
   Social Meaning + Typography 6
   Visual Metaphors and Analogies 11
Cultural Context 14
Power Structures 31
Recontextualization 36

CHAPTER 2
Spatial Context 41

Visual Space 41
   Kinetic and Expressive Type 43
   Sound, Shape, and Speech 51
   Concrete and Visual Poetry 55
Physical Space 59
   Material Meaning 60
   A Known Social Context 62
   History and Material Meanings 65
   Material Metaphors and Analogies 67
   Architectural Materials 71
Public Space 75
   Place-Based Meaning 75
   Public Type + Community Participation 79
Private Space 89
   Challenging Private Space 92
Personal Space 95
   Apparel and Affiliation 96
   Proximity and Politics 97
Virtual Space 99
   Digital Methods 101
   Augmented Reality, Mixed Reality, and Virtual Reality 103
Gestural Space 105
   The Human Hand 106
   Gesture in and of Letterforms 108
   Gesture of Mark 118
   Gesture and Expression 120
   Corporeality and Performance 122

CHAPTER 3
Temporal Context 129

Time and History 129
    Temporal Influence: Technology and Society 131
    Temporal Influence: Current Events 137
    Typographic Trends 141
Historical Type in Contemporary Use 146
    Revivals and References 150
    Temporal Recontextualizations 155
    History-Inspired Type 158
Voices in Design 166
    Type and Identity 175
Time as Medium 179
Into the Future 188
    Language, Form, and Meaning 189
    Speculative Typography 195
What's Next? 198

Resources for Educators and Students 199
Select Bibliography 201
Index 208

ACKNOWLEDGMENTS

This book is only possible because so many people said "yes." I owe many thanks to Louise Baird-Smith and Libby Davies at Bloomsbury for answering a plethora of questions with great knowledge and patience, to the University of Kentucky's College of Fine Arts for granting me a semester of research leave to make headway on my manuscript, and to my colleagues in the University of Kentucky's School of Art and Visual Studies for their kindness and support. I deeply appreciate each artist, designer, organization, and institution who graciously allowed images of their works to be featured in this text, as well as interviewees who shared their expertise through insightful conversations. Special thanks to the reviewers and readers who generously offered helpful suggestions—especially David Wischer, Lauren Ruth, Shoshana Shapiro, and Jesse Hoyle.

Lastly, I am grateful for the encouragement of my friends, my parents Michael and Fosca Cinelli, and my dear husband, Matthew Nyquist, who means the world to me.

The author and publisher gratefully acknowledge the permission granted to reproduce the copyright material in this book.

Every effort has been made to trace copyright holders and to obtain their permission for the use of copyright material. The publisher apologizes for any errors or omissions, and would be grateful if notified of any corrections that should be incorporated in future reprints or editions of this book.

The third-party copyrighted material displayed in the pages of this book is on the basis of "fair dealing for the purposes of criticism and review" or "fair use for the purposes of teaching, criticism, scholarship or research" only in accordance with international copyright laws, and is not intended to infringe upon the ownership rights of the original owners.

Mia Cinelli is Associate Professor at the University of Kentucky in the School of Art and Visual Studies. Her multidisciplinary work in art and design explores frameworks for meaningful physical and visual interactions.

INTRODUCTION

What we say, how we say it

As a student in my first typography class, I was overcome with a sinking feeling of dread. While my professor knowingly explained the importance of typeface choice, internally, I groaned. What did it *really* matter if something was set in Calibri or Papyrus if it didn't change the wording itself? What did any of this have to do with what it *meant*? I feared this was esoteric nonsense I would never understand, and worried that perhaps I should've studied something else after all.

Thankfully, I stuck with it—but not without uncertainty and confusion. To anyone relatively new to typography or visual communication, it can feel like an insular world of rules to memorize and typefaces to avoid. Fluency of handling and communicating with type is only achieved through practice, including ample trial and error. This learning is both joyful and revealing, creating insight into communication previously hidden in plain sight—but how do we determine what such visual language means?

What is this book about, and who is it for?

Rather than focus on letterform anatomy, best practices for type-handling, and typeface classification systems—which are already covered very well, and in great detail, by other authors—this book explores the variety of contexts which give our typographic choices *meaning*. Explained through specific contextual frameworks, this book showcases an assortment of examples, "closer looks," and interviews, curating a selection of how type is used in a variety of creative outcomes.

This text seeks to inform and inspire students, educators, and creative professionals looking to engage more deeply with the type they use and see in a critical yet approachable manner. Building upon existing knowledge, this book hopes to challenge and expand how its readers consider type in use. If you have a basic understanding of typography and you're interested to learn more about how letterforms communicate, this book is for you.

Typography and the expanded field of art and design

How do we make sense of the many ways language is visually represented as well as its numerous descriptions—including written characters, drawn letterforms, designed typefaces, or text-based art? In order to encompass the wide range of practices and projects included within this text, this book defines typography *very* broadly as the intentional arrangement of letterforms in space. As such, *Giving Type Meaning* uses "type" as an umbrella term, and includes visual text-based representations across a variety of practices, locations, and applications—even those which fall outside the traditional definition of typography as the formatting of repeatable letterforms by graphic designers.

While there are some widely accepted definitions and categorizations in art and design, others are informed by differing philosophies. Some approaches divide art and design on such matters as "function," "expression," or "media." This book does not. Rather than separate *fine art* and *visual communication* as opposing disciplines, this text features examples of letterforms in use ranging from practical to poetic, in what is referred to as "the expanded field of art and design."

This is not to push against specificity altogether, as there are many unique areas of expertise which should be recognized and celebrated as such. Typographers, or those who use and create with type, have a different focus from type designers, who conceptualize and construct typefaces. Their skills and practices differ still from those who specialize in hand-lettering, calligraphy, motion design, printmaking, engraving, mural-painting, graffiti, sculpture, or illustration. Despite their differences, each of these individual approaches engages with ways of creating and communicating with letterforms.

As practices blend and evolve, so too should the language we use to describe them. The *Society of Typographic Aficionados'* annual conference *TypeCon* invites and showcases the innovations and talents of many practices, including those of type designers, calligraphers, sign-painters, graphic designers, and letterpress artists. The annual *Typeforce* exhibition held in Chicago presents a range of letterform-based installations, interventions, and sculptures. In these instances—among many others—the term "type" extends beyond its original definition to encompass a wide field of approaches. Such is the case with this book.

1
Social Context

Context + Meaning

In Michelangelo Antonioni and Carlo Ponti's 1966 film *Blow-Up*, we find our protagonist, a young man, at a rock concert in a small venue. The audience is entranced, and the band—famously, the Yardbirds—reaches the peak of their performance by frustratedly smashing a guitar onstage and throwing its neck out into the crowd. When our protagonist takes hold of it, he suddenly finds himself at the center of a squabble as screaming fans clamor for the guitar neck. He escapes and runs outside, where he tosses the coveted object aside onto the sidewalk; a passerby picks it up and regards it briefly before throwing it back onto the ground, disinterested.

This brief scene brilliantly illustrates the concept of *contextual meaning*. Inside the venue, where an audience has witnessed the instrument breaking at the hands of guitarist Jeff Beck, the object holds proximity to celebrity, becoming a valued artifact of experience. Its social, spatial, and temporal context make it a deeply coveted souvenir. Outside of the concert hall—on the side of banal city street, with no witnesses of its genesis—this context changes, entirely shifting the meaning of the object from desired artifact to disregarded trash. While the object itself did not change, its dramatic shift in context fundamentally altered its meaning.

Context refers to the setting and circumstances surrounding an artifact, event, action, or idea. In design, we use context to determine what visuals and language are appropriate for a specific audience, where an advertisement may live, or how an informative campaign might be interpreted. The context in which a design lives allows us to assign meaning. *Meaning* refers to how something is interpreted or understood. As a concept, it is complex because it is not absolute: how something is interpreted may be informed by authorial intent, but is not intrinsically bound to it. Therefore, what a designer *intends* something to mean does not determine its *actual* meaning—especially when its context changes. Even works which are designed with precise composition,

Chapter 1's image: George Diebold via Getty Images.

immaculate type-handling, and excellent craft can fail in the wrong context. A chic alcohol ad intended for a glossy magazine or city bus stop becomes deeply out of place in a church basement during an Alcoholics Anonymous meeting.

How we determine the meaning of our visual field isn't limited to swapping locations of visuals or objects. In every interaction, individuals use past knowledge and experiences to make sense of what they encounter, dependent on a variety of cultural, social, spatial, and temporal factors. Because of this, sometimes meanings are largely agreed upon, and other times they are hotly contested. There is *always* a degree of interpretation in art and design, and conflict or confusion can occur when what is intended is not what is inferred. This book cannot pinpoint exact meanings in all instances—but hopes to offer some insight as to *how* we make sense of our visual experiences.

It is worth noting that the author of this book lives and practices in the United States, with an approach informed by a Western cultural context—which she acknowledges and strives to challenge and expand. Most of the examples are set in Latin text, in English, and most cultural-specific analogies or scenarios referenced are from the United States or other Western sources. The insights offered by this book are intended to be *one* perspective—but certainly not the only perspective—and cannot claim to offer a comprehensive view concerning all matters of meaning-making and typography. Great design happens everywhere: as such, this text features examples from the international type community, seeking to both highlight and celebrate differences and commonalities in typographic expression and meaning-making. The examples, frameworks, and concepts discussed in this book are not intended to be exclusive or exhaustive, but aim to serve as a primer to both inform and question how we create and understand typographic meaning in a variety of contexts.

As an act, giving type meaning is both objective and subjective. Things which are *objective* are concerned with facts rather than feelings, while things which are *subjective* are a matter of opinion. (It is an objective fact that pineapples exist. It is subjective whether or not you prefer them on pizza.) Typographically, 9-point text on a poorly lit wall intended to direct passengers in an airport is an *objectively* poor choice, as its size is too small in a public environment to be read from a distance, and a lack of contrast keeps important information from being visually perceived and understood. In design, we tend to use both objective and subjective approaches to inform our visual decisions, blending what *works* with what we *like*.

How humans construct meaning is the subject of semiotics and semantics. *Semiotics* is the study of how signs and symbols are interpreted, while *semantics* refers to the study of how meaning is constructed in language and logic. The structures of semiotics and semantics apply to the construction of meaning in visual language—including typography. This is also the concern of *visual rhetoric*, which analyzes how visuals are read and interpreted through semiotics and methods of figurative language.

It is essential to understand that signs and symbols can be read in many ways. A *sign* is anything composed of a *signifier* (the indicator) and its *signified* (the concept represented). Sometimes signs are direct representations, or *icons*, wherein a sign looks like the thing it serves to represent. *Indexical* signs convey meaning by which the signifier (skull and crossbones) is caused by its signified (death or danger). Often, signs are arbitrary, with a non-obvious connection between sign and signifier. These require prior knowledge of their affiliations, such as understanding the symbol of an olive branch to mean peace.

When we encounter words and images, we determine their meaning through denotation and connotation. *Denotation* references what something means in a literal and objective way: when we say "this glue is sticky," "sticky" references the literal description of the adhesive qualities of glue. When we say "This is a sticky situation," "sticky" is no longer a literal description of the situation, unless you are *actually* stuck to something in said scenario. Here, we rely on *connotation*, referring to subjective association. We associate the term "sticky" with something difficult to get out of, referencing a particularly awkward, embarrassing, or convoluted interaction. In viewing design and typography, we construct meaning through both our connotations and denotations. When we see the seal of an official award, it denotes the accomplishment and honor of the award to its recipient. When type emulates a similar visual format, it creates a connotation of quality, admiration, and merit—regardless of whether or not it is true—raising larger questions about ethics, authenticity, and truthfulness in design.

However, because multiple meanings can simultaneously be assigned to any one image, object, or scenario, what is intended is not always what is inferred. Imagine you've planned a surprise party for a friend—but are unfortunately unaware that she despises them. When the event transpires, you interpret it as a successful, joyful celebration. To her, it reads as a mortifying, unexpected gathering at which she is the unwilling center of attention. Thus, the party has multiple meanings. While your good intentions do not mitigate her negative experience, they leave room for growth, sincere apologies, accountability, and consequent action. In design, clear client communication and human-centered research methods help to avoid situations where the actual response does not match the expected reaction. Even with careful planning and a considered context, we can never fully control how our creative work will be perceived in the world.

A CLOSER LOOK:
Multiple meanings

On October 4, 2010, The Gap released a new logo designed by Laird and Partners. Their classic logo (designed in 1986) featured tall, widely spaced white serif text within a blue square. Their newly proposed logo consisted of black Helvetica text against a small, blue square gradient in the upper right corner. This new development was met with immediate backlash on social media, with customers and designers alike chiding the design as "tacky" and "ordinary."

In response to this reaction, on October 6, 2010, The Gap replied quickly via Facebook, thanking the public for feedback on the new logo—and asking them to share their own designs in a crowdsourcing project. This response was not well received. Design professionals offered open letters publicly expressing their disappointment that a multi-million-dollar company expected unpaid work for a crowdsourced logo. Others mused that this was nothing more than a publicity stunt.

Professional and amateur designers posted both sincere and facetious proposals online. On October 12, 2010, after much ado, they reverted back to their previous logo.

Why exactly was this backlash so strong? Many companies—among them Jeep, Target, Knoll, and American Airlines—have employed logos set in Helvetica with resounding success. How then, was the designers' bold intention perceived as bland? In the 1950s, Raymond Loewy, a leading American Industrial designer—best known for his streamlined aesthetic—coined the term "MAYA," an acronym for *Most Advanced Yet Acceptable*. He proposed that successfully evolving design relied on connecting new concepts to established ideas. Ideas or imagery which were too radical were met with resentment, while those making smaller leaps forward were more positively received.

The Gap's previous identity featured tall, chic, serif letters, while its new identity relied on forms which were bold, sans serif, and by comparison, quite squat. This new identity bore little resemblance to its predecessor, likely creating a rift between audience expectation and reality. Consumers longing for the familiar clashed with an anemic re-design in The Gap's proposed logo. Paired with an obtuse corporate response, this catalyzed vastly different meanings to the parties involved. The debacle even earned its own nickname of "gapgate." The graphic identity of The Gap recovered, but a valuable lesson in multiple meanings remains.

Figure 1.1 Ben Pruchnie/Staff via Getty Images.

VISUAL INFLECTION

When we speak, *what* we say is influenced by *how* we say it. In spoken word, our tone of voice is as meaningful as the words we choose, allowing us to discern between sincere apologies and sarcastic rebuttals. Because typography tends to lack an aural component, it relies instead on type choice and placement to create a kind of typographic tone—in what the author of this text calls *visual inflection*. This means that *what* is said is influenced by *how* it is chosen and arranged. For this reason, typography is essential in visual communication, influencing the perception and meaning of written words.

Typefaces and fonts, like people, have unique personalities. They can be uptight, overwhelming, annoying, delightful, or provocative, to name a few. The meanings of typefaces are influenced through their formal design qualities, their social affiliations, and the contexts in which they live. As designers make conscious visual choices in order to more closely align our execution with our intent, we deliberate type decisions until we find the one which feels "right"—but how do we come to that conclusion?

In 2012, writer and filmmaker Errol Morris presented a quiz via the *New York Times* positioned to establish if participants were optimists or pessimists. Readers were presented with an article and asked to determine if they believed its authors' claims were true, and how confident they were in that conclusion. There was, however, a catch. Unbeknownst to the respondents (approximately 45,000 people), the article was randomly presented in one of six typefaces: Baskerville, Computer Modern, Georgia, Helvetica, Comic Sans, and Trebuchet. Instead of investigating optimism vs. pessimism, Morris actually wanted to gauge the perceived trustworthiness of typefaces.

Data from this unconventional experiment revealed that of the typefaces used, Baskerville facilitated the most trust from its audience in believing the article to be true. Why is this? A transitional serif designed by John Baskerville in the 1750s, its formal yet approachable letterforms socially construct an air of informed authority. Setting text in Baskerville imbued the text with similar meaning, making the article appear more reliable or trustworthy. This is a curious phenomenon, because while type choice did not change the *content* of what was written, it did influence the *perception of said content*. Unsurprisingly, the obviously juvenile Comic Sans was perceived as least truthful in this particular investigation.

Baskerville
Computer Modern
Georgia
Helvetica
Comic Sans
Trebuchet

Figure 1.2 Baskerville (John Baskerville, 1750s), Computer Modern (Donald Knuth, *c.* 1992), Georgia (Matthew Carter, 1996), Helvetica (Max Miedinger, Eduard Hoffmann, 1957), Comic Sans (Vincent Connare, 1994), and Trebuchet (Vincent Connare, 1996).

Here, *expectation* may influence inflection in a feedback loop of tradition and presumption. Baskerville appears reliable and steadfast in its even and refined visual features, but these qualities are also informed by expectations of where we have seen similar typefaces in use in the past, and where we anticipate seeing them in the future. When imagining a reputable news source or trusted literature, do you imagine it set in a stable serif or a playful display typeface? When you conjure the idea of a scientific journal, what type choices come to mind for the body copy? If, situationally, a long-line of reliable texts have been set in serif typefaces similar to Baskerville, this may lead to an expectation—accurate or otherwise—that trustworthy information should be set this way, and information set this way is trustworthy.

Today, both individual type designers and digital type foundries—groups or individuals who design and distribute typefaces online—host an abundance of typeface choices, providing artists

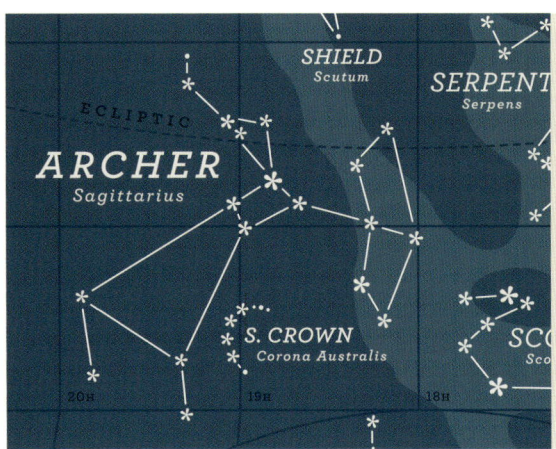

Figure 1.3 Archer by Hoefler&Co., 2016. Reproduced with the permission of Hoefler&Co.

Archer | Hoefler&Co.

Hoefler&Co.'s Archer was originally designed for use by *Martha Stewart Living*, a lifestyle magazine focused on cooking, gardening, entertaining, and decorating. Taking notes from traditionally journalistic typefaces—featuring poised serifs and even, reliable strokes—Archer adds friendliness with playful ball terminals and graceful curves. Social connotations associated with these formal qualities allow us to imbue typefaces with their consequent meanings, leading to its intentionally sweet but sincere inflection.

and designers with ample options for typesetting. Access to digital tools has never been greater, allowing for both novice typographers and experienced designers to create and choose custom typefaces. In this booming age of type design, there are as many trite, poorly constructed letterforms as there are refreshing, well-crafted typefaces. It is up to typographers to choose wisely which type best represents their intended tone.

SOCIAL MEANING + TYPOGRAPHY

Not all type choices are appropriate for all projects. A wedding invitation requires different typographic choices from an accounting firm's annual report, as these typically have different audiences and expectations. How, then, do we articulate an elegant visual choice from a corporate aesthetic, and how might we anticipate that others will share this perception?

People create meaning in art and design by relating experiences, ideas, and values to specific visual choices. This book refers to this as *social meaning*—the understanding of an image or artifact as informed by that which is *social*, of or relating to society, and its consequent interactions, expectations, behaviors, and beliefs. Social meanings exist globally, but are not the same everywhere. Instead, they are bound by societal agreements about what visual representations can mean relative to their use and familiarity, which vary within societies, as well as by time and culture. Consider that many typefaces considered elegant share the visual characteristics of calligraphy, traditionally commissioned for special events or announcements, imbuing their swooping formal qualities with these social affiliations. This differs from "corporate" type, which tends to revel in perceived uniform "professionalism," taking on traits of the historical "anonymous

Figures 1.4–1.7 Artwork by BUCK, shared by permission of the NSPCC.

First Step | BUCK

Based in the United Kingdom, Childline is a service of the NSPCC (the National Society for the Prevention of Cruelty to Children) featuring free, 24-hour counseling services for children and young people under 19 years of age. In *First Step*, an animation created by BUCK, approachable but poignant typography encourages children to reach out to Childline. In this video, there is no voiceover. Instead, the type takes on two visual inflections—the brave but nervous voice of a child, and the clear, trusted voice of a counselor. The caller's typographic voice is obscured in ripples, refracted through objects, and blown about by wind, showcasing just how difficult it can be to talk about sexual abuse. The counselor's voice is written in even, handwritten lowercase, taking on a kind, calm quality. The formal qualities of these letterforms and their respective animations inform their consequent inflections, communicating a message which is gentle but direct.

sans serifs" which have been popular in business branding since the mid-twentieth century. While these affiliations are by no means absolute, their history and sustained use within a society allows designers to predict how similar choices may be viewed and interpreted.

These associations require a common frame of reference for understanding, but social meaning also relies heavily on established design principles, which have evolved from observed experience and psychology, giving guidance as to how compositions might be interpreted by their audiences. Even novice designers know that symmetry has a pleasing, balancing effect, while asymmetry can direct a specific point of interest, provoking thought or focus. Common principles of alignment, contrast and repetition direct visual hierarchy and create structure, movement, and order within visual communication.

Among these principles is *contour bias*. On a deep, evolutionary level, humans are attracted to curvilinear shapes which we unconsciously perceive to be safer or friendlier. We apply these connotations to our entire visual field to assess the meaning or safety of our surroundings. (Situationally, this is the difference between landing on a soft bush or impaling oneself on a sharp stick.) These strong preferences are interpreted *and* perpetuated within societies, creating strong social signifiers from visual choices.

A CLOSER LOOK:
Social connotations

Why does type look cute?
Contour bias informs what we socially consider "cute." The small, vulnerable, or rounded features of babies and puppies activate emotions of care and adoration. Typography intended for, or inspired by, a very young audience may take on the characteristics of young children or babies themselves, featuring toddling, rotund letterforms and bouncing baselines, giving them an adorable, comforting quality.

"Cute" typography often takes on the social association of being 'baby proofed', with forms which are soft and pillowy, without sharp edges. Consider the familiarity of rounded, snuggly text to advertise toys, clothing, and television programs designed for children. To showcase its friendly qualities intended for a young audience, these visual indicators are employed in the logotype for Crayola, whose letterforms feature curved edges and gentle slopes, making them both playful and accessible. More gestural interpretations of "cute" type may reference kids' handwriting drawn with crayon or marker, featuring novice penmanship, wobbling words, or reversed letterforms. Shown here on Crayola's crayon packaging, these earnest, irregular letters socially reference the endearing qualities of their young authors.

Cuteness has other connotations and contexts, such as *Kawaii*, which refers to the Japanese culture of cuteness. In the 1970s and 1980s, popular "cute" handwriting (featuring bubbly letterforms, incorporating illustrations of hearts and stars) by teenage girls helped shape a bias toward objects and imagery with this aesthetic, extending from cartoon characters to garments. *Kawaii* images and typography retain this quality, featuring lovable, marshmallow-like forms—as seen in such typefaces as *Honobono Pop* or *Handy Heart Neo* by Japanese typeface designer Nontynet.

Why do death metal logos look scary?
Consider the sound of death metal. Gnashing chords paired with guttural, indiscernible vocals comprise the intense and divisive aural experience. Unsurprisingly, the visual language of this typography carefully uses design principles to put us on edge. Jagged edges are akin to violence and brutality—gashes, injury, viscera, veins. Barbed points make a reference to sharp, piercing forms, a threat similar to that of the biohazard symbol. In some cases, forms become almost electric, the energy of an uncontrollable scream or tremor. It is unsurprising, then, that so many death metal bands choose to employ these visual qualities. Such features are emphasized through ragged forms

and branching proportions, like those in the typeface XXII Morduk by Lecter Johnson of DoubleTwo Studios Type Foundry.

Because of this expected aesthetic, a viral dissemination of the 2015 *Bay Area Deathfest 2* event poster made the logo for the death metal band Party Cannon particularly well known. In an obvious typographic reference to *Toys-R-Us*, this type stands out among a sea of gore-inspired letterforms, reinforcing the first-most principle of perception and visual communication: discontinuity creates points of emphasis. This successfully demonstrates how expectations of visual inflection and social signifiers do not always align. While the cute and cartoonish appearance of their logo might *imply* a less brutal musical tone, their lyrics and genre are very much death metal.

What gives type a luxurious feel?

Space is paramount in the concept of luxury. We may contrast cramped apartment living with lavish estates, windowless rooms with open architecture. Space is so often the language of wealth—those with means can acquire space, while those without cannot. The weekly newsprint coupon ad is poised to fit as many advertisements and discounts onto one page as possible, a claustrophobic, economic necessity. Advertisements for posh resorts, bottles of perfume, and high-end watches are often minimal, expansive, and uncrowded. Socially, the space created visually and metaphorically in these ads speaks to freedom from constraint, exemplifying a life of unfettered action.

Contemporary type alluding to affluence and luxury is frequently thinner in weight and widely tracked, giving ample space to letterforms. Consider the airy logotype for the palatial Hôtel de Paris Monte-Carlo in Monaco, one of the richest countries in the world per capita. Perfume names, and their consequent

Figure 1.8 Crayola Crayons 8 Count Box image courtesy of Crayola, used with permission. © 2022 Crayola LLC.

Figure 1.9 From https://nonty.net/.

Figure 1.10 XXII Morduk Font by Lecter Johnson. © Doubletwo Studios, 2021. Reproduced with the permission of Lecter Johnson.

Figure 1.11 Logo by Party Cannon. © Party Cannon, 2011. Reproduced with the permission of Party Cannon.

Figure 1.12 © Monte-Carlo Société des Bains de Mer.

packaging, market the sensations of attraction, desire, and elitism, with generous space between—and around—textual components. This is not to say a congested visual field can't be associated with luxury. Historically, wealth and influence were associated with opulence (like Versailles *c.* 1770) but in a culturally dependent, contemporary setting—at the time of this book's publishing—the overly ornate can feel gaudy, tacky, or superfluous.

The social connotations of type are informed by their socially understood visual or spatial context—but also by their authors, associations, and citations. The Greek philosopher Aristotle asserted there were three modes by which to persuade—the rhetorical appeals of *ethos*, *pathos* and *logos*. *Ethos* refers to character, and speaks to an ethical appeal based on the notion that the persuading party or person is credible. Here, the reputation of the speaker influences the written message, imbuing the type, by visual proximity or written attribution, with real or perceived validity. This is, in part, why celebrity endorsements are effective. *Pathos* is an emotional appeal, using emotions such as sympathy, humor, anger, or pride to convince an audience. Type relying on a sensory or narrative experience has the potential to sway an audience via their memorable, emotional response. *Logos* refers to a factual appeal, and relies on logic, facts, and knowledge to persuade, especially by citing sources and showing data.

Combinations of visual inflection, social connotation, and modes of persuasion create endless opportunities for typographic meaning. If intended to be sardonic or ironic, designers may make intentional use of a rhetorical appeal to subvert an expected meaning; the humor of a satirical newspaper relies on the contrast of its ridiculous statements to the poise of its professional appearance. Unfortunately, these methods of persuasion can be used nefariously—such as disinformation campaigns designed to *look* like official election mail, intended to disenfranchise voters. While their modes of persuasion and visual inflections may be similar, their intentions and applications are not.

VISUAL METAPHORS AND ANALOGIES

Metaphors and analogies are powerful tools to create and clarify meaning. When someone affectionately says "my partner is my rock" we easily understand this sentiment. While it hasn't been said directly, we know this statement refers to someone who is sturdy, reliable, and steadfast. Metaphors are concepts which use a non-literal scenario or reference to convey another meaning. Here, the attributes of a rock are attributed to a partner which carries the descriptive meaning for

Figure 1.13 *fART* by Holly Akkerman. © Holly Akkerman, 2020. Reproduced with the permission of Holly Akkerman.

fART | Holly Akkerman
In Holly Akkerman's *fART* installation, the question "What is art" is carefully painted onto individual whoopie cushions. Humorous, vibrant, and socially recognizable, this piece pokes fun at serious questions of artistic merit by mapping the absurdity of a whoopie cushion (source) onto a textual question (target). As a visual metaphor, it successfully fills a pensive inquiry with necessary levity.

an audience. Analogies work similarly, comparing differing scenarios to expose common relationships. Structurally, while a metaphor says A *is* B, an analogy says A *is to* B as C *is to* D—creating a comparison for reference. In an analogy, we can

Figure 1.14 *These Truths* by Brian Singer. © Brian Singer, 2018. Reproduced with the permission of Brian Singer.

These Truths | Brian Singer

Brian Singer's *These Truths* employs visual analogies to create conceptual relationships and realizations. In this installation, the preamble to the United States constitution is displayed on a picket fence enclosing a plot of astroturf. The picturesque "white picket fence" serves as an emblem of the American Dream, representing success, financial stability, homeownership. As the fence slowly fades from white to brown to black, it obscures the message of freedom and opportunity—a reflection on racial and economic inequality in America. In this visual analogy, *visibility* is to *legibility* as *access* is to *opportunity*, prompting an audience to consider: who has access to the American dream, and who has been shut out?

say *caffeine is to coffee as alcohol is to beer*, creating a realization about essential components through their relationship to each other.

Just as metaphors and analogies are used in writing to articulate depth and more nuanced understanding, they are also used visually and physically. In Nazli Cila's *Metaphors We Design By: The Use of Metaphors in Product Design*, she describes how metaphors bridge concepts together to carry meaning. To create metaphorical associations, the visual, physical, conceptual, emotional, or gestural qualities of a "source" can be mapped onto a "target" (the object) to create "meaning transfer." When an object or image is created *in relation to* the features of said source, this affiliation results in a new interpretation or interaction.

Visual metaphors and analogies rely on a cognitive leap, requiring preexisting knowl-

Figure 1.15 Fabel by Typearture. © Arthur Reinders Folmer, 2017. Reproduced with the permission of Typearture.

Fabel | Typearture

However, direct references can be clever and self-aware, such as Typearture's Fabel typeface. At first glance, it simply appears as a playful display typeface composed entirely of animals posed as letterforms. Upon closer inspection, it becomes clear that the characteristics of animals determine their respective characters: rabbits embody the multiply symbol, and the trademark is composed of two small sheep, after Dolly, the first cloned animal. En dashes and em dashes are represented by the sperm whale and blue whale—marine mammals of increasing length. These thoughtful references craft an illustrative typeface while simultaneously creating conceptual depth.

edge from their viewers and a level of poetics to carry a message. When two concepts are simply placed together, they are often too literal, forcing a juxtaposition instead of leaving room for discovery. In a more nuanced method, a typeface lauding the achievement of skyscrapers might use historic sources to create letterforms inspired by text on building awnings, or engage specific proportions referencing vertical construction. In a too-obvious approach, letterforms might be constructed out of skyscrapers themselves, creating a novelty display typeface which leaves little to the imagination. Simply making something *which looks like something else* does not mean the meaning carries over metaphorically or provides additional depth. While there is a time and place for this kind of method, it can often come off as novice or hackneyed.

While figurative language can inform typographic meaning, metaphors and analogies are different from idioms—such as "It's raining cats and dogs"—whose meanings require a specific cultural context for understanding. In Icelandic, the phrase "Ég tók hann í bakaríið" literally translates to "I took him to the bakery." Here, "to bake" is colloquially used to mean "to defeat"—meaning this idiom truly implies "I let him have it" or "I told him off." Therefore, any visual or typographic example relying on an idiom requires careful consideration of audience and culture in order to be fully comprehended.

Cultural Context

All design is understood within a particular cultural context. Type choices which appear obvious to one audience may seem ineffective to another. Preferences in design—including color use, typeface choices, and hierarchy—are all informed by cultural mores, values, and expectations, making cultural context an essential factor in determining typographic meaning.

Global typographers and type designers create and set type in a variety of ways, and in a multitude of languages. Numerous writing systems—which refer to the character sets, scripts, or alphabets which compose a written language—are used to communicate the thousands of languages spoken all over the world. For example: many languages in India, including Hindi, use the Devanagari script, the fourth most commonly used writing system in the world. Korean is written in the Hangul alphabet, developed by King Sejong in the fifteenth century. Many languages make use of the Cyrillic alphabet—including Russian, Serbian, and Bulgarian. The following words (Figure 1.16) are "Typography" in Hindi (in Devanagari script, set in Laila by Indian Type Foundry), Russian (in Cyrillic Script set in Fira Sans by Carrois Apostroph), and Korean (in Hangul, set in Do Hyeon by Woowahan Brothers.)

English is written in the Latin alphabet, but this does not mean that Latin typefaces are limited to the twenty-six letters, ten numbers, and basic punctuation an English-speaking audience may perceive as necessary to communicate. Because *many* languages use the Latin alphabet, any Latin typeface truly intended for multilingual use requires a wide range of special characters, ligatures, and diacritical (or accent)

टाइपोग्राफी

типография

타이포그래피

Figure 1.16 From Adobe Fonts.

Pangrams are phrases which feature each letter in an alphabet at least once, and can showcase specific characters and diacritical marks necessary for a particular language. "The quick brown fox jumps over the lazy dog" is a common pangram for English-speakers. The pangram "Pchnąć w tę łódź jeża lub ośm skrzyń fig" (To push a hedgehog or eight boxes of figs into that boat) highlights a few of the language-specific diacritical marks, such as *L with stroke* (ł) and *ogoneks* (ą, ę) necessary to write in Polish—demonstrating how a writing system can accommodate many languages with thorough character inclusion. In some instances, a single type family can be designed for use in multiple writing systems, creating opportunities for wide global use across cultures and languages.

marks. These additional characters ensure that a typeface will be both writable *and* readable in multiple languages within a variety of linguistic and cultural contexts.

A CLOSER LOOK:

Language, culture, and type

The importance of language goes beyond the exchange of letterforms and phonetics as a means to communicate. Cultural values themselves are embedded in language, revealing who we are and what we value by the way we talk about our environments, our communities, our actions, ourselves, and each other. What happens, then, when the language of a culture begins to disappear?

Lushootseed is a language belonging to the Salish language family, and has been spoken in the Puget Sound region of the Pacific Northwest by Indigenous people for thousands of years. By 2008, the number of native speakers (for whom Lushootseed was their first language) had dwindled critically. Decades of violent assimilation which had forbidden speaking Indigenous languages had resulted in both cultural and linguistic erasure.

ʔ	ʔalʔal	ʔitut	ʔəssasaʔ	
a	ʔacitɬtalbixʷ	ċagʷačiʔb	sʔuladxʷ	
b	biʔbədaʔ	buus	x̌aab	
c ċ č č̓	ʔucut	ċuʔkʷs	čəxʷəluʔ	čaləs
d d̓ᶻ	dayay̓	d̓ᶻədis	sq̓əd̓ᶻuʔ	
ə	ʔətɬəd	sƛ̓əkʷabšəd	saxʷəb	
g gʷ	gədgəd	gʷədil	gʷəčəd	
h	hud	hədʔiw̓	huyəxʷ	
i	ʔi	ʔiišəd	sqibkʷ	
ǰ	ǰəsəd	ǰuʔcut	ǰəsǰəsəd	
k	kəpu	kəlapx̌ʷəlč		
k̓	k̓ədayuʔ	k̓aʔk̓aʔ	k̓əwdxʷ	
kʷ	kʷədad	kʷatač	d̓ᶻubalikʷ	
k̓ʷ	k̓ʷəčəldiʔ	k̓ʷaƛ̓ad	k̓ʷid	
l l̓	lil	stəbtabəl̓	q̓il̓bid	
ɬ	ɬixʷ	ʔəshiiɬ	ʔəsx̌əɬ	
ƛ̓	ƛ̓aƛ̓aċapəd	luƛ̓	ʔəsƛ̓ubil	
m m̓	mam̓ad			
n n̓	miʔman̓			
p p̓	pədƛ̓əs	puʔtəd	sup̓qs	
q q̓ qʷ q̓ʷ	qədxʷ	q̓ilagʷil	buʔqʷ	q̓ʷuʔ
s š	sduhubš	sƛ̓əx̌ʷšəd	ʔibəš	
t t̓	tətupəl̓	təlawil	ƛ̓ilib	
u	buʔqʷ	ċubċub	ʔukʷukʷ	
w w̓	waq̓waq̓	wiw̓suʔ	qaw̓qs	
xʷ x̌ x̌ʷ	xʷiʔ	x̌əqyuq̓ʷ	x̌ʷəl	
y y̓	yayus	p̓uay̓	day̓	

ʔ	ʔalʔal	ʔitut	ʔəssasaʔ	
a	ʔacitɬtalbix̰	ċag̰ačiʔb	sʔuladx̰	
b	biʔbədaʔ	buus	x̌aab	
c ċ č č̓	ʔucut	ċuʔk̰s	čəx̰əluʔ	čaləs
d d̓ᶻ	dayay̓	d̓ᶻədis	sq̓əd̓ᶻuʔ	
ə	ʔətɬəd	sƛ̓ək̰abšəd	sax̰əb	
g g̰	gədgəd	g̰ədil	g̰əčəd	
h	hud	hədʔiw̓	huyəx̰	
i	ʔi	ʔiišəd	sqibk̰	
ǰ	ǰəsəd	ǰuʔcut	ǰəsǰəsəd	
k	kəpu	kəlapx̰̌əlč		
k̓	k̓ədayuʔ	k̓aʔk̓aʔ	k̓əwdx̰	
k̰	k̰ədad	k̰atač	d̓ᶻubalik̰	
k̰̓	k̰̓əčəldiʔ	k̰̓aƛ̓ad	k̰̓id	
l l̓	lil	stəbtabəl̓	q̓il̓bid	
ɬ	ɬix̰	ʔəshiiɬ	ʔəsx̌əɬ	
ƛ̓	ƛ̓aƛ̓aċapəd	luƛ̓	ʔəsƛ̓ubil	
m m̓	mam̓ad			
n n̓	miʔman̓			
p p̓	pədƛ̓əs	puʔtəd	sup̓qs	
q q̓ q̰ q̰̓	qədx̰	q̓ilag̰il	buʔq̰	q̰̓uʔ
s š	sduhubš	sƛ̓əx̰̌šəd	ʔibəš	
t t̓	tətupəl̓	təlawil	ƛ̓ilib	
u	buʔq̰	ċubċub	ʔuk̰uk̰	
w w̓	waq̓waq̓	wiw̓suʔ	qaw̓qs	
x̰ x̌ x̰̌	x̰iʔ	x̌əqyuq̰̓	x̰̌əl	
y y̓	yayus	p̓uay̓	day̓	

Figures 1.17 and 1.18 Lushootseed Sulad Font design by Juliet Shen. © 2009 The Tulalip Tribes. Reproduced with the permission of Juliet Shen.

As a language passed on orally, Lushootseed did not have its own written script until the middle of the twentieth century, when Vi Hilbert (a native speaker of the Upper Skagit tribe) and Thomas Hess (a linguist from the University of Washington) worked to create one. This complex task devised a phonetic means of writing Lushootseed using a modified Latin alphabet with glyphs from the International Phonetic Alphabet. This original Lushootseed font was adapted using a version of Times Roman, making it a functional—but somewhat visually overwhelming—typeface.

For the language to continue and thrive, Lushootseed language teachers required a clearer font for teaching it to children. In 2008, artist and designer Juliet Shen was commissioned by the Tulalip Tribes of Washington state to design a new font for the Lushootseed language. Tasked with redesigning this font with Unicode compliance (a universal character encoding system which allows for consistent use of text across applications), she sought inspiration from the environment of the Puget Sound, as well as the material and aesthetics from Salish artwork. She strategically developed rounded, legible letterforms as though they had been crafted from wood rather than metal, creating continuous letters which looked connected to both the language and the landscape. These decisions culminated in the 2009 design of a new Lushootseed typeface with two variations: Lushootseed School and Lushootseed Sulad.

Since then, the Lushootseed typeface has become part of a recognizable visual identity for the Tulalip Tribes, and is frequently used in language education and bilingual signage. While the typeface was commissioned to be proprietary, the Tulalip Tribes have made both the fonts and a digital keyboard available to download through their website—furthering accessibility and availability. This connection between cultural and linguistic preservation highlights the importance of cultural context, writing systems, and visual inflection. Here, two vocabulary word lists showcase two different typefaces: the original Times New Roman Lushootseed, and Juliet Shen's Lushootseed Sulad.

Both cultural contexts and specifics of writing systems predicate design preferences and expectations. For instance, hierarchically, type in the West is taught with a left-aligned, top-down preference. This bias exists for languages such as English, German, or Spanish, which are read from left to right. In languages such as Hebrew, Arabic, or Farsi, which are read from right to left, the alignment preference switches to right-aligned.

The design values of any particular culture are shaped by numerous factors—including geographic location, belief systems, or historical precedence—but these are not uniform across any one culture, as no one group is monolithic. A cultural expectation might vary significantly between urban and rural locations, or by religious or ethnic affiliations. When discussing culture, it's important to note the difference between *inter*cultural context and *intra*cultural context. The prefix "inter" simply means "between," in the way we might refer to *inter*disciplinary practices or *inter*national relations. *Inter*cultural refers to

Figures 1.19 and 1.20 *A Book about Food*, by Hedai Offaim, designed by Keren & Golan Graphic Design Studio, Lunchbox press, 2015.

A Book about Food | Keren & Golan Graphic Design Studio

A Book about Food, by Hedai Offaim, designed by Keren & Golan Graphic Design Studio, elegantly demonstrates how design hierarchy is specific to language. This cookbook, designed in Hebrew, opens from left to right and features text and image layout following a right-aligned preference across each spread. If the type in these images does not look like layout you normally see, take note—it may only appear visually flipped *to you* based on *your* cultural and linguistic preferences. Look closely at the layout of the book you are presently reading and consider: what language is it set in, and how does this determine the typographic or visual hierarchy you expect it to have?

matters between two different cultures. "Intra," however, means "within"—so *intra*cultural describes matters occurring inside the same or similar culture.

In addition, *sub*cultures refer to unique movements and values within a specific culture, while *counter*cultures directly oppose a culture's mainstream or traditional approaches. Typographically, these values may manifest through the use of materials or design choices which seek specifically to disrupt or challenge conventional expectations or aesthetics. Historically, zines—small, Do-It-Yourself magazines—have been a popular means for democratizing publication and communication within specific groups, including subcultures or countercultures. Made and distributed by their creators, zines represent the perspectives and passions of their respective communities. Historical examples include *Spockanalia*, a Star Trek fanzine from the 1960s, the British Punk zine *Sideburns* from the 1970s, or *Vice Versa*, a 1940s American periodical (authored by Lisa Ben) focusing on lesbian identity.

When *inter*cultural context and *intra*cultural context is considered for typography, it is important to note that not all visual communication within a specific culture will look the same, and broad generalizations about cultural context do not uniformly apply in individual circumstances. While cultural values *do* manifest visually, no national or cultural identity can be fully distilled into a single aesthetic or idea (see "Type and identity" in Chapter 3). Typographic expectations, and

Figure 1.21 Manofim 2015 Jerusalem Contemporary Art Festival by Tirza Ben Porat and Naama Tobias. © artist, 2015. Reproduced with the permission of Tirza Ben Porat and Naama Tobias.

2015 Manofim Jerusalem Contemporary Art Festival | Tirza Ben Porat and Naama Tobias

Tirza Ben Porat and Naama Tobias's catalog for the 2015 Manofim Jerusalem Contemporary Art Festival features a vibrant color palette, abstract forms of a rising sun/moon, and type set in three major languages spoken in Jerusalem—Hebrew, Arabic, and English. Using Hebrew as the leading text, this guide is opened from left to right, and read from right to left. This publication deftly handles type across multiple languages, with each appearing in a consistent order, creating a strong and clear typographic hierarchy.

the many factors which inform them, will vary between communities and groups, even within one country or region. In the United States, produce-stand signs for an Amish community in rural Ohio will undoubtedly look different from Juneteenth celebration posters in Atlanta, Georgia, signage in downtown Las Vegas, Nevada, or lettering on a mural in Chicano Park in Logan Heights, San Francisco, California. In intracultural communication, groups with similar cultural values and expectations may choose to use similar design choices by which to express themselves, as informed by local histories, climate, geography, immigration patterns, and shared preferences.

Figure 1.22 From the Martha Blakeney Hodges Special Collections and University Archives, UNCG University Libraries.

WUAG "In Print" Zine | WUAG staff
Typically produced with very little funding, the frequent use of collaged or handwritten text, photocopied graphics, and novel compositions pushed back against expected formats and professionally produced content, such as this 1989 zine for the University of North Carolina Greensboro college radio station WUAG. This gave creators agency in visual communication—frequently for the purposes of activism or sharing essential information—while simultaneously establishing emblematic aesthetics often affiliated with particular groups or subcultures.

Figure 1.23 Finlandica by Helsinki Type Studio. © Niklas Ekholm, Juho Hiilivirta, Jaakko Suomalainen, 2015. Reproduced with the permission of Helsinki Type Studio.

Finlandica | Helsinki Type Studio

Commissioned by the Prime Minister's Office as part of Finland's visual identity, Finlandica was designed by Helsinki Type Studio in 2015. Informed by the natural environment, industrial history, and cultural values of Finland, its even construction embodies the unique cultural quality of "Sisu"—a stoic, resilient determination. Thoughtfully designed with effective use in mind, Finlandica is easy to read at large and small sizes, making it functional, versatile, and reliable. While clean and considered, details on the letterforms are intentionally quirky and playful—giving this practical typeface an approachable feel.

When communicating with type, designers should consider with whom, and for whom, they are designing. If intended for an international audience, have, or will the works be translated? What pattern of reading can be expected? Designers should also carefully consider personal cultural expectations and biases when viewing and evaluating work from cultures which differ from their own, making note that while individual cultural expectations for typography may be valid—it does not make them universal. In addition, thoughtful consideration should be made concerning where, and by whom, typography was crafted, and the variety of cultural factors which have influenced its aesthetic, use, or value.

Across much of the Middle East, a rich history of calligraphic practice is fostered by

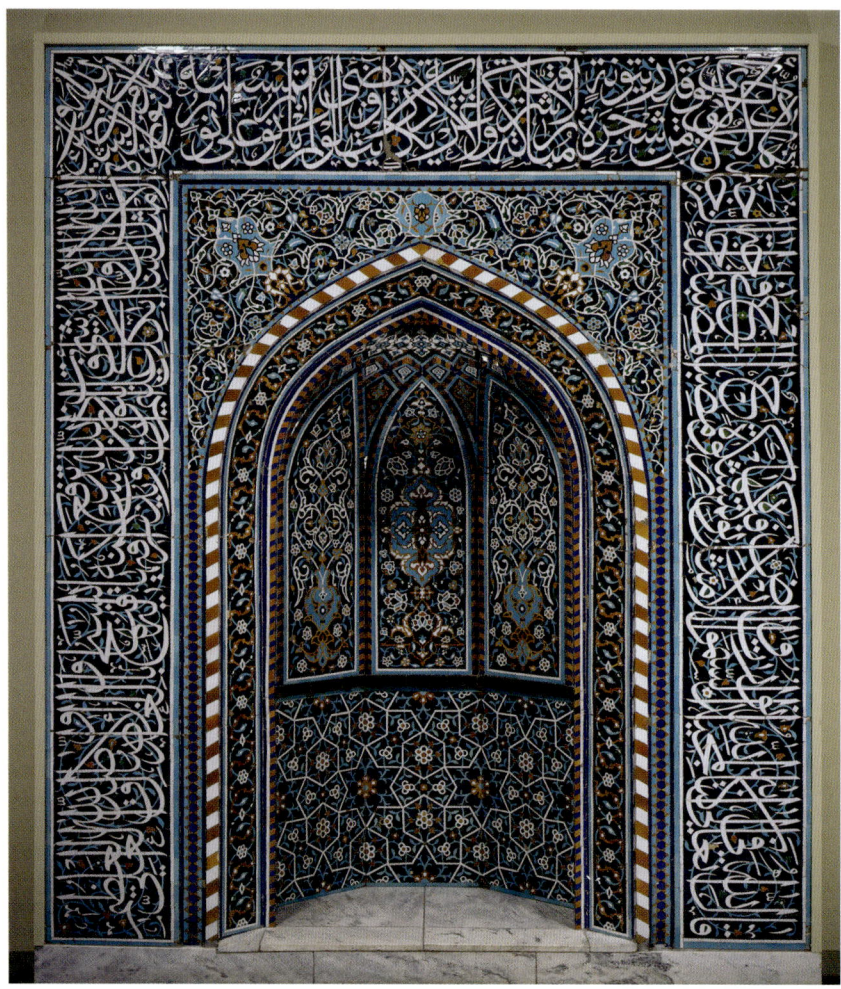

Figure 1.24 From The Cleveland Museum of Art.

Prayer Niche (Mihrab)

Calligraphic tiles and complex tessellating mosaics adorn the perimeter of this *mihrab*, or prayer niche, originating from Isfahan, Iran. Within a mosque, a *mihrab* is situated toward Mecca, the holy city of Islam. Here, verses from the Qur'an are written in *thuluth*, a specific form of Arabic script.

a religious norm. In Islam, it is forbidden to portray or illustrate the image of Muhammad, as this is seen as idolatry. Therefore, Mosques are often adorned with complex tessellating geometric tile, frequently alongside panels of intricate, decorative calligraphy. In addition, poetry and verses of the Qur'an are often written in graceful, ribbon-like script, including the Persian *Nastaliq*, a specific calligraphic style. Arabic calligraphy is considered and extensive in

Figure 1.25 *Regard Each Other as Brothers* by Josh Berer. © Josh Berer, 2021. Reproduced with the permission of the artist.

Regard Each Other as Brothers | Josh Berer

Josh Berer is a calligrapher and craftsman specializing in Arabic calligraphy. Trained through an extensive process, his calligraphic works are detailed in both their construction and material choice in deep respect for the work and its meaning. His work *Regard Each Other as Brothers* is completed on hand-dyed *ahar* paper (made specifically for Islamic calligraphy), bordered with original *ebru*, or paper-marbling. According to the artist, this piece is known as a *kitaa*, a style of calligraphy which pairs two kinds of Arabic calligraphy: larger sections of *Sulus*, with smaller, internal sections in *Nesih*. The non-text images, or *Koltuk* illuminations, are based on illustrations by British illustrator and draftsman Frank Steeley, from 1903. The black calligraphy (*Nesih*) is a passage from *A Treasury of Virtue* by Imam Ali Ibn Abi Talib. The white calligraphy (*Sulus*) inspires the title of this piece, and reads: "Do not envy each other, bid against each other, hate each other, or shun each other. Servants of God, regard each other as brothers"—*Hadith of the Prophet, Riyad al-Saliheen*.

Figures 1.26 and 1.27 (opposite) *Moonrise* Music Album Design (2014) and Iran Silk Screen School Poster Design (2015) by Homa Delvaray. © Homa Delvaray. Reproduced with the permission of Homa Delvaray.

Moonrise and Iran Silk Screen School | Homa Delvaray

Homa Delvaray is an Iranian visual artist and graphic designer whose expansive practice includes posters, sculptural installations, artist books, and graphic identities. In many of her works, historical architectural features and traditional motifs from Iranian-Islamic art are recontextualized and reimagined with contemporary elements, creating both visual and conceptual complexity. This confluence of cultural influence can be seen in her 2015 poster for the Iran Silk Screen School, where both Latin and Persian text engage with a richly illustrated visual field of flora and fauna. In the 2014 design for the album *Moonrise*, vibrant colors and tessellating tile letterforms make references to elaborate building details, crafting striking layers of harmony, motion, and depth.

both its history and approach, and features many unique, specific styles of lettering. Informed by these cultural values, geometric patterns and ornate visual fields are often—but not always—present in design and typography across the Middle East.

Figure 1.28 "Mirsaal bilingual typeface" by Rana Abou Rjeily/copyright owner/2011.

INTERVIEW

Rana Abou Rjeily | Mirsaal

Can typography or type design contribute to cultural connections? How do the relationships between culture and history influence how a typeface is made, used, and interpreted across unique languages and writing systems?

Rana Abou Rjeily is a graphic designer, educator, and author based in Beirut. With a BA from Notre Dame University in Lebanon and a Master's degree from Central Saint Martins in London, her clever creative work ranges from designing typefaces, branding, and publications to co-founding Lebtivity, a major online social calendar for events in Lebanon. Released in 2011, her book *Cultural Connectives: Bridging the Latin and Arabic Alphabets* seeks to compare Latin and Arabic letterforms through the design of her original typeface Mirsaal. In this interview, edited for clarity and length, she shares insights into Arabic letterforms, explains how history and culture impact design, as well as shedding light on her own design process.

For readers who might be less familiar with Arabic script, what are some differences and similarities between Latin and Arabic alphabets?

That's a very large question. Both the Latin and Arabic alphabets descend from the Phoenician alphabet [an early ancient writing system], but Latin has the opposite direction from left to right, and Arabic kept the original right to left direction of writing. Another thing is the arrangement of the alphabet itself; we adapted the order of mnemonic sound arrangement [for Arabic], but the Arabic alphabet has several different sounds and letters that don't exist in English and vice versa. The alphabet in Arabic is mostly based on consonants, inherited from the Phoenician alphabet; there are many more vowels in Latin.

So, talking about consonants: we have diacritics in Arabic which don't always exist in Latin—they can be added on top of and below the Arabic script. We have diacritics that are sometimes there, and other times omitted for the reader to guess from context. Of course, Arabic kept its cursive nature when written and typed, whereas most Latin scripts lost this. The letterforms are connected, which is a big difference, and sometimes this makes it a bit harder for people to learn. Because of this, when you look at the rhythm of typography between Arabic script and the Latin alphabet, there is different stress in the stroke. In the Latin alphabet, it's mostly vertical because of the way you carry the pen [to write the forms]. In Arabic, you get this more horizontal stress because of the cursiveness, calligraphic history, and the angle/how you carry the pen. These are things I can think of right now—I'm sure there are many more!

What challenges or opportunities do these qualities present when designing digital typefaces?

Because Arabic is a cursive script, you end up designing many more glyphs for a single letter than you do in Latin; each letter in Arabic has an initial, medial, final, and freestanding form. This is a big challenge in Arabic for type designers—and designers in general—as well as for people who are learning the language. There's also the positioning of short vowels [written as diacritics]; this can be challenging because you have to monitor and adjust all the positioning of the short vowels with the actual glyph. Moreover, in Arabic, you can have the equivalent of ligatures in Latin—this *too* expands the number of glyphs.

Finally, one really very important thing to mention is that in Arabic the baseline is not always horizontal. The "baseline" can be more diagonal, like in Farsi, etc., so when designing, this can be challenging, yet offers many opportunities for playful designs.

Could you tell me about your typeface, Mirsaal? What was the inspiration behind this project, and what was its design process like?

Sure! It started as part of my experience of being in London. I used to spend a lot of energy trying to explain Arabic to my fellow classmates and teachers, and I found the easiest way was to compare it to Latin, which everyone in the UK knows. I compiled all these small differences which were obvious to me as an Arabic speaker and as someone who also knows English and French. When I spoke with my professor at the time, this was highlighted, and I decided to create a typeface which could ease the introduction of Arabic to non-Arabic speakers. So, I went to schools to research how Arabic is introduced as a second language and did much more research comparing both languages to see the main differences.

After that, I researched historical trials that other designers, architects, or type designers did to simplify Arabic. One of them was Nasri Khattar [1911–98], a very famous Lebanese architect, typographer, and type designer. He is quite famous for his trial on Arabic typography which Latinizes the alphabet to make one shape per letter; instead of having all these glyph variables, you only have one. His main concern was to find a way to adapt Arabic to the typewriter, because at that time you had very limited keys and could not have all the Arabic forms. Unfortunately, his proposal was not adapted, and later came the computer with more flexibility—but this concept kept lingering on through generations. Later on, Mourad Boutros and Cecil Hourani did something similar in simplifying the form and having one glyph per letter: this letter does not change its place wherever it stands in the word.

My design is based on this because I really believe introducing Arabic requires a simplified typeface; the letterforms still have a lot of Arabic characteristics in their stroke and forms, but instead have one form per letter. When I worked on Mirsaal, I designed it in a way where letterforms can be connected just like regular cursive Arabic—with fewer forms, as I mentioned—and at the same time, the same typeface could be used with much more letter spacing so it becomes detached, resembling Latin type. In this way, people can be introduced to it gradually. Later, I worked on the Latin version of Mirsaal because I decided it would be used in a book; I used all my research comparing Arabic to Latin and used Mirsaal in *Cultural Connectives*.

Usually, in the world of type design, you create an Arabic typeface for an existing Latin font which is quite famous, so what I did at the time was interesting and exciting by creating the Arabic typeface first, then the Latin to support the Arabic in the book.

Language can be both a bridge and a barrier. How do you think typeface design or typography can contribute to understanding across cultures?

This is a tough question. Because typography is basically working with forms and symbols, a lot of people are now experimenting with approaching typography from a *visual* standpoint. They are doing things similarly to what I did with Mirsaal; understanding the script by introducing them to the shapes and comparing them to other things we are familiar with. In that sense, typography can be playful and be used to break, a little bit, those cold barriers between cultures.

Lebanon is a multilingual country. In the Middle East, typography and type design are important because we often use Arabic script and the Latin alphabet at the same time, on the same page, in the same ad, etc. Even in our spoken Levantine Arabic, we integrate different languages—so I can be saying a sentence and have three different languages in it. Multilingual typography in the Middle East is important because it brings cultures together. You see it everywhere—in branding, publications, newspapers, ads.

There is the concept of "match-making" in type design between Arabic and Latin—which is taking a Latin typeface, looking at its structure, and then creating the Arabic equivalent—like Mirsaal Arabic and Mirsaal Latin. They can coexist on one page and have a similar visual balance, style, rhythm, contrast, etc. That's one approach for designing Arabic and Latin simultaneously. At the same time, Arabic can be used in its more calligraphic style, as opposed to Latin, and this creates a nice contrast as well. You can bring both cultures together through type by making them more similar—but at the same time you can use them each in their different visual style, using that contrast to create interesting compositions and visual language.

In what ways do regional histories or cultural values influence contemporary design or typography from Beirut, or Lebanon more broadly?

That's a vast question! When I started graphic design, we highly relied on books from Europe. We learned about Swiss typography, the grid system, Jan Tschichold—and then Arabic was introduced much later, in the second or third year. We were always trying to fit Arabic into these Western systems. We still do this! But lately we're becoming much more aware of the uniqueness of the script and visual culture and trying to integrate that as well.

A lot of research is being done on Arabic book design through history. They have different grid systems—or maybe no grid systems at all—and this is being much more used now. But at the same time, these were not documented, so we highly rely on Latin designs to create our own. Another important point to mention is that Arabic type developed in the Middle East and *specifically* in Lebanon; Lebanon has the first printing press in the Middle East, in a convent! We're always adapting technology from Europe

Figures 1.29 and 1.30 "Flow of the Arabic script" and "Mirsaal simplified letterforms" by Rana Abou Rjeily/copyright owner/2011.

and everywhere else in the world, and it's not just a problem for Arabic—it's a problem for several other scripts as well, because we lose some of the genuine characteristics of the script. When letterpress was introduced to the Middle East, we had to adapt the alphabet in Arabic into the metal letterforms. Therefore, we see so many Arabic typefaces with one single baseline. In Arabic calligraphy—and there are so many kinds, of course—most of them do not have a strong baseline, so in adapting Arabic to the letterpress, we lost some of its characteristics.

Later, type designers looked at these typefaces and designed their own. It's only recently that typographers and type designers from the Middle East became much more aware of researching calligraphy and trying to integrate Arabic "script grammar" in their work—a term which was introduced to the typographic scene by Thomas Milo. It's mostly referring to how the word-shaping changes according to the sequence of letters coming in a word.

Recently, type designers are looking into that, and are creating designs which are much more authentic and truer to the origins of Arabic calligraphy. Research is being done in visual culture in Lebanon and the Middle East and is being *much* more used as inspiration in type design and brand identities. This is quite an interesting time, I think, for Arabic typography.

Power Structures

Visual communication occurs within, and not outside of, power structures. *Power structures* refer to the hierarchy or frameworks for authority or governance within a society; familiar examples include the ability of a municipal government to pass ordinances, or the understood hierarchical social agreement between mentors and mentees. Power structures influence perception, participation, and how visual communication is shared and accessed. How we choose, refer to, and identify type is informed by existing hierarchies; what we consider to be in "good taste" and socially acceptable is embedded in both our language and expectations, influenced by societal levels of who holds power and who does not.

For centuries, philosophers, sociologists, and artists have been theorizing on the concept of taste, which refers to both the subjective quality of determining what one does and doesn't like, but also refers to a social concept of generally agreed-upon values by which something is "good." This has been historically difficult to define. Eighteenth-century philosophers David Hume and Immanuel Kant shared a philosophy that some works of art were in fact better than others, but notably disagreed on notions of what and who could set the standard for good taste. In the late twentieth century, French sociologist Pierre Bourdieu correlated notions of taste to class and social stratification. His theory asserts that those from a background with more cultural capital—composed of education level, mannerisms, skills, dress, credentials—were most likely to have authority and influence over what is accepted as "good taste," while those with less cultural capital were more likely to accept this distinction. Bourdieu theorized that cultural capital could be used to attain greater economic capital, increasing opportunity for social mobility.

Taste is not innate to any particular group; it is shaped by social, educational, and cultural influences. Bourdieu's research showed that groups within similar social strata (upper-class, middle-class, and working-class people) tended to have similar tastes. Preferences among the upper class often reflect time and leisure with an emphasis on learning to interpret abstraction, while those among the working class tend to value functionality, narrative, and popular culture.

But what does any of this have to do with social meaning and typography? Affiliating design solutions which look "classy" vs. "cheap" as "good" or "bad" are socially constructed and perpetuated, historically determined by upper-class taste. These associations embody wealth and status as paramount, showcasing an express or subtle contempt for those with less power or privilege. Consider the financial resources required for custom design work, "bespoke" typefaces, or high-end font bundles as opposed to what is default and on hand in Microsoft Word. If cultural capital is associated with exclusivity, default typefaces may be perceived as less sophisticated because of their wide attainability across a variety of applications. Because cultural capital is often inherited (parents who take their children to the theater, enroll them in schools with advanced programs, and expose them to diverse art, music, and food), a system of inequality is perpetuated. Those from wealth use their access to culturally transmitted notions of taste to maintain or gain power. This may be as subtle as knowing which typefaces indicate class-based "sophistication," whose use on a résumé or cover letter can further their advantage for opportunity.

A CLOSER LOOK:
Typographic similarities

Bourdieu's research built upon the theories of American economist and sociologist Thorstein Veblen. In 1899, Veblen coined the term *conspicuous consumption*, which refers to public display of consuming luxurious, expensive, and often superfluous goods and services as a means to demonstrate status and prestige—which those in the middle and lower classes may seek to emulate, despite an economic inability to do so.

The penchant for status through consumption is evident through the design of a wide range of consumer products, showcasing how typography can be representational or aspirational. Most supermarkets carry both "name brand" and "generic brand" products at different price points, giving customers options about what they buy based on how much they

Figure 1.31 Fred Dufour/AFP via Getty Images.

"Superme"
From movie props to feigned reproductions, typographic similarities can be used to create copies of real items and their corresponding social meanings. Here, a counterfeit bag attempts to carry the fashionable qualities of the brand *Supreme* by emulating its color scheme and typography, featuring recognizable stark white text against a bright red ground. While the typeface choice and spelling are obviously inaccurate, the iconic visual *reference* remains, despite its inauthenticity (see "History and material meanings" in Chapter 2).

want—or can afford—to spend. The packaging for these items is frequently designed to highlight their similarities, particularly typographically; their visual parallels highlight proximity to "the real thing" by offering the look of brand-name products at a lower cost.

The relationship between identity, brand similarity, recognition, and visual culture is pervasive, giving insight as to why counterfeit goods featuring emulations of brand-name labels and logos remain such a thriving commercial enterprise. In this context, similar typography offers the feel or association of luxury without the price—or quality. This desire also explains why expensive retailers still offer authentic but affordable merchandise in the form of keychains and garments; if you can't afford to drive a luxury car, you can still feature their name or logo on your T-shirt (see "Personal space" in Chapter 2).

The advantage of wealth and cultural capital also impacts participation in design as a profession. Access to typefaces and the software used to make or use them costs money, as does a formal art and design education. Even publicly available lectures or online tutorial videos still require a stable internet connection, a safe environment, and time to commit to learning instead of earning. Opportunities to compete in design competitions (whose winnings offer inclusion in consequent archives and publications) require knowledge of the competitions themselves as well as the ability to afford frequently steep entry fees. This creates barriers for entry for those without cultural capital *or* disposable income, further limiting participation while simultaneously highlighting the inherent difficulties and complications of working and designing in a capitalist, consumer-driven society.

This is not to say *all* power structures or hierarchies are problematic. There is a marked and important difference between an expert and a novice, between peer-reviewed journals and shared social media posts. However, this knowledge does not mean that power structures shouldn't be questioned: designers should engage with critical thinking and consider *how* hierarchies influence educational systems, lived experience, and determinations on how expertise is defined and acquired—especially through frameworks which differ from their own. The larger question then pertains to access and opportunity; when what is considered *good* is created and perpetuated by an affluent ruling class, influence becomes inaccessible.

This book—written earnestly in pursuit of education, but distributed commercially—cannot and will not attempt to cover these complex issues with any claim of completeness, but instead seeks to ask: who has been excluded from the discourse or decision-making due to oppression or socioeconomic constraints? How do we mitigate these inequalities moving forward, and how can power be reclaimed or more equally distributed? (see "Voices in design" in Chapter 3).

Within art and design, written messages—and their consequent typography—can be leveraged to conspicuously (or covertly!) maintain or challenge existing hierarchies. Designers have addressed these queries through their practices and projects, addressing power structures in both the production *and* perception of visual language. Because power structures influence dissemination of visual communication, organizations and individuals can use their voices wisely and creatively to establish effective avenues for access. When strategically applied, typographic communication can subvert, clarify, amplify, or unite.

Figures 1.32–1.33 "There Is No Planet B" taken April 23, 2015 and "No Water for Profit" taken January 26, 2016. Photos by Joe Brusky/Overpass Light Brigade. Reproduced with the permission of Joe Brusky/Overpass Light Brigade.

Overpass Light Brigade

Within current power structures, widespread public messaging is expensive, and significant sums of money are required for extensive campaigns, broadcast advertisements, or billboard space. How, then, do working- or middle-class people convey messages beyond the realm of social media? Formed by artists Lane Hall, Lisa Moline, and photographer Joe Brusky in the state of Wisconsin in 2011 as part of protests calling to recall then-governor Scott Walker, the Overpass Light Brigade protests injustice and reclaims public messaging through community organizing. Referring to itself as "The people's bandwidth," this do-it-yourself approach uses individual lighted letters to create large-scale messages. Constructed from corrugated plastic, wood, and battery-powered string lights, these letters are held by individuals and can be infinitely arranged to show phrases on public highway overpasses. These wide-reaching messages promote equality, community, and environmental justice. Here, typographic meaning is created through both their phrasing and their construction: values of solidarity are inherent to the project itself, as this communication is only made possible through mutual cooperation and commitment.

Figure 1.34 Guerrilla Public Service by Richard Ankrom. © Richard Ankrom, 2001. Reproduced with the permission of Richard Ankrom.

Guerrilla Public Service | Richard Ankrom

How can a typographic intervention reclaim power to create a positive impact? In 2001, artist Richard Ankrom made note of particularly confusing signage on a California highway in Los Angeles. Knowing that it could be clarified with additional information, he decided to enact a solution in a generous act he called "Guerilla Public Service." Meticulously following the exact size, material, and typeface specifications for constructing state highway markers, he covertly designed, fabricated, and *very* carefully installed additional elements—the Interstate 5 emblem and directional text—to the existing highway wayfinding. This stealthy installation was documented from multiple perspectives by friends and signed by the artist. As a helpful addition, it successfully clarified directions for passing motorists, and went unnoticed by officials until the story was leaked to the media—but the signs were not removed. In 2009, the California Department of Transportation replaced this intervention with a new sign of their own which incorporated clarifying components from Ankrom's solution. Simultaneously bypassing *and* respecting regulations, this typography defied bureaucracy to better serve the public.

Recontextualization

Recontextualization takes a familiar artifact, event, action, or idea and changes its context to create a different meaning or interaction. Even a subtle change in material, scale, text, or space can significantly alter perceptions. Recontextualization can be saccharine or serious, overt or subversive. It can spark recognition and create humor, like it does with parody—when an idea is imitated in an exaggerated, irreverent way. Symbolism, visual metaphors/analogies, cultural context, and social meaning create concepts and scenarios which can be juxtaposed, remixed, or reimagined.

As a means of art-making and visual communication, recontextualization is a common feature of Postmodern art and design. *Postmodernism* and *Modernism* are wide concepts, difficult to discuss and define in their entirety, as they exist as unique temporal eras and schools of thought, as well as specific movements of art, design, architecture, and literature. Modernism is associated with a rejection of what had historically come before—the conservative and traditional—in pursuit of rationality, idealism, universal truth, and societal progress. As a converse school of thought which followed in the second half of the twentieth century, Postmodernism challenged these ideals, asserting that *Modernism* did not lead to progress or betterment of society. Instead, *Postmodernism* proposed that truths may *not* be universal and rejected singular definitions. Visually, this manifested in remixing, parodying, and combining new and historical elements and materials into new hybrid combinations or contexts. The materials, concepts, and methods which comprised "high art" and "popular culture" were combined into new works. While *Modernism* and *Postmodernism* refer to specific historic movements and periods in time, their concepts and methods remain in use in contemporary practice.

Recontextualization functions differently from *appropriation*. Appropriation is the act of taking an idea, image, or artifact for use without permission of its owner or author. Artists and designers often borrow and remix visual or structural elements to reference a specific piece or to craft a homage to a particular movement or style. While appropriation can be an effective visual tool, it can also present significant challenges. As a general rule, content belongs to those who created it. Copyright and intellectual property laws protect the original work of creative practitioners and prohibit others from using specific imagery and typefaces without permission or licensing. Font files are typically accompanied by a license outlining their permitted terms of use, including if the typeface can be used for personal or commercial purposes, or how many computers it can be installed on at any given time. In determining successful visual choices, it is best practice to ensure your typefaces have appropriate licenses for their intended use.

In addition, cultural appropriation is problematic. *Cultural appropriation* occurs when culturally specific symbols and aesthetics are recontextualized without attribution or acknowledgment of their sources—especially when the culture in question is, or has been, oppressed or marginalized. Typographic tattoos featuring Chinese characters and Polynesian symbols became popular at the turn of the twenty-first century, often because they looked "cool" or "exotic"—

Figures 1.35–1.36 *Populists are not my people* by Daan Lievense. © Daan Lievense, 2017. Reproduced with the permission of Daan Lievense/Galerie ALB, Paris. *One Small Moment* by Daan Lievense. © Daan Lievense, 2020. Reproduced with the permission of Daan Lievense.

Populists are not my people and One Small Moment | Daan Lievense

The work of Vienna-based artist Daan Lievense relies on the imagery of common objects, shifting language to contradict the original, anticipated message in poetic and often unexpected ways. In *Populists are not my people*, the common LED "OPEN" sign is subtly changed to "NOPE" a visual and linguistic shift representing the artist's reaction to contemporary politics. *One Small Moment* repurposes the popular hanging foil "happy birthday" letters with a poignant commentary on illusions of control and the fleeting nature of humanity.

Figure 1.37 *We walk the world two by two* (Jerry) by Chloë Bass. © Chloë Bass/Elsewhere, 2016. Reproduced with the permission of Chloë Bass.

We walk the world two by two (Jerry) | Chloë Bass

Cast-metal markers are often erected to commemorate historical events, and are frequently spotted beside highways, in old towns, or near city courthouses. In this site-specific series titled *We walk the world two by two*, artist Chloë Bass recontextualizes the familiar format of cast-aluminum plaques by featuring specific, personal histories of the residents of Greensboro, North Carolina. The design and placement of these permanent installations create new discoveries from otherwise overlooked intimate histories, drawing attention to a series of small but significant moments on South Elm Street. On this particular plaque, the emotional impact of a beloved local dog is preserved for posterity.

effectively erasing their historic meanings while simultaneously "othering" cultures and people.

Cultural norms, expectations, and imagery are constantly shifting, and *cultural appropriation* is an evolving term. In contexts where power structures are more balanced, the updating and remixing of cross-cultural imagery is that of sharing or borrowing. When there is inequality of power structures, especially where there is a history of marginalization and discrimination, cultural appropriation becomes oppression—an act of *taking*. Artists and designers have an obligation to practice in a way which is respectful, thoughtful, and well considered. When framing intent and design decisions, designers should carefully consider power structures, privilege, and the cultural origins of their visual choices. Just because something *can* be used does not mean it *should*.

Figures 1.38 and 1.39 *Hell Is Other People* and *Fancy Fuck* by Julie Jackson. © Julie Jackson, 2013/2010. Reproduced with the permission of Subversive Cross Stitch.

Subversive Cross Stitch | Julie Jackson

Traditionally featuring alphabets, bible verses, and pastoral scenes, cross-stitch samplers have been historically perceived as wholesome or domestic craftwork. Established in 2003, Subversive Cross Stitch reclaims this medium for unexpected, comical, and sardonic messages. As both an action and artifact, these patterns facilitate a way to vent, resulting in a visual and social recontextualization which is both cathartic and entertaining.

Figure 1.40 *Exist/Exit* by Mary Willette © Mary Willette, 2012. Reproduced with the permission of Mary Willette.

Exist/Exit | Mary Willette

Recontextualizations can be subtle or overt in their approach. Presented in the context of an everyday egress, artist Mary Willette's subtle *Exist/Exit* sign employs a quiet, poetic power for those observant enough to notice. The unexpected addition of one letter changes the meaning of familiar signage: shifting from a message of *leaving* to *living*.

2
Spatial Context

Visual Space

In order to understand visual space, we have to understand perception. If you look up from this book straight ahead at the space in front of you, you'll encounter your field of vision—the space you can visually perceive—from the horizon spanning out to the surrounding edges of your peripheral vision. This is made possible by light and brightness, which allows us to differentiate between figure and ground. Often referenced as positive space/negative space, figure/ground refers to the ability to differentiate an object or element from what is around it. Here, the figure refers to the object or element which draws our focus or has our attention, which can vary by circumstance, interest, or partiality.

Figure/ground relationships are what allow us to perceive (or not perceive) hierarchy in our visual field. Clear figure-ground, created by hierarchy of size, style, color, or brightness, allows us to differentiate a vibrant red stop-sign from the rest of the intersection. Conversely, figure-ground ambiguity, by which we *cannot* determine an object or element from what is around it, is what makes camouflage possible. Your ability to (visually) read the words on this page relies entirely on your ability to differentiate between the groups of letters and the page—the figure from the ground—and construct meaning from their particular arrangements (see "Language, form, and meaning" in Chapter 3).

This perception is informed by Gestalt theory, a framework for making sense of our visual field. Among other things, Gestalt psychology, established by German psychologists in the early twentieth century, is concerned with how we perceive forms and their relationships to each other—as informed by their visual contexts and the predictable ways in which our brain draws these conclusions. Gestalt principles are specific, observed frameworks for perception, and include such principles as proximity, continuation, closure, and similarity. These allow us to analyze individual elements to create or navigate patterns and groupings, which often translate socially: you

Chapter 2's image: Image Source via Getty Images.

might understand that a duo is a romantic couple due to their intimate proximity to one another, or you can identify the group of players belonging to a single sports team by the similarity of their jerseys.

In typography, Gestalt principles allow us to determine hierarchy, imply motion, and create ambiguity within a visual space. We assign meaning to these arrangements and visual relationships, allowing us to represent ideas, relationships, actions, and objects through thoughtful compositions of letterforms. These are, of course, the basics of all typographic composition: the ways in which artists and designers may effectively use space, size, and placement to effectively communicate.

Figure 2.1 *Jazzy* by Gen Ramírez ©, 2020. Reproduced with the permission of Gen Ramírez.

Figure 2.2 Design of book «*TTANZIT*» by BOWYER. © BOWYER, 2016, Republic of Korea. Reproduced with the permission of BOWYER.

Jazzy | Gen Remírez

Gen Ramírez's energetic and vibrant *Jazzy* makes skillful use of Gestalt principles. This word is easy to read, even though the shapes comprising its letterforms don't *actually* connect. Why is this? The swooping forms of these components facilitate *continuation*, where individual parts of letters are perceived as whole given their arrangement and alignment. This is also evidenced in the words' respective flourishes. In addition, *similarity* allows us to view similar shapes as belonging together more so than disparate shapes. Due to their visually related forms, we are able to discern a congruous word from repeated, familiar strokes.

«*TTANZIT*» | BOWYER

BOWYER's «*TTANZIT*» book cover uses *proximity* to craft clear Hangul characters effectively and creatively. Although each character is composed of many blue squares on a white ground, their visual proximity to each other allows perception of whole, individual characters which compose the title—all while maintaining a chic and pixelated appearance. As the cover for a book on workplace experiences at tech companies, this method of engaging the proximity of pixels is both visually engaging and conceptually relevant.

Figures 2.3 and 2.4 Nextbus by Nancy Wu. © Nancy Wu Design, 2011. Enoki Solutions by Nancy Wu. © Nancy Wu Design, 2016. Reproduced with the permission of Nancy Wu, Nancy Wu Design.

Enoki Solutions and Nextbus logos | Nancy Wu

Nancy Wu's direct and clever typographic work uses Gestalt principles to create layers of meaning and discovery. The Nextbus logo features closure to create a capital letter N—creating an opportunity for an intriguing figure/ground relationship between the directing arrows and the respective letterform. The Enoki Solutions logo works similarly, making use of *figure-ground reversal*. At one glance, the work appears as an organic, lowercase e; at another, the figure and ground swap, revealing a delicate enoki mushroom, the organization's namesake.

KINETIC AND EXPRESSIVE TYPE

Pioneering English photographer Eadweard Muybridge is best known for capturing individual frames of movement, producing sequential images of running horses. When viewed in quick succession via a zoopraxiscope (a device he invented for projecting moving pictures), these individual frames amounted to an animation, creating the illusion of movement. While this might seem banal today, in the 1870s this was revelatory—a major event in the development of film and animation. This photograph shows documentation of real animal locomotion, but when viewed as single frames still *implies* movement. Things which are *kinetic* refer or relate to motion, which leads to the question: does kinetic type *actually* have to move?

This book nestles kinetic works under two categories: actual and implied. Typically, works labeled as kinetic are referring to type in motion or "motion type"—which moves on screen or in virtual space, and is intended to be viewed as such. Within this printed book, however, no works are truly in motion, as even the most animated pieces have been reduced to sequential stills on paper. Kinetic typography which is *implied* isn't actually animated, but makes use of Gestalt principles and compositional strategies effectively to create semblances of—or references to—movement within static images. Images frozen in

Figure 2.5 A galloping horse and rider. Eadweard Muybridge, 1887. Wellcome Collection.

motion, images "bouncing" across the page, or images viewed in sequence may not move in the literal sense, but still communicate similar ideas through their form and placement.

Kinetic type uses motion as a means to gain attention and create specificity, relying on metaphors of movement to carry meaning. Rapid maneuvers, deliberate trickling, or slow crawls denote unique pacings and evoke different responses physically and emotionally. High-speed events—such as riding a rollercoaster—tend to increase adrenaline, making them scary, invigorating, or exciting. Elements moving in the same fashion may evoke similar feelings, while objects and events which move at a glacial pace may kindle the opposite. Today, most movies and TV shows begin with title sequences, introducing the cast and crew and setting the theme of the program typographically, adding layers of meaning and inflection through the pace of their presentation (see "Time as medium" in Chapter 3).

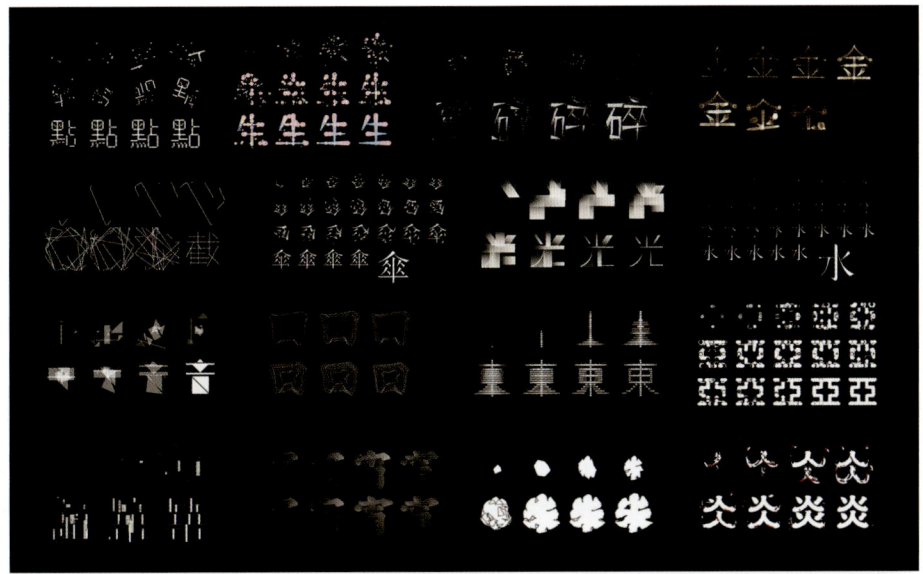

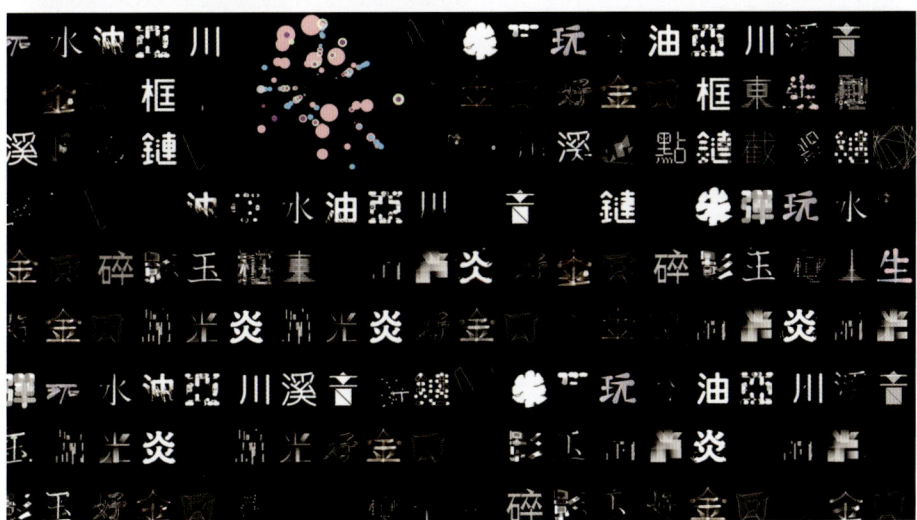

Figures 2.6 and 2.7 *Motion Type Project* by Ting-An Ho. © Ting-An Ho, 2016. Reproduced with the permission of Ting-An Ho.

Motion Type Project | Ting-An Ho

The letterforms of the Latin alphabet differ from Chinese characters in both their construction and meaning. As such, the methods for creating Latin letterforms in motion aren't always useful or appropriate for Chinese characters. Manifesting as a resource website, workshops, and multiple exhibitions, Taiwanese designer Ting-An Ho's *Motion Type Project* proposes new methods for representing Chinese characters through motion type. This project features a rich visual catalog of methods and examples, representing animation techniques which complement and illustrate a character's meaning. For instance, the character for *cut* (截) is animated using sharp, slicing mono-weight strokes, which intersect to form the character. The animation style for flame (炎) mimics gestural pen strokes, with this particular motion sparking and flickering like fire.

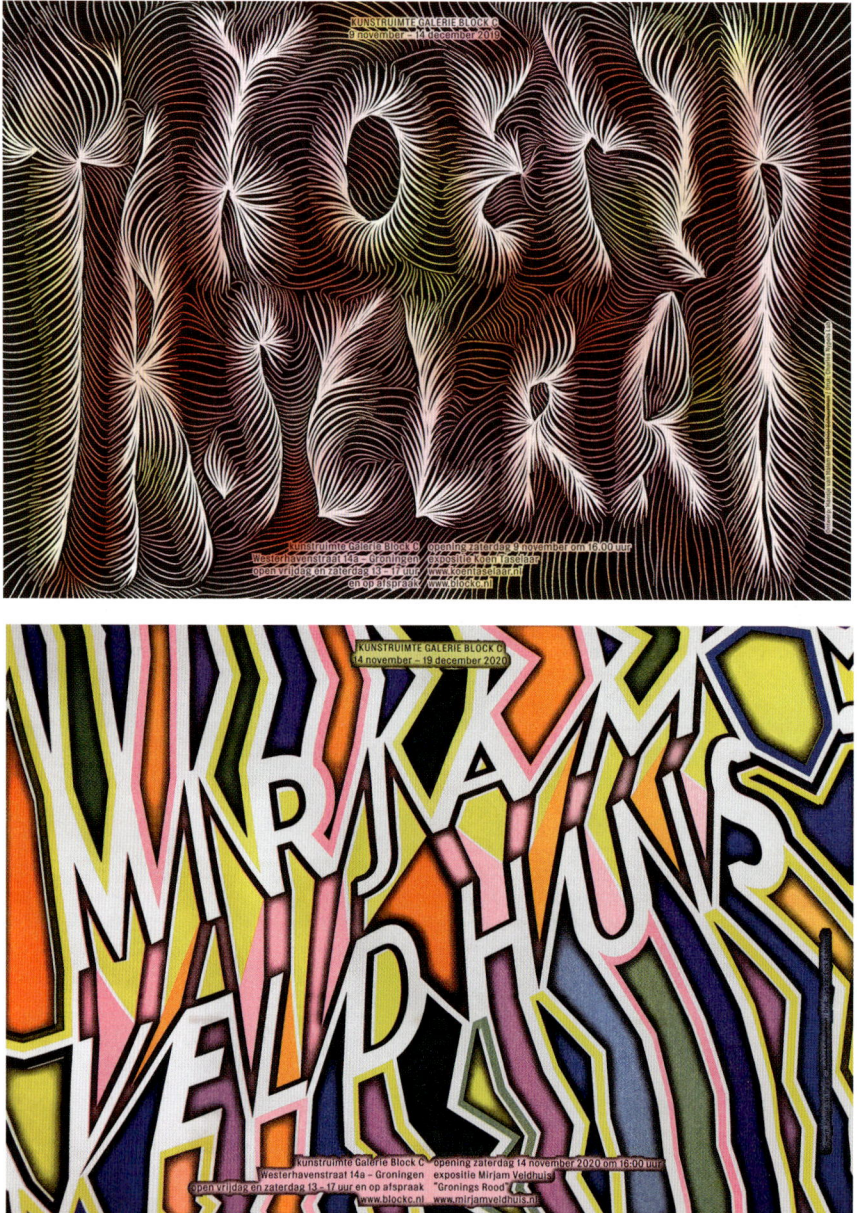

Figures 2.8 and 2.9 Posters for Galerie Block C by Hansje van Halem, 2019. Reproduced with the permission of Hansje van Halem.

Galerie Block C posters | Hansje van Halem

Designed by Hansje van Halem, these event posters for Galerie Block C showcase vibrant typographic explorations. Here, letterforms are electric and expansive, stretching out in all directions, as if vibrating or reaching—evoking a certain exhilaration and anticipation for the gallery's event. These riveting and deeply energetic letterforms *imply* motion, even though they are intentionally still images.

Kinetic type is inherently expressive, but not all expressive type is kinetic. Expressive typography is a broad category by which type becomes the main means of portraying a concept, using its placement and visual qualities to communicate or represent ideas, actions, objects, or relationships. This relies heavily on the use of Gestalt principles to connect form and meaning, associating type choice and placement with intent and analogy. Splitting, spreading, shearing, scaling, layering, reversing, jumbling, scrambling, shrinking, and even—on rare occasions—stretching individual words can create meaning by associating socially recognizable scenarios or events with similar visual representations. Therefore, a long pause, the reunion of old friends, a bitter dispute, or a sudden ending can all be implied, and consequently understood, through the intentional arrangement of letterforms.

All type is expressive on some level—but each application expresses different things, and some more strongly or effectively than others. While the term "expressive typography" may be affiliated with dynamic placements or witty letter juxtapositions, its use extends to applications which may be more subtle, but still emotive, in their approach.

Figures 2.10–2.13 *The Expanse* Opening Credits Sequence. © Expanding Universe Productions, LLC 2019.

The Expanse Title Sequence | Expanding Universe Productions, LLC

The Expanse is a sociopolitical sci-fi drama, set hundreds of years in the future across asteroids and planets in the vastness of space. The expressive typography of its title sequence hints at its context and narrative through visual references to objects and occurrences. In tandem with images of quickly evolving planetary landscapes and perpetual motion, text appears letter by letter, changing in style, becoming more recognizably futuristic. Their size is dwarfed by the enormity of the cosmos and features the familiar underscores of digital file naming. In a poetic shift, the title of the show subtly expands in space, as if unconfined by gravity. This increased tracking moves individual letters away from each other, breaking the X of EXPANSE into two halves—a visual allusion to action, direction, or opposition.

Figures 2.14 and 2.15 Advertisement for Pyribenzamine by Herb Lubalin, 1957. Mother & Child logo by Herb Lubalin, with lettering by Tom Carnase, 1965. Reproduced with the permission of The Herb Lubalin Study Center.

Break up Cough advertisement and Mother & Child Logo | Herb Lubalin

Herb Lubalin was an acclaimed designer, art director, typographer, and type designer best remembered for his innovative and deeply expressive typography. In his 1957 advertisement for Pyribenzamine, Lubalin's expressive type emulates an action. Here, the word "cough" has been punched through to symbolize the phrase "break up," showcasing the effect of the cough medicine's strength. His Mother & Child logo from 1967 uses perceptive placement of letterforms to represent a relationship. To showcase the special connection of maternity and the relationship of mothers to their children, the ampersand and "child" are encompased in a metaphorical womb, the counter of the O.

Figure 2.16 *Take up More Space* by Dani Molyneux, Dotto Studio. © Dotto, 2019.

Take Up More Space | Dani Molyneux

Dani Molyneux's *Take Up More Space* visually embodies the action of an empowering phrase. This strong, expressive type branches confidently to occupy the visual space of this poster. As a foil to frequently repeated, limiting sentiments, this mantra is a bold statement, encouraging viewers not to minimize themselves, their opinions, or their accomplishments.

Text arranged in a radial or dilatational layout—moving away from a central point, or outwards in concentric arcs—can subtly or overtly imply a ripple, meditation, or focus. Even the static, immovable typography of corporate banks and institutions are expressive in their predictable presentation and stable baselines. Because letterforms can be arranged in every imaginable way relative to each other and their respective reader, the possibilities for expressive type are endless.

Figures 2.17 and 2.18 Dead-Alive and Real-Fake by Yash Mathur. © 2020, @yvm_design.

Dead-Alive and Real-Fake | Yash Mathur

As part of an intriguing series of typographic dualities by Yash Mathur, relationships of opposite definitions are represented through expressive visual outcomes. By effectively using figure-ground relationships and utilizing extended stems of letterforms to create two words from one, Real-Fake and Dead-Alive make visual use of opposing ends, facilitating new textual ways of viewing familiar dichotomies.

Figure 2.19 Coconut Milk by Grinning Face by Leo Burnett Toronto. © Leo Burnett Toronto, 2019. Reproduced with the permission of Leo Burnett Toronto.

Coconut Milk by Grinning Face packaging | Leo Burnett Toronto

Grinning Face Coconut Milk only contains two ingredients: coconut and water. Because these ingredients naturally separate, it needs to be shaken first before it can be enjoyed. Considering this action relative to its product packaging, Man Wai Wong (via Leo Burnett Toronto) devised a package design which represents an action in a clear, expressive, and informative way. By showcasing energetic, playful, and jumbled letters, people are encouraged to shake the bottle and its contents.

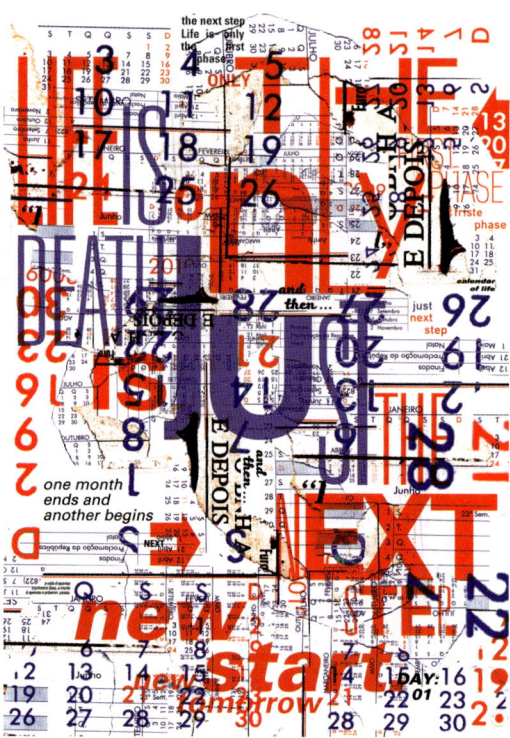

Figure 2.20 *Next* by Olavo D'Aguiar. © Olavo D'Aguiar, 2013. Reproduced with the permission of Olavo D'Aguiar.

Next | Olavo D'Aguiar

Intentional placements denote specific actions or attitudes: spirited placement, directional changes, or intentional overlaps within a visual space can create compositions which range from frenzied to overwhelming. In Olavo D'Aguiar's detailed and frenetic poster titled *Next*, an overlapping collage of tickets, signage, calendars, and paperwork highlights the constant, overwhelming, and unwavering pace of time. Overlaid subtle messages live alongside large, thin text, calling attention to time and its relationship to life and death. Here, visual complexity creates a rich composition implying an absolute urgency: *What's happening now? What's happening next?*

SOUND, SHAPE, AND SPEECH

If type implies motion, can type imply sound? In a series of experiments repeated across cultures and languages, researchers presented respondents with two shapes: a sharp jagged form beside a smooth, rounded one. When asked to assign the words "kiki" and "bouba" to these respective shapes, participants overwhelmingly agreed: kiki sounds sharper, and bouba sounds rounder. This realization—dubbed the bouba/kiki effect—revealed that the relationship between sound and shape is not arbitrary. As letterforms are tied to the sounds they denote and words they form, we may consider the relationship between sharp characters and sharp sounds. The characters K and X, for instance, typically feature steep inclines and pronounced points, while B and O feature more gentle, curvilinear attributes.

Socially, there also tends to be a connection between sound, shape, and *size*. Even common phrases referencing sound, like a "huge thunder clap" or "enormous applause" indicate that something louder is understood as something bigger. THIS MAY EXPLAIN, AT LEAST IN PART, WHY CONVERSING THROUGH ALL CAPS CARRIES THE VISUAL INFLECTION OF SHOUTING—and consequently illustrates why this approach should never be used in email correspondence.

Figures 2.22 and 2.23 Goertek typeface by Kontrapunkt. © Goertek, 2018. Reproduced with the permission of Kontrapunkt.

Goertek typeface | Kontrapunkt

The relationship between size and sound is also showcased in visual representations of sound waves themselves; when visualized, loud sounds have greater amplitude, occupying a greater visual space. Kontrapunkt's sound sensitive typeface was designed in collaboration with Nippon Design Center of Japan for Goertek, a Chinese audio tech company. By using innovative OpenType technologies, this typeface reacts to sound input, visually responding to changes in frequency and volume in its environment. When used in digital signage, these changes create site and sound-specific text for this multi-weight typeface, a clever visual representation of the sonic spaces it inhabits.

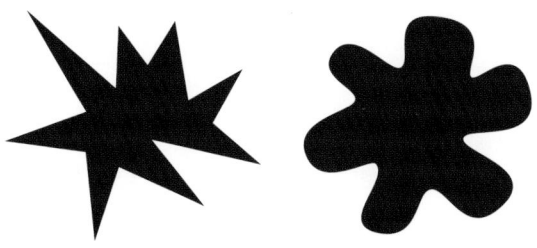

Figure 2.21 The author's visual interpretation of Kiki and Bouba, respectively.

However, this particular visual inflection is entirely dependent on expectation and context of use. The all-caps line-up of band names on a promotional poster or signage on a building's storefront do not automatically denote an inflection of a raised voice, as this use may not induce the same sudden tonal change implied in a conversational context,

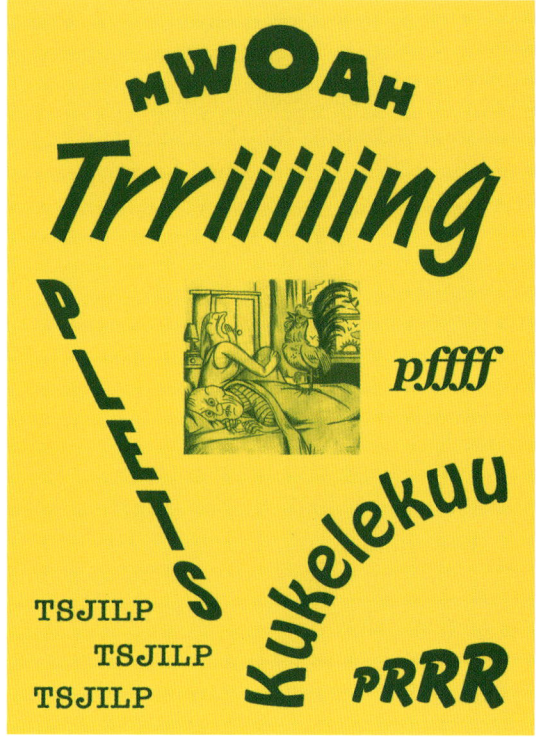

Figures 2.24–2.28 In uw kot, Mondomatopee, Overlap, and Overtreffende trap. © Broos Stoffels & Lukas Verstraete, 2019.

Onomatopee | Broos Stoffels and Lukas Verstraete

Onomatopoeias are words which phonetically resemble the sound they reference—such as *achoo*, *boom*, or *clang*. In Broos Stoffels and Lukas Verstraete's collaborative book *Onomatopee*, expressive type and illustrations work in tandem to create scenes of recognizable sounds. The expressive type effectively varies in its word and letterform choice, size, and placement to create reflections of volume, speed, pitch, and pace, while detailed illustrations give context to where, when, or from whom these sounds are produced or encountered.

or in extensive body copy, where lowercase is generally used, expected, and disrupted by all-caps text.

In the relationship between shape, sound, and speed, characters can also reflect the length of time required for speaking, reading or thinking. Note the differences between hyphens, en dashes, and em dashes: hyphens are used to quickly connect compound words, requiring less time to read or consider, such as the words "high-tech" or "ex-president." En dashes are slightly longer, denoting a duration. This serves as a substitute to the word "to" or "through," as used in July 8–10, or Monday–Friday. Em dashes—shown here denoting a change of thought—are even longer, reflecting the time required to shift between ideas.

When translated to type referencing speech, all of these factors play into visual translations of speed, volume, pitch, and pace. Much in the same way that text with frenetic placement can set a frenzied pace, a jumble of text can create a visual representation of a verbal cacophony, indicative of overlapping voices. Large, bold text can imply shouting, and repetitions of words reflect repeated phrases or echoes. Speed can be implied through direction, proximity, and letter spacing; exceptionally tight or wide tracking can imply quick or meandering paces of speech. Volume can be indicated by letters increasing in size, or imitating the direction of a shout. Consider the large, uneven textual formatting of sudden sounds or interjections in traditional comic books expressed as *AARRRGGHH!*, *POP!*, or *BANG!*

A CLOSER LOOK:
Jazz typography

Connections between sound and shape can create long-lasting social connotations—like typography affiliated with jazz. As a musical genre, Jazz developed within African American communities as a distinct musical style, encompassing numerous sub-genres—including fast, frenetic bebop, and smooth, melodic cool jazz, which became widely popular in the mid-twentieth century. On posters and album covers, visual and typographic choices mirrored jazz's unique musical qualities: bounding and overlapping letters, shapes, and silhouettes were frequently used along with faceted visual elements referencing syncopated rhythms, overlapping melodies, and musical improvisation.

These expressive visual choices sought to represent the sound and feel of jazz in the 1940s and 1950s, but have earlier origins and influence in the twentieth century as informed by culture and identity. Jazz album covers often featured cubist approaches, like those frequently employed by painter Pablo Picasso, whose works were inspired by African sculpture. African American artists and designers during (and following) the Harlem Renaissance explored similar visual choices and compositions, including designer Aaron Douglas, whose work featured bold, overlapping shapes and silhouettes inspired by both cubism and African art, and Jacob Lawrence, whose "dynamic cubism" paintings captured both the challenges and vibrant spirit of his community in Harlem.

With these aesthetic influences, playful, angular, cubism-inspired letterforms and colorful, jostling sans serif letters were commonly set in reference to the cadence of complex notes. In addition, wedge-serif letterforms—which feature sharp, bulky serifs—were frequently used and arranged, often with intentionally uneven baselines, lilting in a gestural reference to rhythm. Some of these letterforms were hand-drawn, giving each glyph an even more improvisational quality, as shown in this 1947 Bix & Tram album cover by illustrator Jim Flora, which features energetic, stylized figures and equally engaging text. Despite their use in the mid-twentieth century, plenty of these commonly used typefaces were designed and released much earlier, in the late nineteenth or early twentieth century—such as Stephenson Blake & Co.'s *Wide Latin from 1883*, shown here as "Lining Wide Latin" in a type specimen book from 1908.

While commonly seen on jazz albums, these type choices were not exclusively used in this capacity, and appeared on many other applications at that time in styles consistent with popular typography of the 1950s (see "Typographic trends" in Chapter 3). However, the association of bouncing, wedge-serif letterforms with jazz has been perpetuated through use—perhaps due to their accentuated serifs, whose forms are analogous to the bells of trumpets, trombones, and saxophones.

While influenced by mid-century trends, these specific visual and typographic choices have become emblematic *and* enduring across eras; this relationship of sound and shape has become socially affiliated with the specific concept of jazz. These forms continue to appear in contemporary use in a variety of media. In the title sequence for *Monsters Inc.* from 2001, colorful, overlapping shapes dance and pulse to the jazzy, upbeat musical introduction by Randy Newman—appropriately matched by joyful wedge-serif type with hand-rendered qualities. This choice highlights how a confluence of historic, aesthetic, and kinetic references can continue to visually express concept, tempo, and tone.

Figure 2.29 BIX & TRAM by Jim Flora, 1947, illustrated Columbia Records album cover. © The Heirs of James Flora. Reproduced with the permission of JimFlora.com and the Heirs of James Flora.

Figure 2.30 *Specimens of Point Line Type: Borders Ornaments Brass Rules &c. &c* by Stephenson, Blake and Company, Ltd; Sir Charles Reed & Sons. From archive.org.

CONCRETE AND VISUAL POETRY

Specific syntax, rhyming-structures, and diction are used intentionally in written poetry, which relies on both word choice and word placement to create meaning. Punctuation is integral in shaping intention: A series. Of words. Broken. By periods. Might create. A strange. Start-and-stop. Feeling. Using alliteration can spark a continuous flow or conceptual link—a sinuous strand of similar sounds suggests a smooth sensibility. In addition, the length of a line carries meaning, directing the reading pattern of an audience. Short lines in rapid bursts can imply more urgency, while varying line-lengths may represent a more conversational or captivating pacing.

Historically, artists and designers have experimented with poetic structures and typographic placement in an attempt to respond to, critique, or influence societal events. Near the turn of the twentieth century, futurists concerned with the connections between speed, industrialization, and societal revolution experimented with free-verse poetry and kinetic typography. (In some of its most well-known examples, however, notable Italian futurist F.T. Marinetti problematically tied notions of modernity and progress to Mussolini's harmful fascist politics.) Dadaists used similar typographic explorations in a different conceptual pursuit. They embraced absurdity and used unexpected printed compositions and methods of collage as a response to the horrors of the First World War.

The field of visual poetry primarily uses visual representations of poetics through shape or otherwise expressive arrangements of text. Here, the visual arrangement of words in relation to their verbal or spatial reading pattern contributes to an audience's understanding of pacing, content, or authorial intent. Visual poetry may use words in combination with images, or sometimes letterforms used in these compositions might not form recognizable words at all. Words formatted into representative shapes have existed for centuries, and have been referred to as "shaped poetry" or "pattern poetry," serving as precursors to concrete poetry.

Concrete poetry is much more elusive in its definition, but seeks to categorically distinguish itself from both visual poetry and text-based visual art.

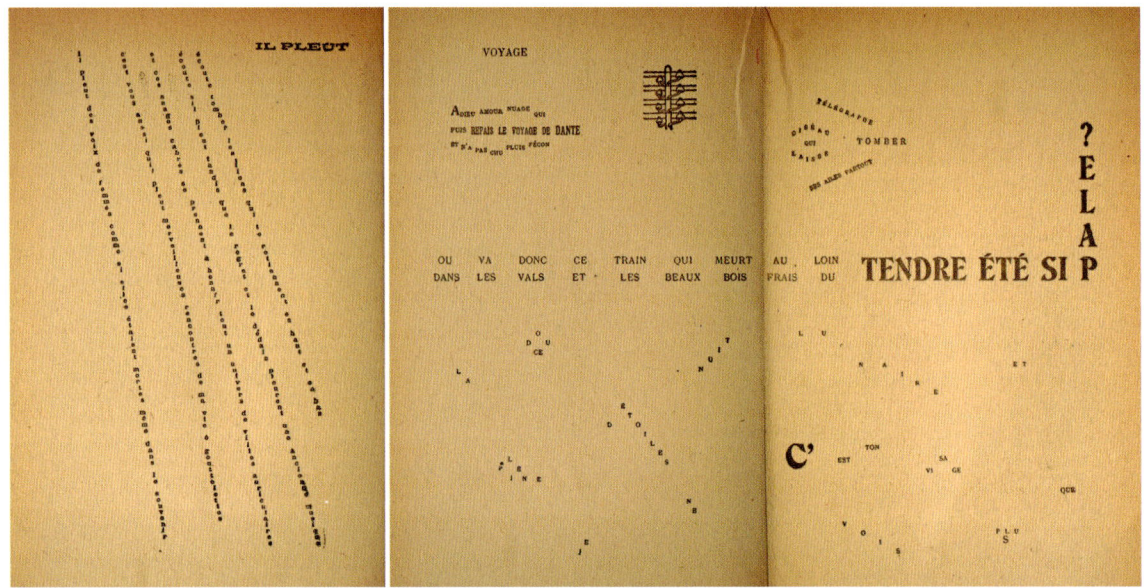

Figures 2.31 and 2.32 *Calligrammes: Poèmes de la paix et de la guerre, 1913–1916,* by Guillaume Apollinaire, Paris, Mercure de France, 1918. Digitized by Duke University Libraries.

Calligrammes | Guillaume Apollinaire

Before concrete poetry became a recognizable term in the twentieth century, French poet Guillaume Apollinaire explored the relationship of type, image, and meaning as it pertained to poetics. He coined the term *calligramme* (calligram, in English), a way of formatting text into an image which represented the subject matter of the poem. His book of poetry, *Calligrammes: Poèmes de la paix et de la guerre (1913–1916)* (*Calligrams: Poems of Peace and War (1913–1916)*) features works about longing, romance, and his experience as a soldier during the First World War. It was published the year of his death from the Spanish flu, in 1918, following a war injury. In his work "Il Pleut," individual letters collectively form streaming drops of rain. In "Voyage," he references traveling by train, alluding to tracks formed by parallel lines of text, as well looking at stars in the night sky, with textual constellations comprising the lower half of the poem.

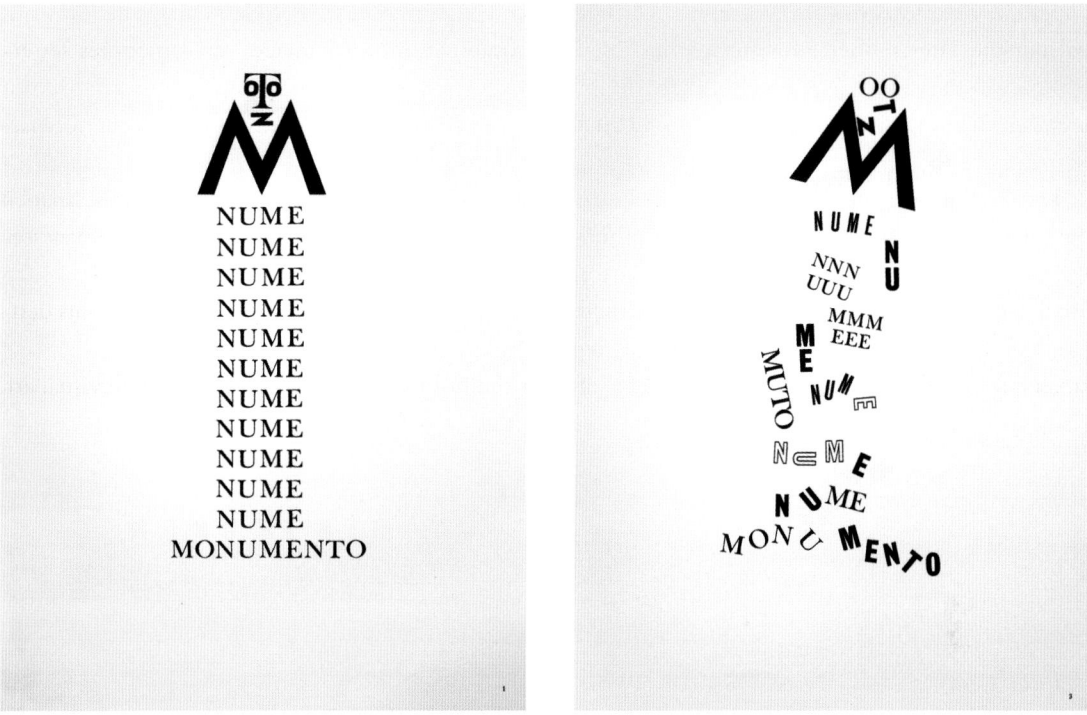

Figures 2.33 and 2.34 *History of Monument*, Mirella Bentivoglio (with Annalisa Alloatti). © Mirella Bentivoglio/De Luca Ed., Rome 1968. Courtesy Archivio Mirella Bentivoglio, Roma.

Storia Del Monumento | Mirella Bentivoglio

The work of the late Italian artist Mirella Bentivoglio engaged with language and its visual representations in a variety of forms, including sculpture and concrete poetry. In her 1968 work *Storia Del Monumento* (*History of Monument*) in collaboration with Annalisa Alloatti, a monument is formed from the text MONUMENTO. Over the course of six pages, this collapses into individual words and shapes until it is unrecognizable as itself—but becomes something else entirely. Through the disintegration of a familiar icon, new phrases arise. As individual words appear from the text MONUMENTO, their meanings are informed by, or question that which is, monumental. The work's introduction page includes translations: NUME (GODLIKE), ME NON TU (ME NOT YOU), MENTO (I LIE), MUTO (DUMB: or I AM CHANGING), and TEMO (I FEAR). These fracturing typographic compositions interrogate language and conceptual affiliations through a single-word narrative and its respective visual transformation.

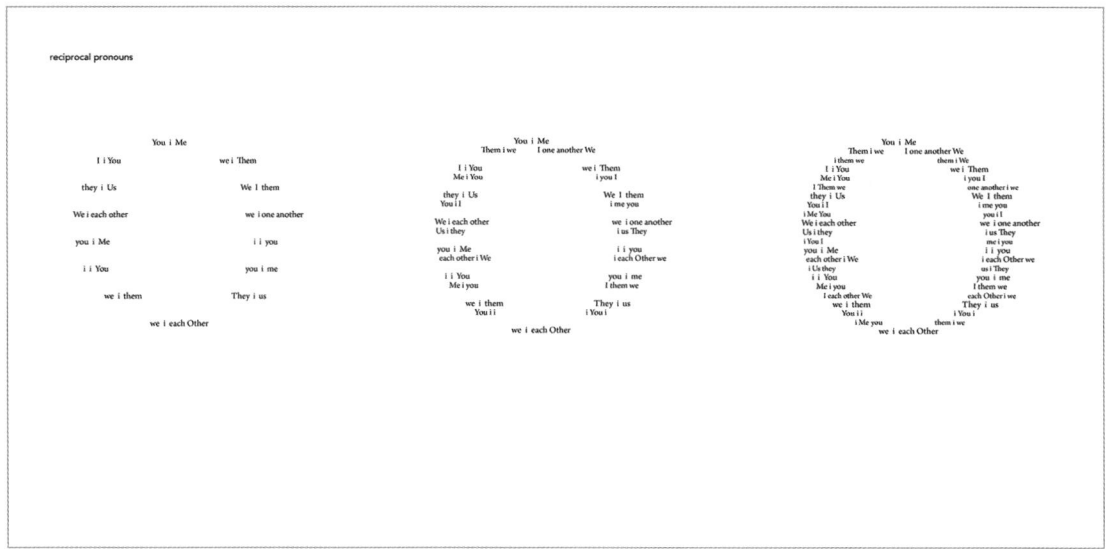

Figure 2.35 *reciprocal pronouns* by Chantal Gibson. © Chantal Gibson, How She Read, 2019. Reproduced with the permission of Caitlin Press.

reciprocal pronouns | Chantal Gibson

The textual sculpture *reciprocal pronouns* is from *grammar of loss*, a section of *How She Read* (Caitlin Press, 2019) by artist, educator, and author Chantal Gibson. This reflective book of poetry is informed by personal narrative and explores the representation of Black women across Canadian culture. Here, the artist uses typography as a decolonizing agent, disrupting the expected formatting of lines, paragraphs, or stanzas. This layout, which builds across multiple pages, calls attention to the act of reading itself. It seeks to dismantle how we have been taught to use grammar and English—especially with its history as a colonizing language. While the poem may be interpreted in many different ways, its arrangement challenges readers' assumptions about how it should be read. Intentionally, to undo conventions, there are no instructions. There isn't a right answer to where it begins or if it ends. The text's circular form may suggest the face of a clock, signifying a relationship to time. Other readings might engender notions of a meditative process, a circular argument, or a perpetual rumination on race and identity—how we regard ourselves and one another.

While the term "concrete poetry" was used in the early twentieth century, its core development occurred through an international movement spanning the 1950s through the 1970s. Generally, concrete poetry is concerned with *unifying* the meaning of a word to its closest visual representation, merging them into something "concrete." This makes the visual composition of the poem integral to its purpose; its intent becomes lost if the textual element is separated from its composition, such as if the poem is read out loud. Despite the nuances in their definitions, both concrete and visual poetry rely on the arrangement of words and letters within a visual space to convey particular meanings.

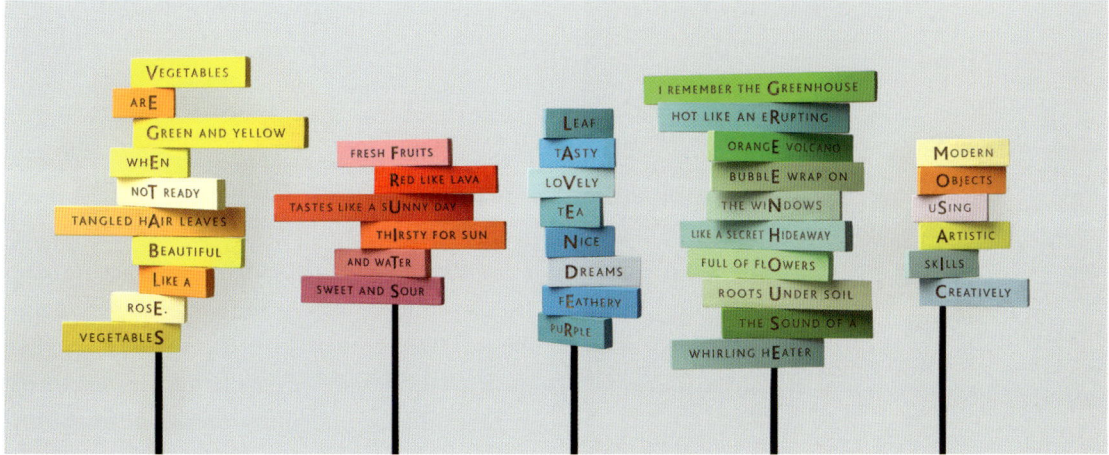

Figure 2.36 *Planting Poetry* by Burgess Studio. © Burgess Studio, 2013. Reproduced with the permission of Burgess Studio.

Planting Poetry | Burgess Studio

While many examples exist on-screen or in printed books, visual poetry can also live in a physical environment. Burgess Studio's playful *Planting Poetry* series takes the form of sculptural *mesostic*. A *mesostic* (sometimes listed as a mesostic poem) is a type of poem which follows a format of one word running vertically, with lines of the poem intersecting horizontally (though not symmetrically) using letters of the core word, which typically serves as the title. These works were designed in conjunction with the *Ministry of Stories*, a charity which seeks to inspire young people through creative writing mentorships and workshops. With assistance from professional poets, children wrote original poems which were then designed, laser-etched, constructed, and installed at Mary's Secret Garden in Hackney, London, composing a poetry trail. Together, the whimsical formatting of the text and a cheerful color palette create endearing works to be discovered.

Physical Space

If you've ever stubbed your toe, you already understand the bounds of physical space. In this realm, everything in three dimensions (with height, width, and depth) is bound to the laws of reality and physics. Typography in physical space often manifests as works which are tactile or sculptural. While media such as prints, paintings, or digital images are traditionally defined as two-dimensional, they still *exist* in three dimensions, requiring tangible materials or physical viewing devices—like a laptop or canvas—in order to be created and viewed.

Interactions with objects in physical space creates opportunity for movement, texture, and tactility. Our senses of smell, touch, sight, taste, and sound are informed by interactions with external stimuli through the experiences of our bodies within a real space, sparking an emotional response. Even digitally mediated interactions—like watching a movie or attending an online

Figure 2.37 Rolfo Brenner/EyeEm via Getty Images.

Spatially informed text

Spatial contexts—both visual *and* physical—also inform how type is situationally designed and constructed. Letterforms used in road-marking are unusually large and tall, with stretched forms and bulky serifs, and applied with a reflective paint. In other circumstances, this choice would be quite strange. In the context of a roadway, however, the unusual length of these letterforms aids legibility from a distance, and at extreme angles, by people on bikes and in vehicles. These considerations of physical space allow these signs to appear as recognizably proportioned text in the intended audience's field of vision, alerting them of specific speed limits or when to slow down for upcoming train tracks, pedestrian crossings, or school zones. Viewed from above, this 30 km/hour speed zone in Germany showcases the elongated letters necessitated by its physical context and viewing angle.

seminar—still interact with physical reality. These bounds are perhaps most obvious if you are sitting behind a tall person in the theater or you've managed to crack your computer screen before an online event.

The meaning of typography in physical space is informed by how it's made, what it's made from, the place it occupies, or what it's near to. Its physicality (understood physical or tangible qualities) and/or its proximity (the context of its physical space or its placement in relation to other things) influences interactions with the work and its consequent interpretation.

MATERIAL MEANING

What something is made *from* influences what it means. Inherent qualities, material analogies/metaphors, and references to objects or artifacts with known social contexts all influence the intention and interpretation of material meanings in typography. When we encounter words constructed from, or in conversation with, specific materials, how do we understand what they mean?

First, consider the inherent meaning which all materials possess: the qualities of a substance which are inseparable from the ontology of the thing itself. Steel is extremely durable and melts at a very high temperature, but if untreated and exposed to air and water, it rusts. Water at room temperature is wet. When heated, it becomes steam, when frozen, it forms ice. These are entirely obvious statements, but inherent material qualities are vastly important, as they determine how and when materials are chosen—and what these applications convey. Our understanding of material qualities informs everyday decisions about taste, safety, familiarity, and cultural significance. No reasonable person would lace-up ice skates to glide on a lake on a hot summer day, and we would be remiss to hop on an extremely rusted, brittle bicycle. These inherent material meanings transcend physical descriptions to become social meanings, unifying both the physical and emotional qualities referenced, such as strength, durability, tenderness, warmth, or fragility. This is why a fuzzy fleece blanket elicits a very different emotional response from hard concrete.

Material meanings and interpretations are also socially constructed. A *social construct* is when a meaning is agreed upon and perpetuated in ways which are both culturally and temporally specific. As an example: in the West, the emotional and financial values of diamonds are relatively new, and entirely socially constructed. This is the result of a very effective twentieth-century marketing campaign purporting diamonds to be remarkable and essential symbols of a couple's love. Persuaded by this, diamonds became the go-to gem for engagement rings, with size, quality, and cost of diamonds serving as symbols for status or commitment. In reality, diamonds are *not* particularly rare—but their socially constructed symbolism has become culturally ingrained and sustained. In this way, material meanings cannot be determined by inherent material qualities alone.

Therefore, the emotional qualities we assign to material qualities are, in some instances, largely arbitrary—after all, cash is just paper, and gems are just rocks or minerals—but their socially agreed-upon meaning makes them particularly valuable within a specific society. Because these social meanings persist, a typographic work constructed of money or real diamonds would hold significant economic and societal importance—at least, at the time of this book's publishing. Because social constructs shift over time, the emotional and economic value of objects and materials are liable to change, transforming consequent meanings. Sought-after materials like diamonds may ultimately meet the fate of Beanie Babies in the United States in the 1990s or tulips in the Netherlands in the 1630s. As such, a shift in social constructs would render previously desirable material-based typography as both unremarkable and unvalued.

Materials are so strongly tied to meaning that even without their physical presence, *implied* visual references are used to carry their associations. Across a range of digital applications, filters, textures, and patterns seek to emulate physical qualities, using textural references for a variety of surfaces and substances—such as glass, fabric, glitter, or soil—making social inferences to material meanings. This further translates emotional references to craft and materiality through implied visual contexts (see "Virtual space" later in this chapter). Consider the plethora of vectored logos which convey a "rubber stamp" texture, implying a social and material origin, or the number of display typefaces which feature a woodgrain or concrete texture to imply something natural or strong.

Informed by social expectations and cultural contexts, connotations of craft and material meanings communicate intention and quality. Even in familiar typographic applications of print and package design, choosing the appropriate paper stock is imperative for practical production and use, as well as for communicating effectively. The power of material meanings is evident through craft and construction, as demonstrated through a simple material change. A large newspaper produced with cardstock would be comically clunky or annoyingly cumbersome, and even a beautifully designed business card would feel lackluster, at best, if printed on flimsy paper.

A KNOWN SOCIAL CONTEXT

The meaning of an object or material may be informed by its inherent or socially constructed qualities, but also by its known social context: presumptions or prior knowledge such as where it lives, how it is used, who it is used by, and the connotations associated with each. When used in typography, letterforms made from office supplies will inevitably conjure different affiliations than those constructed from jalapeño peppers, leather boots, hypodermic needles, or beach glass. As you read that last sentence, it's likely you made immediate associations between these materials and what they imply from their social context. Informed by your personal experiences and preferences, these connections impact how you understand what this typographic communication means.

However, a social context must be *known* in order for an inference to be made. For example, if we consider text constructed from plastic sequins, with knowledge of their social use, we might affiliate them with their material qualities (shiny, light-reflecting), common applications (costumes, flashy attire, formal wear), their spatial or situational context (theaters, parties) as well as who might use them (performers, dancers). These associations are incredibly subjective, and rely heavily on cultural and temporal knowledge in addition to familiarity with the social context of the object or material in question.

As a result of their known contexts, objects or materials can represent larger concepts extending beyond their more literal presentations. Linguistically, this is referred to as a *metonym*. A Metonym is a figure of speech by which a person, place, action, or object becomes a shorthand for something larger than itself, the whole of which is not directly depicted. Common examples include "suits" (businesspeople), "the crown" (royalty), and "the White House" (the US Government). Typographically, and informed by a known social context, this may manifest as a visual substitution—using text made from fresh vegetables as a way to mean *health*, or ruled paper for *education*. Semiotically, because a single *signifier* can represent many differing *signifieds*, any material-based choice can be informed by—but not limited to—a particular social meaning. Flames may mean *passion*, but might also mean *hell*.

Therefore, when objects and materials with a known social context are used in typographic applications, their associations and consequent meanings should be carefully considered. In these instances, meanings can *transfer*—allowing the work to be read through the additional context of its material's overt *or* implied affiliations.

Figures 2.38 and 2.39 *THEY DON'T SPEAK FOR US* by Adam Farcus. © Adam Farcus, 2018. Reproduced with the permission of the Advance Art Museum, Changsha, China. *THE KNOWN SUN SETTING* by Adam Farcus. © Adam Farcus, 2019. Reproduced with the permission of the artist.

Signs | Adam Farcus

Adam Farcus's work often explores emotional responses as they relate to concerns such as climate change or social justice. In their series *Signs*, large, hand-painted Arial Bold text adorns a series of bedsheets. These appropriated, overheard, or original poem fragments are protests which purposefully use ambiguous language, prompting a viewer to ask: "*Who* doesn't speak for us?" or "What does 'the known sun setting' mean?" Subtle but salient, the known social contexts of these materials inform and influence how the work is read. Protest signs are sometimes painted on bedsheets, and bedsheets are indicative of a familiar, calm or intimate space. Thus, these messages reference feelings which permeate our lived experiences in all areas, even places we perceive as being safe and comfortable—like our beds.

Figure 2.40 Jeffrey Gibson, *YOU'LL BE GIVEN LOVE*, 2020, 47 x 48 x 3 in (119.4 x 121.9 x 7.6 cm). Courtesy of the artist and Roberts Projects, Los Angeles, California; Photo Max Yawney.

YOU'LL BE GIVEN LOVE | Jeffrey Gibson

Jeffrey Gibson is an American artist of Choctaw and Cherokee heritage. His paintings and sculptural works employ materials and methods of traditional Native American art in combination with queer iconography, aesthetics from geometric abstraction, and appropriated text from popular culture. In his textual and sculptural work *YOU'LL BE GIVEN LOVE*, the use of repurposed trading post weaving, acrylic felt, nylon thread, artificial sinew, glass beads, plastic beads, nylon fringe, and cotton canvas imbues its intricately beaded text with new meanings as informed by the social and cultural contexts of these materials. Featuring a lyric from *All Is Full of Love* by Björk, this detailed material and textual recontextualization prompts dialogue between global art and Native American aesthetic histories, probing questions of Indigenous representation, personal identity, contemporary art, and cultural production.

Figures 2.41–2.43 Waste typography B, Waste typography C, and Waste typography H by Monique Goossens. © Monique Goossens, 2017. Reproduced with the permission of Monique Goossens.

Waste typography | Monique Goossens

When materials with a known social context are used in typographic communication, they inevitably inform the message of the work, but not always in the way a viewer might expect. Even recognizable materials with strong associations can be re-framed or recontextualized to create new interpretations. Artist and designer Monique Goossens frequently challenges expected meanings by constructing letterforms from surprising substances, such as human hair, fish, or frogspawn. Through careful composition, these works interrogate the relationships between their visual qualities and material meanings. In Waste Typography, something previously disregarded is strategically transformed into something thoughtfully formed and considered, using refuse to craft intriguing and engaging letters.

HISTORY AND MATERIAL MEANINGS

Imagine you've discovered a faded and brittle ocean liner ticket in an old book. Materially, it's not worth much to you: the historical typography might be of visual interest, but it's otherwise just water-damaged paper. What would happen, then, if you were to discover that this unimportant ephemera is actually an original ticket to the Titanic in 1912—an artifact which survived in the pocket of a passenger, waterlogged and distressed, as witness to a major historical event? Immediately, this ticket transforms from useless paper to treasured object, highlighting the power of history and "lived" experiences in material objects.

The emotional (and often monetary) value of objects or materials are entwined with their origins and history. This backstory becomes an essential part of its narrative, especially when publicly shared, understood, and re-applied in another context. If a typographic installation is constructed with debris from a well-loved razed building, fur from an extinct animal, leather from world cup winning soccer balls, or with wood from an endangered rainforest—these materials can elicit a strong positive or negative emotional response in reaction to their respective histories. Here, the historical context of a particular material embeds an added layer of significance to the typography.

This is why a genuine autograph adds meaning to a photo, and why counterfeits and forgeries purporting to be real are so devastating to collectors and museums, creating major conflict

Figures 2.44 and 2.45 *Defiant Gardens* by Dario Robleto. © Dario Robleto, 2010. Collection of the Mint Museum, Charlotte, NC. 79½ in. × 61 in. × 4½ in.

Defiant Gardens | Dario Robleto

Dario Robleto's works are detailed and poetic, making thoughtful use of material histories to imbue their structures with additional depth and meaning. His sculptural work *Defiant Gardens* is constructed from the following, as listed from the artist: "cut paper, homemade paper (pulp made from soldiers' letters sent home and wife/sweetheart letters sent to soldiers from various wars, cotton), thread and fabric from soldiers' uniforms of various wars, carrier pigeon skeletons, WWII-era pigeon message capsules, dried flowers from various battlefields, hair flowers braided by war widows, mourning dress fabric, excavated shrapnel and bullet lead from various battlefields, various seeds, various seashells, cartes de visite, gold leaf, silk, ribbon, wood, glass, foam core, and glue." These materials—especially those which witnessed the horrors of war and the depth of loss—saturate the piece and its textual elements with reverence. Profound and pensive in its testament to remembrance, its materiality sparks a transference of meaning and an impetus for empathy.

Figure 2.46 Nicola Costantino Lecture Poster by Sharleen Chen and Dasol Jung. © Sharleen Chen and Dasol Jung, 2015. Reproduced with the permission of Dasol Jung (http://dasoljung.com/) and Sharleen Chen (http://sharleenchen.com/)

Nicola Costantino Lecture Poster | Sharleen Chen and Dasol Jung

The work of Argentinian artist Nicola Costantino probes that which is desirable or repulsive through bodily materials and cast likenesses, such as molds from human skin and stillborn animals. To advertise the event of her artist talk and evoke the feeling of her work, multidisciplinary designers Sharleen Chen and Dasol Jung collaborated on a promotional poster using pig intestines, a pig snout, chicken feet, and a pig heart to form the name of the artist and respective visual embellishments. As viscera from a butchered animal, the material histories of these items mark the life and death of a living creature in an unexpected context, facilitating a strong emotional reaction. Charged with these material histories, an elegant script becomes simultaneously gruesome and appealing.

over issues of perceived and actual authenticity. However, *authenticity* itself is a nebulous term. We might talk about a restaurant having *authentic* Vietnamese cuisine, or remark on the *authenticity* of a politician's impassioned speech. We may comment on the *inauthenticity* of an intentionally worn mass-produced metal sign, signaling visual references to age without *actually* being old. Of course, the use of this term is relative to what something *claims* to be. A new, metal sign *purporting* to be antique is disingenuous; a new, weathered sign among identical others at a department store simply references connotations of its visual language without relying on a true material history. While the definition of *authenticity* refers to facts which can be verified, its common use often refers to what we *perceive* as real—which is not always the same.

MATERIAL METAPHORS AND ANALOGIES

Inherent and socially constructed material meanings are integral to language, especially in idioms, metaphors, or analogies: "People in glass houses shouldn't throw stones;" "Variety is the spice of life;" or "He has a heart of gold." We understand these phrases because of their cultural familiarity, but also because of the inferences made between materials and their respective social meanings. In typographic applications, material qualities and methods of craft can serve as metaphors or analogies on their own, embedding integral meaning in a poetic way.

Material metaphors and analogies showcase conceptual similarities through material choice, construction/destruction, or consequent action. These can be complex, requiring multiple layers of comparison in order for a meaning to be understood. If a word is made from fresh daisies

Figures 2.47 and 2.48 *And Yet* by Keetra Dean Dixon and JK Keller. © 2011. Reproduced with the permission of Keetra Dean Dixon.

And Yet | Keetra Dean Dixon and JK Keller

And Yet is a 150lb. typographic sculpture by artists and designers Keetra Dean Dixon and JK Keller. This evocative object is a visual manifestation of process, showcasing methodically poured wax in layers over positive type forms which are later removed. This is then cut to reveal a shiny, visually rich surface. The act of physical layering creates evidence of time passing, serving as a material analogy to a rumination or an emotional dwelling. As these wax strata ripple out from the original word, they form a robust geode-like structure from an initial thought, a tangible reflection of both process and feeling.

Figures 2.49 and 2.50 *Handprinted Alphabet* by Evelin Kasikov. © Evelin Kasikov, 2011. Photos by Juliet Sheath and Evelin Kasikov. Reproduced with the permission of Evelin Kasikov.

Handprinted Alphabet | Evelin Kasikov

Embroidery and cross-stitch practices are delicate, requiring careful stitching to create a uniform image. In *Handprinted Alphabet*, artist and designer Evelin Kasikov uses embroidery thread and paper as both a craft and material analogy, emulating the many, tiny components easily overlooked within a standard CMYK printing process. Using meticulously stitched cyan, magenta, yellow, and black thread, these works are constructed with care and exactitude, moving "printing" from a mechanized process to a precisely crafted endeavor.

to intentionally wilt and decay, it uses the short life of flowers to represent something beautiful but ephemeral. This serves as an analogy when applied to the text itself. If the words "beauty" or "success" wilt, it illustrates this concept—implying that those things too may be desirable, but fleeting.

Focusing on *how* something is made can also create material analogies. Something meticulously constructed through accumulation of many small objects or actions might speak to slow growth, labor, persistence, or community. References to ideas or objects ceasing to exist may take on the form of an object disappearing, like a knit word unraveling as its concept becomes undone.

Figures 2.51 and 2.52 *DNR (No Code)* by Corbett Fogue. © Corbett Fogue, 2013. Reproduced with the permission of Corbett Fogue.

DNR (No Code) | Corbett Fogue

In healthcare, DNR stands for Do Not Resuscitate, a written patient directive indicating that in the event they should need resuscitation, it should not be initiated, giving individuals agency over their end-of-life terms. Corbett Fogue's *DNR (No Code)* uses a material analogy to create a poignant typographic installation. Over the course of the exhibition, helium-filled balloons reading "DO NOT RESUSCITATE" slowly sink to the floor as their helium dissipates. They are not refilled; they do not rise. These material choices illustrate a powerful and personal reflection on death and loss.

Figure 2.53 *This Time Just the Girls* by Rachelle Vasquez. © Rachelle Vasquez, 2020. Reproduced with the permission of Rachelle Vasquez.

This Time Just the Girls | Rachelle Vasquez

This typographic piece serves as a response to how often women and girls feel obligated to apologize—even when there is no apology needed, or others should apologize instead. In a personal effort to recognize how ingrained this feeling is, artist Rachelle Vasquez took note of her own apologies and those of women around her. A different typographic "Sorry" was crocheted each time until she lost count, demonstrating how ubiquitous these apologies were. Sewn into a blanket, this selection is a physical manifestation of this emotional weight. Each stitch serves as a material analogy to the exhaustive labor of perpetual penance. This piece is a message: women should live their lives freely and confidently—without apologizing for it.

ARCHITECTURAL MATERIALS

Anyone who has ever set foot inside a grand concert hall, pristine museum space, or ornate place of worship can speak to the power of material choice and designed environments in setting the tone of a space. For type *in* architectural spaces, and for letterforms constructed *from* architectural materials, these choices are imperative in crafting messages or communicating a space's intent. Typography constructed from architectural materials creates social signifiers for its audiences. Letterforms in or made from stone, metal, wood, resin, or concrete tend to denote stability or longevity, qualities which are inherent to strong substances. When typographic signage, sculpture, or architectural features require significant exposure to the elements—such as those which are outdoors, on the facade of a building—traditionally architectural materials become obvious choices for durability.

Environmental graphic design typically refers to works which are part of a built environment, such as wall text, wayfinding, or signage, which give specificity to a particular location. When type is used in an environmental or architectural context, it impacts the meanings of the spaces it inhabits. An unfamiliar office building can be made navigable by clear hallway signage, while a banal waiting room can be brightened with a hand-painted typographic wall mural (see "Place-based meanings" later in this chapter). In this context, considerations of scale are essential, especially if the works are going to be viewed from a distance, or with particular lighting. Any typography within an architectural context has the potential to be enormous or all-encompassing, especially if the message is several stories tall.

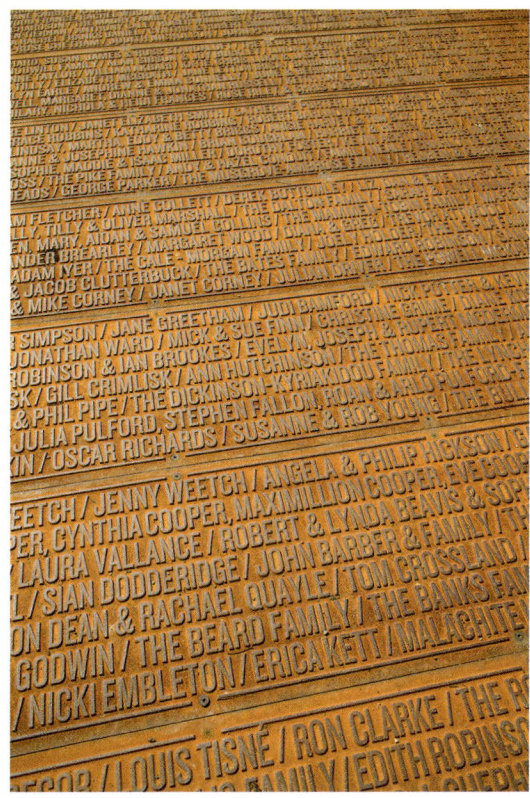

Figure 2.54 *Walk of Art 2* by Gordon Young in collaboration with Andy Altmann. Photography by Josh Young, 2019. Reproduced with the permission of Yorkshire Sculpture Park.

Walk of Art 2 | Gordon Young

In collaboration with Andy Altmann, Gordon Young's *Walk of Art 2* features a plethora of names set in cast iron along a 100-meter-long pathway leading to The Weston, the visitor center of the Yorkshire Sculpture Park in West Bretton, Wakefield, in West Yorkshire, England. Listing the names of the organization's contributors, these plates were meticulously cast and securely set into place. This typographic walkway is both practical and expressive, honoring those who "led the way" through their contributions to the sculpture park. Its material choice is durable and long-lasting for its outdoor location, while its surface features facilitate audience participation: visitors can delight in finding a recognizable name, or may create a rubbing from the raised text. *Walk of Art 2* is a successor to Young's earlier work *Walk of Art* (2002) in which names of donors were cut into stainless steel.

Figures 2.55 and 2.56 *One More Wall Well Done* by Martijn Sandberg, 2016. Photo by Peter Cuypers. *Silence Please Science Please* by Martijn Sandberg, 2017. Photo by Martijn Sandberg.

One More Wall Well Done and *Silence Please Science Please* | Martijn Sandberg

Martijn Sandberg often works with site-specific, architectural typography. His installation *One More Wall Well Done* is located on the southern face of the First Building in Rotterdam, the Netherlands. This large installation, measuring 11.5 ft × 88.5 ft (3.5 m × 27 m), uses brick relief to spell out a phrase on the building's exterior facade. Permanent and impressive in its scale and material, this message uses the medium of an architectural wall to reflect on the hard work of finishing an artwork, celebrating both construction *and* creation.

In addition, his work *Silence Please Science Please* merges a typographic message with a particular architectural function. This installation is in the Gorlaeus Building at the University of Leiden, which houses the Faculty of Science. This series of white-coated perforated aluminum panels is both an artwork and an acoustic wall, featuring a contemplative phrase which can be read in any direction. Measuring 65.5 ft × 23 ft (20 m × 7 m) and prominently featured in an academic building, it architecturally and emotionally supports the pursuit of knowledge by its viewers. Silence is important for studying and creativity, but also reflects the concentration required by scientific research.

A CLOSER LOOK:

Permanent typography?

How do you send a message to the future? This is the quandary of any monument-maker or headstone-carver, whose typographic and material choices are designed and constructed to outlive them. Gravestones, monuments, and memorials are all intended to preserve the memory of a particular person, event, or value for future generations. As such, they are most often constructed from materials which are intended to withstand the test of time—but what happens when they don't?

Widely used in the 1800s, Didone typefaces, informed by the names and qualities of typefaces Didot and Bodoni, are characterized by high contrast and unbracketed, hairline serifs. Their bolder variations, called *fat faces*, originated at the beginning of the nineteenth century. In the United States, gravestones carved in the mid-nineteenth century through the turn of the twentieth century often featured typography similar to what was seen in common print advertisements of the era—which included fat face letterforms.

Because sandblasting wasn't invented until 1870, headstone typography relied on the expertise of engravers and the labor of hand-carving. Softer stones, such as slate, marble, or locally available limestone (especially in the American Midwest) made carving delicate ornate letterforms easier. However, the combination of softer stone and delicate hairline serifs has proved problematic, as typography intended to be permanent has become less timeless than intended. On many headstones of this era, over 100 years of weathering and acid rain has worn down these delicate features, making the names, dates, and relations on many historical headstones increasingly difficult to decipher. Thankfully, this issue is less common on contemporary headstones, which are largely made from more durable granite, or may feature cast bronze plaques, securing legible text for years to come.

What happens, then, when permanent materials require revision? The Gettysburg National Military Park in Gettysburg, PA, features approximately 1,328 monuments, markers, and memorials commemorating the places, people, and actions of the harrowing 1863 battle. One such monument is the

Figures 2.57 and 2.58 Headstone typography. © photos by Mia Cinelli, 2021. Reproduced with the permission of The Lexington Cemetery.

Nineteenth-Century Headstone Typography

These images of nineteenth-century engraved letters (from headstones in The Lexington Cemetery, in Lexington, Kentucky) show their consequent weathering over time. Because thinner hairline strokes are more delicate, they disappear first. Consequently, important information like dates may be misread—such as this date from 1844 which appears more like 1S11. The large text on this 1862 headstone is faded, but still visible. Unfortunately, the delicate, smaller subtext on this headstone has become so eroded it can no longer be read.

Pennsylvania Memorial, the largest of the state memorials in the park, which features large, cast-metal tablets of names designed and crafted with extreme durability in mind. A close look at these textual portions of the monument reveals that while most of these names still exist with complete clarity—some have been carefully but noticeably filed off—erasing a previously present, permanent name. Why is this? At the time of its commission, surviving soldiers assisted in assembling the names of those individuals on duty near, or engaged in, the battle. When the Gettysburg Battlefield Memorial Commission asked surviving veterans about errors in 1910, corrections were made to the monument in 1914 with the knowledge from those who had witnessed the events firsthand. Consequently, and perhaps ironically, this clarifying information resulted in the removal of text intended to be everlasting.

These examples speak to the complexity of architectural materials and their relationship to typographic meaning relative to permanence. Durable materials yield durable messages—shedding light on a question on the type of our present. What architectural materials available today will best carry our typographic messages forward into the future? Furthermore, what messages do we want to send?

Figures 2.59 and 2.60 The Pennsylvania Memorial. Photos by Jason Martz, 2022, courtesy of National Park Service, Gettysburg National Military Park.

The Pennsylvania Memorial, Gettysburg National Military Park
Cast-metal plates feature names on the Pennsylvania Memorial at Gettysburg National Military Park. These images showcase both the corrections made in 1914 and the physical effort inherent in altering an otherwise long-lasting material.

Public Space

Notions of public and private spaces are determined by who has access, when, and by what means. Public spaces typically refer to places which are intended to be open and accessible to everyone, such as city parks, public squares, roads, woods, or beaches. These areas often become social spaces, hubs of community events and outreach, making them ideal locations for protests, vigils, or marathons. It is important to note accessibility remains a challenge in many public spaces, rendering them out of reach to specific communities: if a town square only has steps to enter the plaza, or a city beachfront has no wheelchair access—is it truly public and accessible to everyone?

At times, public spaces can be converted to private spaces through the establishment of a physical or monetary barrier. A public park may set up seating and charge admission to view an outdoor theatrical production, creating temporarily a private space by which access is restricted. Even within otherwise private spaces, people can generally determine what is public and private through social norms. At a friend's apartment for a dinner party, the living room, kitchen, and bathroom are openly navigated. However, moving the event into someone's bedroom would feel invasive, breaching the socially acknowledged norm of what private and public spaces are in that particular circumstance.

Social constructs of space are complex and subject to power structures and cultural standards. In Sweden, the "Right of Public Access" grants citizens and visitors the right to camp or traverse wherever they would like, with the exceptions of private gardens, on land being cultivated, or within a specific distance of existing dwellings. While a source of pride for the Swedish, this concept may feel completely unfamiliar to another cultural audience. In addition, the concept of public or private *land ownership* itself is indicative of a larger power structure: across the globe, designated public or private spaces are on land stolen from Indigenous people, the result of forced removal by colonizers.

When typography exists in public spaces, it creates opportunities for wide viewership and interaction, both desirable and destructive. Typographic signs, installations, and sculptures are subject to human interventions, weather, ecological conditions, as well as space-based histories and constraints—highlighting the opportunities and challenges inherent in public space.

PLACE-BASED MEANING

All places have unique meanings informed by culture, history, and geography as interpreted by their respective residents and visitors. Because *where* something lives impacts *what* it means, typographic applications in physical spaces have the capacity to influence—and be influenced by—the particular places they inhabit. While these meanings are subjective, there is always a negotiation between what a space represents, what type in use communicates, and how these indicators influence or override one another.

For this reason, the same message is likely to elicit different meanings in different locations. A "THANK YOU" banner hung at an office retirement is appropriately celebratory; if unfurled on Omaha Beach in France (the site of the Battle of Normandy, in which thousands lost their lives during the Second World War) its meaning shifts, becoming an earnest, solemn, or poignant display of gratitude. While not every space has a known past, sites of major events are all but inextricable from their histories. As such, typography *within* those spaces is subject to the same historical impact and consequence, undoubtedly influencing how the work is viewed and understood.

In less emotionally or historically charged places, typography may have greater opportunity to define and influence space. These can be permanent or temporary, like the projected works of American artist Jenny Holzer, whose work includes larger-than-life textual projections which drape buildings or cities in evocative phrases such as "YOU ARE MY OWN." These texts shift the perception of the places they cover, *and* are informed by such, if only temporarily. Works which are *site-specific* are intentionally created for particular locations, reflecting on or responding to the geography, architecture, or history of an environment. Their specificity binds them to their location, as their intended meaning is contextually dependent on their precise physical surroundings. Spaces can also be activated by site-specific *typographic interventions*, which integrate images or installations within built or natural environments, often covertly.

A CLOSER LOOK:
I amsterdam

What happens when a typographic installation and public location influence each other in an unexpected way? In 2004, creative communications agency KesselsKramer developed an identity campaign for their home city of Amsterdam, using the play on words "I amsterdam" to celebrate pride in its cultural characteristics and diverse population. As part of this campaign, a massive three-dimensional sculpture of the *I amsterdam* logotype (set in clean, solid Avenir), was placed near the entrance to the renowned Rijksmuseum on the Museumplein, a public space surrounded by several major museums.

This particular placement—and its consequent impact—showcases the power of type in public space. Intentionally set in close physical proximity to several popular cultural institutions, the sculpture's location catalyzed a perfect opportunity for audience engagement. However, because of its conspicuous size, physical interactivity, and public accessibility, this installation became its *own* tourist destination. Shown here in this photo, visitors to the city frequently flocked to the Museumplein to climb the letters, peek through their giant counters, or stop for a photo opportunity. This confluence promoted positive interaction with the city's graphic identity while attracting visitors to a well-known location's beloved establishments. How, then, did this immensely popular sculpture come to be removed in 2018?

As visitor interactions with the *I amsterdam* sculpture changed, so did the public place it inhabited; the space of the Museumplein was transformed by the work itself. Because of the letters' popularity, the location became perpetually crowded with visitors vying for a photograph, sparking debate on the impact of mass tourism on the city and its local residents. As reported in the Dutch newspaper *Het Parool* in 2018, Femke Roosma, a member of the left-wing party *GroenLinks*, cited concern that the *I amsterdam* campaign promoted "the city as a product," and that the letters valued "individualism" rather than "solidarity and diversity."

A motion to remove the letters was submitted to the city, and consequently approved. In December 2018, the *I amsterdam* sculpture was officially removed from the Museumplein. According to the official *iamsterdam* website, "These letters were removed at the request of the City of Amsterdam because they were drawing too big of a crowd to an already limited space" while noting that visitors can still find *I amsterdam* sculptures at Schiphol Airport, as well as in touring locations around the Netherlands.

The rise and fall of an iconic textual sculpture highlights the dynamic relationship between type and the public place it inhabits. While the letters may be gone from the Museumplein, their popular impact lives on. Cities around the globe have emulated this approach by designing and installing their own similar city-specific typographic sculptures—like "We Ramallah" in Ramallah, Palestine or "ONLY LYON" in Lyon, France.

Figure 2.61 Photo by Jennie Remida on Unsplash.

Figures 2.62–2.64 PENSAR/SENTIR by Boa Mistura. © Boa Mistura, 2014. Reproduced with the permission of Boa Mistura.

PENSAR/SENTIR | Boa Mistura

Boa Mistura, a Madrid-based creative team, specializes in large-scale, site-specific typographic murals and interventions. In Panama City, Panama, *Ciudad del Saber* (City of Knowledge) is home to a range of government and academic organizations. Repeating architectural features on the facade of a 1965 house-of-worship turned exhibition-center created a unique surface for exploring multiple perspectives. Carefully planned and painted to account for scale and vantage points, this large 98 ft × 25 ft (30 m × 8 m) installation changes depending on the view. From one direction, it reads PENSIR (think), from another, SENTIR (feel). According to the artists, this intersection of *thinking* and *feeling* results in *wisdom* and *knowledge*. Crafted with students from Isthmus of Panama School of Architecture, these vibrant texts are informed by both their visual and conceptual overlap and their location within a learning environment.

Giving Type Meaning

Figure 2.65 Photo by Sifan Liu on Unsplash.

Black Lives Matter Mural | District of Columbia Department of Public Works and MuralsDC

In the summer of 2020, a series of global protests against police brutality and racism were catalyzed by the murder of George Floyd in Minneapolis, Minnesota, in the United States. That June, a section of 16th Street NW in Washington DC was painted with the phrase "BLACK LIVES MATTER," along with the three stars and two stripes of the DC Flag. Produced by the District of Columbia Department of Public Works and MuralsDC, its resonance lies in both its scale and location; its 40-foot letters live a mere two blocks from the White House. This mural visually and emotionally activated the space, which was officially renamed Black Lives Matter Plaza. Variations on this mural have since been adapted by various organizations in cities around the globe—including in New York City, on Fifth Avenue, in front of Trump Tower, intentionally challenging political power structures with its placement and proximity.

However, the mural faced criticism from advocacy groups as being performative—focusing on visibility rather than real policy change. To voice this concern, the DC Chapter of Black Lives Matter modified the mural and added their own text: erasing the stars to create an equal sign, the mural then read "BLACK LIVES MATTER = DEFUND THE POLICE." In August 2020, this portion of the mural was paved over following planned road work, according to city officials. These actions demonstrate how debates about power, visibility, and equality manifest typographically in public space. It raises the question: who determines what public messaging should be visible in a public space, and what is its true impact?

PUBLIC TYPE + COMMUNITY PARTICIPATION

Public spaces are ideal for commercial and utilitarian signage like billboards and street signs, as their locations are accessible and can easily reach a wide audience. While type in public space has the ability to inform and direct, it can also represent collective values or individual voices—especially when it is the result of community initiatives rather than corporate messaging. Because public spaces are frequent gathering locations for friends or organizations, these spaces are prime locations for public engagement, inclusion, and interaction.

Works relying on community participation create meaning through both their physical *and* social contexts. When created and accessed in a public space, typography has the power to activate, disrupt, or embellish otherwise overlooked areas. Whether part of an individually led project or collaborative art initiative, the act of creating something together ties individuals to a shared experience. When successful, this collective action builds teamwork, trust, and connection between participants. These experiences also empower individuals to become stakeholders in their communities, expressing themselves through direct involvement in how their public spaces look and function.

Figures 2.66 and 2.67 *Our Shoulders*, The Whispers Project by Amanda Grondal, Eli Horn, and Jordan Bent. © Eli Horn/Amanda Grondal, 2012. *The Morning of the Sale*, The Whispers Project by Paul Antony Carr, Eli Horn, and Jordan Bent. © Eli Horn/Paul Antony Carr 2012. Reproduced with the permission of Eli Horn.

Whispers | Amanda Grondal, Eli Horn, Jordan Bent, Paul Antony Carr

As painted prose, *Whispers* recontextualizes a history of advertising text and expectations of public signage to amplify poetics and creative writing. Together, Amanda Grondal, Eli Horn, Jordan Bent, and Paul Antony Carr worked closely with community members to solicit new original works from local writing groups in Vancouver. These texts were painted as typographic installations on the sides of buildings in a custom typeface referencing commercial hand-lettering. Appearing in unexpected public contexts, these installations are informed by the community they inhabit—transforming ordinary spaces through poetry, igniting opportunities for conversation and discovery.

Giving Type Meaning

Figure 2.68 *BLACK IS* by Ciara LeRoy. © Pretty Strange Design/Ciara LeRoy. Poetry contributed by Terrill Thurman. 2020. Reproduced with the permission of Ciara LeRoy.

BLACK IS | Ciara LeRoy

Ciara LeRoy is the artist behind Pretty Strange Design, specializing in vibrant and invigorating hand-lettering, embroidery, and mural work. Painted on a brick facade in downtown Lexington, Kentucky, her piece *BLACK IS* is a public typographic mural celebrating Black lives. This mural engages with the community through both its public placement and its development. Lines of poetry were contributed by Terrill Thurman, and the artist surveyed Black residents of Lexington for additional words to include in the mural, which are *beautiful*, *unapologetic*, *innovative*, and *resilient*. This public message is proud, positive, and determined in its proclamation: Black Lives Matter. As a message of celebration and encouragement for the Black community, it is also a call to non-Black residents to dismantle systems of racism, inequality, and oppression.

Figures 2.69 and 2.70 *You Are Beautiful* ® by Matthew Hoffman. © Matthew Hoffman, ongoing project est. 2002. Reproduced with the permission of © Matthew Hoffman, You Are Beautiful ®.

You Are Beautiful | Matthew Hoffman

You Are Beautiful began in 2002, when Matthew Hoffman, a Chicago-based artist and designer, printed 100 stickers featuring a simple but encouraging phrase: "you are beautiful." Sold or given away to others, their dissemination was the result of sharing and sticking— peppering the public landscape with a kind and direct message, transforming otherwise banal objects into beacons of positive encouragement. Since then, it has grown into a global undertaking fueled by community participation. The text on these small but powerful stickers has been printed millions of times in over 100 languages; the project now includes public sculptures, signs, murals, billboards, and products. Here, the classic silver sticker showcases the power of typographic interventions, while a large-scale *You Are Beautiful* sculpture brings a warm, vibrant message to a public waterfront.

Giving Type Meaning

Figure 2.71 *Before I Die* by Candy Chang. © Candy Chang, 2011.

Before I Die | Candy Chang
Following the death of a loved one, Taiwanese-American artist Candy Chang painted a pensive prompt on the side of an abandoned house in her neighborhood in New Orleans, stenciling the words "Before I die I want to ___" onto exterior walls coated with chalkboard paint. This public pondering was immediately filled with responses by the community, and continued to grow into a public forum of personal goals, hopes, and dreams. Reflecting a shared humanity, this public installation provided a cathartic way to reflect. Through shared online resources and encouragement of the artist, thousands of *Before I Die* walls have been created in over 75 countries, facilitating frameworks for connection.

Figure 2.72 Sidewalk Poetry is a program of Public Art Saint Paul (PASP) and the City of Saint Paul. PASP City Artist Marcus Young began the program in 2008 under his trademark name of "Everyday Poems for City Sidewalks." Images reproduced with the permission of Public Art Saint Paul (PASP).

INTERVIEW

Public Art Saint Paul | Sidewalk Poetry

How might city infrastructure become an avenue for discovery? In what ways can typography in public spaces spark elation or connection?

In partnership with the City of Saint Paul, Minnesota, in the United States, Public Art Saint Paul (PASP) is a private nonprofit organization working to create spaces which are more beautiful and inclusive through public art initiatives. Artist and educator Aaron Dysart serves as their City Artist; in this position, he works to coordinate communication between artists and the city and uses the "systems of the city as his media," taking into consideration how infrastructure and actions can be creatively shifted or engaged to create a more equitable and just society. In this interview, edited for clarity and length, he discusses the detailed planning and positive impact of Sidewalk Poetry, an ongoing public art project in which original poems are stamped onto city sidewalks.

Could you tell me a little about how this project first began—and how it manifests now?

Sure! Sidewalk poetry began as a project of a past City Artist-in-Residence, Marcus Young 楊墨. As I understand its origin story: as he was walking down the sidewalk, he began to think about how contractors often put a little stamp in the corner of the concrete, stating when it was stamped and who stamped it. He thought, "if we can stamp a name in there, why can't we stamp poetry?" and approached public works. In our city—as in most cities—there is a sidewalk reconstruction program, where an inspector goes through the city and flags sections of sidewalks that need to be replaced because they've cracked, or roots have pushed them up, etc. Marcus's thought was: wouldn't it be great if while we fix the city, we publish poetry at the same time? This project began in 2008 under his original title "Everyday Poems for City Sidewalks." To source poems written by Saint Paul residents, they ran a contest helped by the Saint Paul Library.

Regarding how it is implemented now, one of my roles [as City Artist] is to oversee the stamping of the poems. We hire a coordinator who goes out with our collection of stamps and follows the sidewalk crew around for the summer. I think we have close to 70 poems in our collection. [We've created] about 1,200 stampings across the whole city. These poems, once they're made into a stamp, are used repeatedly—basically indefinitely.

That's incredible! Is the location of each poem relative to its surroundings intentional or arbitrary? What physical considerations are made relative to their placement?

So, the answer is both. From a systems standpoint, where the poems are located can only follow the sidewalk reconstruction program, which distributes them fairly equally around the city. What I love about this is no matter how much political power you have, or how much money you have—you don't get a poem unless your sidewalk's getting fixed, as determined by the sidewalk inspector. It follows the system of the city.

When there is a sidewalk being reconstructed, I charge our stamping coordinators (who for the last two seasons, both write poetry themselves) to take in the area and consider what makes sense based on the content in the collection. We don't want the same poem stamped again and again, and we should continually rotate through our collection. There is a maximum of three poems per full city block. I feel my role is to try to hold to Marcus's artistic intent here regarding surprise notions of joy.

If there is a poem on every sidewalk panel, they become common and therefore overlooked, so this notion of surprise and being a bit more sparse—as opposed to pure numbers—is much more important.

Each panel is considered by physical limitations of the project area. Some of the bigger stamps require a person on either end to use, but if it's up against a building, you can't get somebody on the other side. As far as type layout, I charge our coordinators to think of the text block within the panel of the sidewalk, and to work with the public. If somebody requests a specific poem, we'll do our best, but we don't take the whole collection with us—it just doesn't fit in the truck.

The production process is also really complicated: concrete dries at different times based on temperature, air, humidity, and how much it's mixed. We had a heart-wrenching thing where a coordinator had a poem stamped in front of a poet's house. When they stepped away, a squirrel had walked all over the wet concrete, so they had to brush it all out … and the poem was gone. It's one of these things that's super beloved, but also kind of fickle—which makes it all the more special when it actually happens.

This project relies heavily on community participation. How are these poems selected?

For the first few years of the project—beginning in 2008, through 2013—we held a contest every year through Public Art Saint Paul, where a panel of poets selected the poems. It's actually really hard to get selected. We typically select at least four and at maximum eight poems out of 600–700 applicants. It's considered a really big honor to have your poem selected. There is a maximum character count, poems cannot be religious or political (as these are stamped on city property) and applicants have to be residents of Saint Paul. The last competitions were held in 2015, 2019, and 2021. Public Art Saint Paul hires someone to put that panel together—typically local spoken-word artists or poets who have a different background or orientation than perhaps our staff at Public Arts Saint Paul.

How has the Saint Paul community responded to these works?

To say this program is beloved is an understatement. Where else can you get people literally freaking out that their sidewalk is being redone because they might get a poem in front of their house? We have people who are desperate to get a poem. One thing we do is that if you don't want a poem, you won't get one. Everyone getting their sidewalk redone gets a flyer, and if they call into the city and say "I don't want one" they won't get one. But when people do request it, which is much, much, much more often, we do our best.

People get really excited to have a poem stamped on their sidewalk, but there is a lot of excitement for people to submit their poems as well. People want to know where their poems have been stamped. I have such beautiful stories from the stamping coordinators of people "cheersing" beers over finally getting a poem in front of their houses. People cheering—it's super exciting.

Are all the poems set in the same typeface? What typefaces were chosen, and how were they selected?

No—but I can't give you the name of the typefaces because I'm not a typographer. In my role, I work with graphic designers on this project to create stamps out of a specific type of plastic that needs to go into concrete. The type is mostly sans serif, and a bit simpler, because the less complicated it is, the less the concrete will move. I try to shoot for letters which are at least an inch tall, if not taller, for legibility, and a lot of kerning goes on because we're pushing this material around. Lastly, we look at the interiors of letterforms—like those of o's and a's—because if those pillars [of concrete] are too narrow, they're going to snap off when we are shoveling snow. My concerns are a bit more physical. I ensure that the stamps will be legible, hold up, and stamp well. I teach art and design, and know enough about type to know that I don't know enough about type; I hire experts and give them free rein with these constraints, asking them to figure out which font works best with the content.

In the last two iterations, we finally went to non-English languages, which had been a desire ever since the program started. There wasn't any sort of political will why we hadn't—it was the notion that many non-English languages use a lot of different accent marks, and there was a concern about its legibility in the material. We now have Spanish, Hmong, Dakota, and Somali. The Dakota is very accent heavy, so we've worked with our designers to ensure the letterforms fit with this materiality. It's one of the more exciting things we've done. It was finally just making sure we were working with the right materials so it was actually legible within the concrete.

What does Public Art Saint Paul hope these poems mean to visitors who discover them for the first time?

I'll return to Marcus's artistic vision here: it's this notion of small art and unexpected joy. Myself and the other folks at Public Art Saint Paul are much more interested in this notion of integrated public art. Rather than focus on the big, fancy thing that's in front of the expensive building that only a few people get to see, we consider how art can be integrated into the fabric of our lives. When smaller, it actually gets into neighborhoods where people don't expect it.

It's a happy and unexpected moment, to be walking, to look down, and see a poem.

If you look at the map of where poems are, it's the entire city, rather than where just a few people live. To me, it's much more egalitarian and creates a broader impact.

If you think about it, most of our lives are kind of in that middle ground—where it's not absolutely terrible, but it's not euphoria and transcendence.

Those moments are here and important, but the vast majority of our lives are our day-to-day, and that's where art belongs as well. I think what we're trying to do is reimagine the critical infrastructure of our lives. I am an advocate in this city for art, but also for this way of thinking—to try and create a city that people want to live in. If our bar is purely utilitarian, asking "is it going to work?," I think we can do better than that—like getting people excited about new sidewalks, because new sidewalks are awesome! Infrastructure and city systems support our lives, but we only think about them when they're broken. How can we think about them when they're joyful as well?

Figures 2.73–2.75 Images reproduced with the permission of Public Art Saint Paul (PASP).

Private Space

Private spaces are created by barriers to entry or access, making their limited accessibility a tenet of their definition. However, this isn't inherently negative: privacy is important, and is required in many spaces for commerce, security, or personal reasons. After all, *absolutely no one* is excited about finding themselves in a public bathroom stall with a door which does not latch.

Galleries and museums occupy a unique position as spaces which are sometimes private, and other times public. While museums and galleries both offer exhibitions of creative works, there are subtle differences to their intentions. Broadly speaking, art museums tend to be more educational in nature and often house permanent collections which may include both contemporary and historical works. Commercial galleries typically showcase works through exhibitions with opportunities or intentions to sell the pieces on display. In either of these contexts, both the architecture and accessibility of these spaces contribute to the meaning of works they choose to display.

Artists exhibit their works in museums and galleries for many reasons—including their social and spatial advantages. Socially, visitors to museums and galleries do so with the express intention of viewing, experiencing, or purchasing art, making these contexts ideal for engaged viewers or economic opportunity. Curators and museum docents can expertly explain histories and contexts of work, and in many spaces, community programming offers opportunities for school groups or new visitors to interact with exhibited work. The physical context of a museum or gallery's built environment allows for typographic installations and experimental practices which are simply not possible in other spatial contexts. Blank walls, large adaptable spaces, dedicated project rooms, and professional lighting systems create flexible locations for creating and viewing text-based installations, performances, or artworks.

To many people, most exhibition spaces appear as pristine, white-walled, impartial venues, providing a neutral space to view art—but this does not consider the many facets of an organization's context. While manicured surfaces and ample space may provide a less cluttered visual field, museums and galleries are *not* actually neutral spaces. The makeup of the museum's board, what is shown in exhibitions—by whom—and the provenance of their collection all contribute to a museum's stance on current social and political issues. Museums are reflective of the people who run them, which means that as the individuals who compose museum teams change, so do the works shown in the museum—reflecting new ideas or values over time. Ergo, the spatial *and* social contexts of museum spaces are entwined with the meaning of works displayed within them.

Though many museums feature substantial and accessible online viewing, any work existing in a museum collection is only *physically* available to those who can enter the space itself. Therefore, access facilitates or limits viewership. Many museums charge for admission, but others are free due to sponsorships or governmental support, especially for young people, which increases the circle of viewers who can see, discuss, and interact with works of art. While financial barriers to entry do serve as limitations, they are the reality of many arts institutions who rely on these monetary resources to exist and support exhibitions. When artworks are purchased by private *individuals*, access to works may disappear entirely at the discretion of their owners.

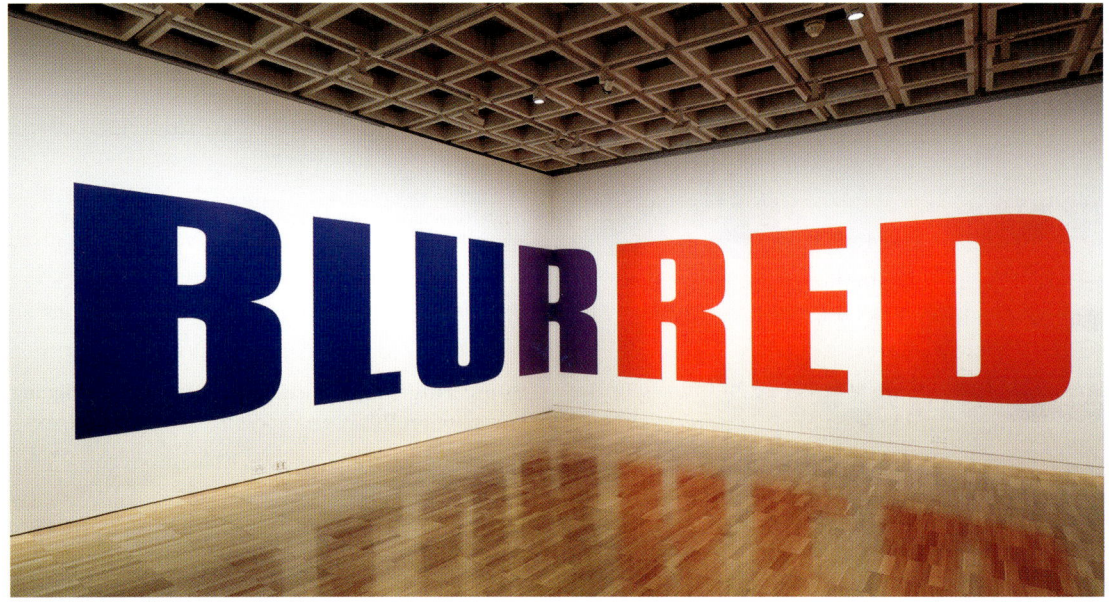

Figure 2.76 *BLURRED* by Kay Rosen. © Kay Rosen, 2004. Reproduced with permission of the artist and Sikkema Jenkins & Co., New York. Installation view: Colourwheel, Art Gallery New South Wales, Sydney, 2015. Photo: Mim Stirling.

BLURRED | Kay Rosen

Kay Rosen's text-based work explores the intersections of language, form, and meaning. Her large wall-painting *BLURRED* features text which can be read on multiple levels, and in a variety of ways. Language of transition is expressed in a gradient from blue (BLU) to red (RED), referring to both the word choice and hue-structures represented. Its spatial placement is also important: it is intentionally installed into a gallery's corner wall, at a large, architectural intersection. The single purple R lives in this junction, connecting the two halves and two colors. Perhaps referencing opposing political parties, this installation invites contemplation of values, identity, diplomacy, or transition.

Figure 2.77 LAWRENCE WEINER, & GIVEN & REPLACED, 2009. Language + the materials referred to, dimensions variable. © Lawrence Weiner; Courtesy Lisson Gallery.

& GIVEN & REPLACED | Lawrence Weiner

The conceptual works of the late Lawrence Weiner have been shown globally in major museums, though they are not exclusively intended for private or gallery spaces: others have lived in a variety of contexts, such as in outdoor parks or on facades of buildings. In all instances, language is explored as its own material to create sculpture, through evocative depictions of descriptive or poetic phrases. Many of these works are set in a custom typeface designed by the artist, called Margaret Seaworthy Gothic.

Figure 2.78 *Pay Nothing Until April* by Ed Ruscha. © Ed Ruscha, 2003. Reproduced with the permission of Ed Ruscha Studio.

Pay Nothing Until April | Ed Ruscha

With a practice informed by both fine and commercial art practices, Ed Ruscha's text-based artworks have been associated with the pop-art movement of the 1960s. His works often recontextualize promotional language of advertising into the context of paintings, using rectilinear letterforms of the artist's own creation, which he calls *Boy Scout Utility Modern*. In his 2003 work *Pay Nothing Until April*, everyday text is set against a majestic mountainscape creating an intriguing juxtaposition. While we expect to see advertising text on billboards, its presence on a painting in a gallery challenges audiences to interpret these phrases as informed by their new context.

Figure 2.79 Nari Ward, *We The People*, 2011. Shoelaces. 96 in. × 324 in./243.8 cm × 823 cm. In collaboration with The Fabric Workshop and Museum, Philadelphia. Collection of Speed Art Museum, Louisville, KY, 2016.1. Courtesy the artist and Lehmann Maupin, New York, Hong Kong, Seoul, and London. Photo by Will Brown.

We The People | Nari Ward

Nari Ward is a Jamaican-American artist who often recontextualizes found or discarded materials to discuss topics of race, consumer culture, and poverty. In his work *We The People*, a plethora of differing length shoelaces are installed via holes in a gallery wall to form a recognizable, historic phrase—the preamble to the United States constitution. Making use of recontextualization as well as material and spatial meanings, the diverse, individual strands serve as a metaphor, intentionally open to interpretation by the numerous visitors who encounter and interact with this large (96 in. × 324 in. (2.4 m × 8.2 m)) and detailed work. The reinterpretation of this text poses questions to its viewers: at the time of its writing, who did *We The People* refer to? Who does it refer to now?

CHALLENGING PRIVATE SPACE

What should be private and what should be public? Socially, what is understood as private space, and what happens when that space is disrupted? What are the consequences when a public space suddenly becomes inaccessible? These queries are in perpetual flux with shifting societal values and power structures. While some text-based works *live* in private spaces, others explore the concept of private space itself. Textual installations, interventions, and performances can purposely question the concepts of private and public space and their respective notions of access, information, or transparency.

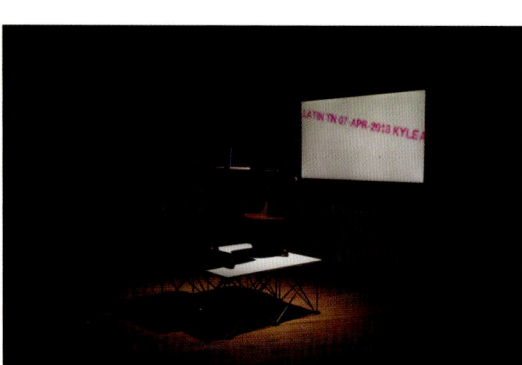

Figures 2.80–2.82 *Alternative Rule* by Matt Kenyon. © Matt Kenyon, 2020. Reproduced with the permission of Matt Kenyon/S.W.A.M.P. (Studies of Work Atmosphere and Mass Production).

Alternative Rule | Matt Kenyon

At first glance, *Alternative Rule* appears to be an ordinary piece of penmanship paper, like those frequently found in elementary school classrooms. These standard sheets feature familiar solid and dashed lines, giving guidance to small hands learning to write. However, in this work created by designer and new media artist Matt Kenyon, these ruled lines contain microprinted names and dates of the many children who have been victims of gun violence since the 1999 Columbine High School shooting. Recontextualizing a form of common ephemera as both a commemoration of loss and an agent for change, viewers are encouraged to write to their respective representatives using the paper, urging them to take action against gun violence. This action interrogates private space by subversively placing this powerful, poignant work onto the desks of government officials—questioning how and where a memorial to an ongoing tragedy should live.

Figure 2.83 *TSA Communication* by Evan Roth. © Evan Roth, 2008. Reproduced with the permission of Evan Roth.

TSA Communication | Evan Roth

Airports are complicated locations. In an age of increased security measures, expectations of public and private space often collide in the security screening line. Named for the agency of the United States Department of Homeland Security's Transportation Security Administration (TSA), Evan Roth's *TSA Communication* explores this complexity through a typographic intervention. Cut sheets of stainless steel placed in a standard carry-on bag communicate provocative messages about privacy, such as "mind your own business" or "nothing to see here." When scanned, they appear on the screen of a TSA agent, obscuring the bag's contents. This prompts a bag search, facilitating a new interaction between artist and agent. Intended to be earnest, discursive, and performative in their very nature, these interventions prompt conversation on issues of free speech, privacy, and security theater.

A CLOSER LOOK:

Graffiti

For millennia, humans have been visually altering surfaces. From petroglyphs to carved stone, publicly marking our names, relationships, or ideas into or onto our surroundings seems nearly instinctive, transcending time, culture, material, and language. Even graffiti, from the Italian word *graffio*, or *scratch*, speaks to the origins and intent of such surface manipulation. However, the meaning of such markings can vary widely as informed by their respective spatial and social contexts.

Why is a city-sponsored mural lauded as public art, while an equally impressive, unsanctioned composition scorned as graffiti? Here, meaning is formulated through a matter of space, permission, and power structures. Where an image is made, who it is made by, and who does (or does not) approve it, all inform the labels of *public art*, *street art*, *graffiti*, and *tagging*. While *public art* is a broad category of creative works which live in public spaces, *street art* tends to refer to works outside of traditional exhibition spaces, existing publicly on or within the built landscape. As broad categories, public art and street art are defined by their location, but can vary in their respective *authorization*. After all, street art can be public art—but not all public art is street art.

Though graffiti has taken many forms throughout history—and lacks an absolute definition—its contemporary understanding refers to text or images marked in public locations *without permission*. *Tagging* exists as a graffiti practice by which a particular artist's name (often an alias) is written or adhered to a surface or structure as a way to mark territory or one's presence. While there are many catalysts for their creation, these works often speak to establishing power by reclaiming space. Sharing an idea or identity publicly can foster a sense of individual agency. In this context, private property in public space—such as overpasses, train cars, or building facades—become ideal, albeit illegal, canvases. When created without authorization, these works are both defined and contextualized by their relationship to the power structures of ownership and permission.

Therefore, what graffiti *means* is complicated and rarely concrete. Because of its often-illicit origins, graffiti is frequently affiliated with vandalism, gang territory, or architectural

Figures 2.84 and 2.85 Photos by Mia Cinelli, 2021.

Graffiti

Because those creating graffiti can face arrest or hefty fines, it works in the best interest for those covertly leaving their mark to do so expeditiously, often under a pseudonym. Easily attainable markers or spray paint can facilitate quick mark-making, frequently affiliating graffiti with its common means-of-making in the twentieth and twenty-first centuries. These methods and materials have informed the gestural forms and recognizably stylized letters which can be difficult to discern. Typographically, works or typefaces emulating textual graffiti reference the act of its making *and* respective spatial contexts—alluding to something spirited, subversive, or edgy.

neglect. However, there are many intersecting historical and social factors which catalyze how, why, and when people choose to mark text in public space—far more than can be discussed in this text, alone. As such, graffiti can exist as many things, including as a form of activism, giving a platform to voices which might otherwise lack a visible avenue for communication (see "Power structures" in Chapter 1 and "Public type + community participation" in this chapter). In addition, because graffiti directly addresses both space and power dynamics, it has been unfortunately used for purposes of discrimination and intimidation. Not all graffiti is good in its content *or* concept—especially that which contains threats or hate speech, which are never acceptable.

The meaning of graffiti is partially informed by its covert genesis. An enormous tag or typographic piece is impressive through both its scale and *existence*, the result of an effort to create something unsolicited in a public context. The presence of graffiti in public space by private or obscured authors presents an unusual quest for attention of their makers—a desire to be seen, but not always known. Therefore, the private and public negotiation of which spaces belong to whom contributes to what graffiti communicates. The discourse of *what* public space should look like and *who* has a voice in their built environment prompts continued questions on how permission, public space, private property, and personal expression intersect.

Personal Space

Who are you, and how do you let other people know who you are? Clearly, self-identity is demonstrated in a variety of ways, including what we believe, how we behave, and the cultural activities we recognize and participate in. In 1959, sociologist Erving Goffman's book *The Presentation of Self in Everyday Life* outlined what has become known as *self-presentation theory*—an individual's desire to influence how others perceive them. Depending on the audience and context, individuals change their self-presentation in an attempt to impact how others may regard them. Situationally, people tailor how they speak, how they act, and what they wear in order to facilitate a particular impression. Therefore, when we think about what we want our presence to communicate to others and what we want our identities to *mean*, the curation of our personal spaces becomes deeply important.

Colloquially, "personal space," refers to proximity to our bodies or the immediate space we inhabit. When we choose to include typography in our personal spaces, it influences our self-presentation, becoming an integral part of our self-expression, a shorthand for who we are and what we believe in. This is particularly evident in how our public affinities shape our identities. Consider the sports teams you support, the brands you like, your political party, or your institutional affiliation. When you share these associations with a wider audience through typography in your personal space, such as through logos on your clothing, stickers on your computer, or a lawn sign in your yard—you do so with the understanding that they are social signifiers, communicating to others who you are and what you value. In many instances, their intimate physical proximity to your body or personal space implies a connection, fondness, or closeness.

While we use personal typography to represent our own personalities, we also use these signifiers to determine the beliefs of others. However, it's important to discern that perception is not always reality, and the entirety of someone's personality is rarely distilled to their personal effects. People are complex. Their beliefs and behaviors are often at odds with each other, reinforcing the notion that the identities we project aren't always a reflection of reality.

APPAREL AND AFFILIATION

Why do you want to wear brand-name apparel? Individuals purchase recognizable, brand-name clothing and accessories for a variety of reasons, including aesthetics, quality, or preference of fit—but the personal performance of identity is difficult to ignore. We associate the qualities of particular brands with real or aspirational social status or personal qualities. By including these brands in our personal spaces or on our bodies, we choose to affiliate ourselves with them and their respective associations.

In choosing to sport a Coach bag, we may suggest we value exclusive, high-end accessories, demonstrating affluence or a commitment to sharp fashion. Choosing Nike apparel might seek a particular affiliation with determination, speed, and athleticism. Conspicuous brand-name placement on clothing, bags, or other garments highlights the power and presence of brand typography as a label of expression and personal identity (see "Power structures" in Chapter 1). Personal typography communicates the intent of its wearer, but can also be influenced *by* their persona. Celebrities wearing brand names can associate a brand with prestige, further creating a connection between idolized personality, typography, and identity (see "Social meaning + typography" in Chapter 1).

Engaging with particular personal typography can also speak to belonging, representing your identity as part of a larger group. This can be entirely practical, like donning a shirt labeled "volunteer" at a charity outing—or it may be personal, such as wearing a specific athletic jersey to identify oneself as a fan of a specific team. By portraying this typography on our bodies, we communicate a value or persona in which others can respond to. Consider the ubiquity of the "graphic tee" as both a casual fashion statement *and* identifying garment. Personal typography can spark recognition and connection, facilitating immediate affinity for a stranger who loves the same TV show or attended the same university, as communicated by the typography on their hat, shirt, or keychain.

Retailers and organizations, too, understand this connection between typography, personal proximity, and identity, and can use it strategically to promote their endeavors. Promotional giveaways or conference swag—such as pens, koozies, or tote bags—may be frequently used or worn to symbolize affection or involvement in an event while promoting its visibility through use. Even items like shopping bags can use personal typography to give their carriers a sense of pride—such as the prestige one might feel toting an iconic robin-egg blue Tiffany and Co. bag down a busy city street.

Figure 2.86 Freitag Bags: F201 PETE, F49 FRINGE, F303 HAZZARD by Freitag. Photo by Oliver Nanzig © 2019. Reproduced with the permission of Freitag.

FREITAG

In 1993, Swiss brothers Markus and Daniel Freitag developed the first FREITAG bag: a well-designed, water-repellant messenger bag made from used truck tarpaulins, bicycle inner tubes, and car seat belts. Since then, their production of one-of-a-kind bags has expanded to include a range of products, including backpacks, phone cases, and laptop sleeves. All are adorned with the robust FREITAG logo in a prominent, outward-facing position, ensuring they are easily identified. An individual may choose to use a FREITAG bag because they enjoy the quality or look—but also because the brand qualities resonate with their sense of self and how they wish others to perceive them. Especially popular among designers for their unique patterns and sturdy construction, donning a FREITAG bag or accessory may publicly associate its wearer with an appreciation of design as well as a commitment to sustainable practices.

PROXIMITY AND POLITICS

Our personal space is our proverbial soapbox, serving as a way to express our personal or political beliefs. Bumper stickers, yard signs, buttons, sashes, and garments all have the potential to showcase who you are and what you stand for. While this might seem like a recent phenomenon, personal typography has long-since designated personal and political affiliations: even in the 1780s George Washington's presidency was supported by metal buttons reading "LONG LIVE THE PRESIDENT."

While many places offer freedom of speech—including personal typography as political statement—not all spaces do, and not in all circumstances. For example, the connection between personal space and political space is so compelling that what you wear to or near a voting location during elections in the United States is subject to some states' specific electioneering laws. At the time of this book's writing, according to The National Conference of State Legislatures (NCSL) and The National Association of Secretaries of State (NASS), (two nonpartisan organizations for elected officials in the US), fifteen states have laws limiting where political apparel can be worn as part of prohibiting electioneering activities within a specified distance of a polling place. These laws have been the subject of much debate regarding the protections (or limitations) of free speech and the desire to create spaces without political persuasion or intimidation. Nonetheless, they highlight the importance of site-specific meaning and the power of personal typography.

Personal space can extend beyond what we wear or surround ourselves with, to how we adorn our bodies, themselves. While the existence of a physical body is often affiliated with movement and gesture in a variety of scenarios (see "Corporeality and performance" later in this chapter) the relationship to typography *on* the human body provides unique opportunities to shape perceptions of ourselves—personally or politically—and how we communicate this to others. For instance, the connection of tattoos as a part of one's body may speak to *closeness* on multiple levels.

Figure 2.87 Richard Hamilton Smith via Getty Images.

Figure 2.88 *Disarm Hate* by Ida Woldemichael. © Ida Woldemichael/Everytown for Gun Safety, 2017.

Bumper Stickers

Our transportation choices are a result of a culmination of many factors, such as what we can afford, what is available, and what is most appropriate for our respective needs and climates—but they also serve as a means of self-presentation. As our vehicles speak to our choices and identities, so do the bumper stickers we adorn them with. This public display of typography is a direct reflection of a desire to shape how others view us—even if that interaction only comes from sharing a parking lot or roadway. Here, our vehicles become media for messages—showcasing support for political candidates, hobbies, businesses, or locations, giving passers-by information about who this car belongs to and what is important to them.

Disarm Hate Subbrand | Ida Woldemichael

Everytown for Gun Safety is an organization working to prevent gun violence in America. In the United States, the majority of hate crimes are directed against religious minorities, communities of color, and members of the LGBTQIA+ community. Everytown for Gun Safety's *Disarm Hate* campaign works to enact policies to keep guns out of the hands of individuals convicted of hate crimes. To promote awareness and education, branded collateral for *Disarm Hate* designed by Ida Woldemichael includes buttons, clothing, and tote bags. By wearing these bold, direct typographic statements, a personal space becomes political—showcasing their wearer's values and catalyzing conversations on ending gun violence in the United States.

The phrases "they were near to me" or "I hold this close to my heart" reference emotional proximity—but tattoos can represent this in a truly physical manner. Typographic tattoos of names, mantras, phrases, and dates speak to a desire to connect these things to our most personal selves by permanently marking them on our bodies, the epitome of nearness. Consider how frequently typographic tattoos are commissioned for remembrance or honoring. Choosing to have a date, phrase, or a family member's handwriting tattooed on your body can serve as a visual signifier or perpetual reminder that a person or memory cannot be forgotten, and is inextricably tied to you and your identity. Tattoos, of course, can also be more casual, or downright flippant, despite their permanence. Just like anything else intended to be long-lasting (see "Architectural materials" in this chapter), its intention can work as expected, or otherwise backfire. A typographic tattoo might be cherished for life—or may become a daily reminder of heartbreak—especially if the name of an ex-partner is perpetually visible on your arm or leg.

Figure 2.89 Westend61 via Getty Images.

Tattoos

Tattoo meanings are entirely dependent on their cultural and societal contexts. Based on historical precedents, or cultural or religious norms, they are taboo in some contexts and utterly commonplace in others. In this stock-photo, an individual has "ROCK" and "ROLL" tattooed across their knuckles, which may assert their commitment to a carefree life of rock 'n roll defiance—or may simply reflect a love of the musical genre.

Virtual Space

The word *virtual* has several meanings. This includes a nearness or facsimile of something which is *almost-but-not-quite*, such as "the line was *virtually* invisible." Another definition references something produced by means of computing, such as a digital artifact which exists, but not in the traditional *physical* sense. During the Covid-19 pandemic, many school, work, and social activities were largely suspended and "moved online" to prevent virus transmission. This abrupt social shift from in-person to virtual interactions showcased the stark contrast between experiences which happen in real space and those which occur in digital environments. While parts of these new modalities were deeply frustrating due to inaccessibility, technology issues, lack of bandwidth, and an absence of tactile experiences—among *many* other things—others were quite freeing, allowing for new interactions or investigations otherwise impossible in a physical space.

In the context of this book, *virtual space* references digital spaces made possible by hardware and software which complement or transcend the bounds of physical reality. Therefore, the works explored therein focus on typographic applica-

Figure 2.90 From Adobe Fonts.

Impact Meme Text

Consider the internet *meme*, a cultural shorthand often merging image and text to reflect a specific value or comment on a particular situation in a formulaic way. These typographic expressions have become cultural touchstones in a virtual context, and have given new meanings to typefaces used in this capacity, such as the typeface Impact, designed in 1965 by British type designer Geoffrey Lee for the Stephenson Blake foundry. As a strong, tall headline typeface easily accessible in both image and word-processing programs, it became frequently used as the textual element on memes. While a meme is certainly not *established* through its use of Impact, its ubiquity of use is hard to ignore. As a consequence, text set in white Impact with a black shadow or outline culturally references this particular use and context, creating affiliation by association. This is the result of socially recognized viral dissemination in a virtual space.

Figure 2.91 *Subjective letters* | Non Fungible Type by Frank Adebiaye. © Frank Adebiaye/Forthcome, 2021. Reproduced with the permission of Frank Adebiaye/Forthcome.

Subjective letters | Frank Adebiaye

How do we determine value, and what does it mean to *own* something in a digital space? Type designer and founder of Velvetyne Type Foundry Frank Adebiaye's *Subjective letters* is a project which interrogates concepts of ownership and personalization in the context of digital artifacts. Seeking to sell fonts as comprehensively as possible through the transference of a unique font file, *Subjective letters* is a collection of display typefaces with 100 copies each, €20 per font file. Each font comes with a unique glyph (differing from other files) and a distinct number sequence embedded in its metadata to denote the individual nature of the file, as well as to prevent copying. When something like a pen or pencil is purchased, it becomes a tool of creation—but the object itself can be modified, sold, or destroyed by its owner. Here, owners of each unique font file can treat their font similarly, and may sell, gift, or destroy their particular purchase. These exclusive features give near physicality to an otherwise intangible virtual purchase. Thoughtful specificity facilitates a meaningful experience through both the design of the font file as well as its means of purchase—making the transaction itself something personal and precious.

tions made *in* or *for* these spaces. These include the internet (including apps and websites), digital graphics programs, and ways to interact such as virtual reality (VR) or augmented reality (AR). This is not an exhaustive list by any means, as the abilities of—and opportunities for—virtual spaces increase daily.

These contexts influence how type is made, formatted, or experienced—but also how visual language is shared and perceived. In previous eras, reaching a global audience required enormous physical and monetary resources: at present, it simply requires internet access, a strong online presence, and a bit of luck. This rapid pace of distribution yields frequent remixes and adaptations, giving rise to unexpected forms of typographic experimentation and transmission. The freedom and power of virtual space facilitates opportunities for new processes—not just in typography and design—but in systems and structures for commerce, community-building, and communication.

DIGITAL METHODS

Today, a great deal of typographic work takes place in a virtual space involving digital tools, regardless of whether the outcome is physical (such as a printed book) or virtual (a digital typeface). Just as computer-generated imagery (CGI) extends the abilities of practical effects to create otherwise unfeasible environments and actions, creating typography in a virtual space can allow designers to produce new experiments, manipulations, or generative works. These may manifest as animations or renderings produced through coding, algorithms, computer-aided modeling, or graphics programs—all with increased speed and fluidity. While these tools rely on skilled artists and designers for intentional outputs, the use of these digital tools can produce otherwise impossible typographic feats.

This pace is a marked shift from how design work has been created previously (see "Gestural space" in this chapter). Prior to the familiar graphics softwares and layout programs used today, design and typography were largely created through analog means. For example, for much of the twentieth century, many layouts were achieved via *paste-up*, the act of *literally* cutting and pasting text and images to create camera-ready compositions which would be photographed before printing. Dry type transfer sheets, including those produced by *Letraset*, featured a sheet of individual letters which could be burnished onto a surface *one at a time*. While beloved by many for their tactile, nostalgic, and DIY qualities, these methods were limited by their physical and technological bounds, hindering both the scope of a project and its speed of revisions. When accessible, virtual space removes many of these restrictions. Even the ability to instantly *do* and *undo* digitally allows for a freedom of typographic making which was inconceivable in previous decades.

However—there are certain physically achieved outcomes which simply can't be mimicked digitally, and specific digital methods which can't be replicated by any other means. Therefore, both tactile and digital methods are essential in design and typography. Requiring different skills and thought processes, they each carry potential to catalyze unique solutions. In pursuit of their best work, individual creators develop preferences about how they work and which methods are most appropriate for their practices and conveyance of specific meaning.

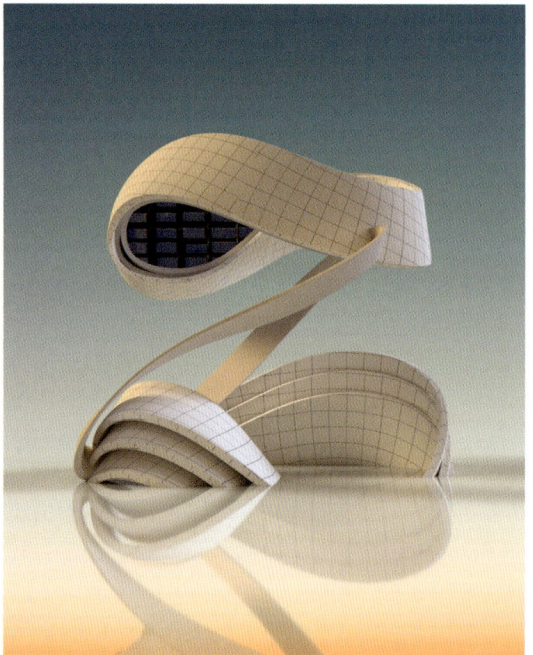

Figures 2.92–2.94 *36 Days of Type 2020* by Anushka Tendolkar. © Anushka Tendolkar, 2020. Reproduced with the permission of Anushka Tendolkar.

36 Days of Type | Anushka Tendolkar

Communication and experience designer Anushka Tendolkar's playful and vibrant letterforms showcase the power of 3D-rendering softwares. Created in Adobe Dimension, these letters make use of a virtual environment to digitally reference artifacts or environments. This allows for experimental forms, patterns, or objects which suspend disbelief, exceeding the bounds of physical reality. Here, 3D renderings of letters serve as a homage to Dan Flavin, Yayoi Kusama, and Zaha Hadid, respectively, in tribute to their popular creations. These works were a part of the global type design project *36 Days of Type*, a collaborative project originally developed by Nina Sans and Rafa Goicoechea, designers from Barcelona. This yearly online design challenge invites creatives to design and share a character of the Latin alphabet (represented through twenty-six letters and ten numbers) for thirty-six consecutive days.

  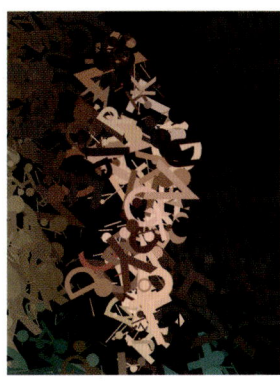

Figures 2.95 and 2.96 *TYPE Portrait: Didot* and *TYPE Portrait: Futura* by Yeohyun Ahn. © Yeohyun Ahn, 2020. Reproduced with the permission of Yeohyun Ahn.

TYPE Portrait: Didot and TYPE Portrait: Futura | Yeohyun Ahn

Selfies are an important form of contemporary self-portraiture, a way of communicating who we are and how we wish to be perceived—especially on social media. A series of *TYPE Portraits* by artist, designer, and educator Yeohyun Ahn showcase visual research in typography through generative selfies investigating identity, communication, and expression. As part of an ongoing series, Yeohyun Ahn began using computational methods to formulate generative typographic selfies in order to call attention to the isolation and marginalization of female Asian faculty in predominantly white academic institutions in the United States. Created in a virtual space, complex selfies generated from recognizable typefaces simultaneously obscure and reveal an identity, embedding qualities of their visual personas. Shown here are examples in Didot (Firmin Didot, 1784), representing vogue sophistication, and Futura (Paul Renner, 1927), regarded as contemporary and efficient.

AUGMENTED REALITY, MIXED REALITY, AND VIRTUAL REALITY

In their most basic definitions, *augmented reality*, *mixed reality*, and *virtual reality* use computer-aided graphics to supplement existing physical spaces, or invent entirely new ones. Augmented reality (AR) refers to digital interventions overlaid onto real-world viewing, while mixed reality builds on these virtual elements, making them receptive to feedback, movement, or interaction in real time. Virtual reality (VR) refers to entirely virtual spaces composed of digital stimuli, which are often accessed via a VR headset by which an individual can view and navigate an enveloping environment, and/or interact with its visual elements.

While these elements are based in virtual space, their interactions still have impact on the physical world. For instance, the *Google Translate* app features the ability to create near-instant visual translations from one language to another, responding to typography on a variety of surfaces such as on signs or packages. When the phone is aimed at text for translation, the

Figure 2.97 *AR Optical Typography* by Andrew Johnson. © Andrew Johnson, 2019. Reproduced with the permission of Andrew Johnson.

AR Optical Typography | Andrew Johnson

Designer Andrew Johnson's work in augmented reality includes experiences in mixed reality—where digital and physical worlds blend, yielding new ways for people, technology, and environments to interact. *AR Optical Typography* examines how these contexts can catalyze new kinds of interactions with typographic communication. These investigations include visual and stylistic changes to digital typography as a response to physical proximity. In this instance, as a visitor approaches this virtual number panel in real space, the size of the numbers increases in response to their location. These inquiries probe the possibilities of adaptive typography in physical and virtual contexts, crafting new possibilities for communication, clarity, and legibility.

translated language appears in augmented reality, changing in real time on screen to provide its user with necessary information. In addition, virtual reality's qualities can be so immersive that it has the capacity to be physically disorienting. Because our bodies attempt to follow our perceived motions and movements through space, those navigating virtual reality have inadvertently fallen off chairs and bumped into furniture while attempting to traverse through a virtual space quite different from the *actual* space they inhabit.

Figure 2.98 *Chalkroom* by Laurie Anderson and Hsin-Chien Huang, 2017. 3D renderings of virtual reality work.

Chalkroom | Laurie Anderson and Hsin-Chien Huang

A collaboration between artists Laurie Anderson and Hsin-Chien Huang, *Chalkroom* is a virtual reality exhibition. Wearing a VR headset and equipped with handheld controllers for navigating, viewers are invited to enter an immersive digital space—a labyrinth-like structure of hallways and towers, where words and stories cover the walls or float through the air. Within this virtual environment, participants can explore its many areas and fly through a tree with leaves of letters. Paired with a pensive, spoken-word aural component (voiced by Laurie Anderson) these fantastical possibilities of virtual reality allow interaction with language and typography in a way which is otherwise impossible in the "real world," kindling a freeing sense of wonder and discovery.

Gestural Space

Gestures carry meaning. A gesture can speak to a physical action, such as a friendly wave or blown kiss—or may refer to a movement through space, either real or implied. It may speak to a metaphorical *or* symbolic action, as referenced in the phrase "that was a kind gesture." Socially, and within a shared cultural context, we understand the connection between gestures and the messages they seek to convey. When letterforms are made or explored through gesture, the inflection of their origins, construction, or movement influences their consequent meaning.

Throughout its history, letterforms have inherently been connected to gestures of making. Consider the language used within contemporary typography as informed by the physical actions of its design and construction. *Setting* type originally refers to the literal act of arranging movable type for composition; even *uppercase* and *lowercase* letters speak to the physical placement and proximity of separate type cases, wherein more frequently used lowercase letters were positioned in a lower, closer case, making them easier to reach. The term *leading* is grounded in the act of inserting pieces of lead between lines of text to format their spacing. Designers speak often

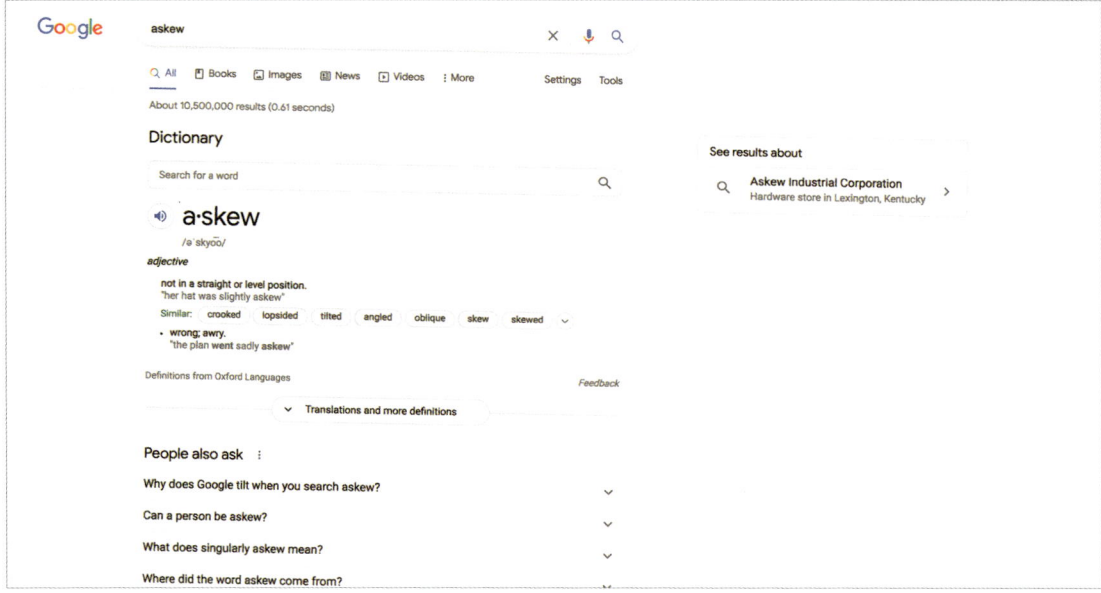

Figure 2.99 Google and the Google logo are trademarks of Google LLC.

"Askew" Google Search result

The use of gesture in typography can be both emotive and informative. When you search the term "askew" on Google, an unexpected and engaging page appears. Playful and illustrative, the textual description and its relevant search results slope slightly to one side, using gesture to both showcase *and* define this word.

of text as something to be "handled"—perhaps informed by centuries of physically handling movable type. While today we understand that a *type foundry* refers to companies or collectives who design and distribute digital typefaces, this definition is a relatively new concept. For most of their histories, type foundries produced typefaces in the form of wood and metal fonts by means of carving, punch-cutting, and casting.

Whether we are hand-drafting letters, manually setting type for letterpress, performing with letterforms, or digitally arranging works on a screen—physical, visual, or metaphorical gestures are inherently entwined in typographic practice.

THE HUMAN HAND

Before computers, typewriters, and movable type, all text was written or marked by hand. For large or intricate texts, such as illuminated manuscripts, this process was laborious and tedious, making the distribution of written information slow and limited—in part because it was only available to those who were literate and those who could afford to commission or purchase such texts. Manuscript handwriting and contemporary typographic communication may seem entirely removed from each other, but how human hands move and write has had a lasting impact on the formal qualities of letterforms. While the history of handwritten Latin letters and their translation to formally designed typefaces exceeds what can be covered in this text, a few brief historical progressions and relationships are important to note.

Early Greek letterforms carved into stone were later used by the Romans, where they were written by hand with a flat-edged brush, developing greater contrast and serifs. These letterforms were also carved into stone, and only featured what we understand today as capital letters. As various regional handwriting preferences and practices emerged and evolved over time, so did *majuscule* (uppercase) and *minuscule* (lowercase) letters, which began being used together. In Europe, during the Renaissance, *humanism* was a significant intellectual movement which featured a revived interest in studying and reproducing cultural ideals of antiquity from the ancient Greeks and Romans. Italian humanists aimed to replicate their letterforms as well through emulating the writing of Roman texts … or so they thought. In reality, they were actually copying the handwriting of manuscripts written by scribes in the eleventh and twelfth centuries in a style called Carolingian minuscule, and mistook them as original, ancient Roman artifacts. These consequent *Humanistic scripts*, written with a broad-nibbed pen and featuring airy yet structured letterforms, were easier to read than the thick, monotone *blackletter*, or Gothic script, popular at the time.

In fifteenth-century Venice, French printer Nicolas Jenson created movable type based on this humanist handwriting style, called Jenson. We now identify this kind of typeface as roman (note the lowercase r), featuring a style of letter with unique qualities which differentiate it from blackletter or italic (see A closer look: *Italics* in Chapter 3). Because Jenson was based on calligraphic handwriting, it features modulated strokes, or lines whose thicknesses vary depending on direction, as if drawn with a flat brush or broad-nibbed pen. This shows a direct impact of human gesture—even on typefaces which are more uniformly drafted and designed. As a typeface, Jenson has been massively influential to type design since. In 1996, Robert Slimbach designed revival Adobe Jenson, a digital version of Jenson, as part of the Adobe Originals program.

The handwritten qualities of humanistic scripts have endured, but are not limited to revivals from history. Visual characteristics referencing the human hand are still evident in both the shape and style of Latin letters today. The contrasting upstrokes and downstrokes of many letters—perhaps easiest to identify on a high-contrast capital V or A—are the result of a calligraphic tradition of right-handed writing with a broad-nibbed pen. Because of their familiarity, the visual weight of this handwritten gesture has come to be preferred or expected, even very subtly on low-contrast typefaces. In addition, evidence of gesture is especially notable in typefaces we categorize as Humanist or Venetian, which feature similar proportions to humanistic scripts as well as reference their

Adobe Jenson

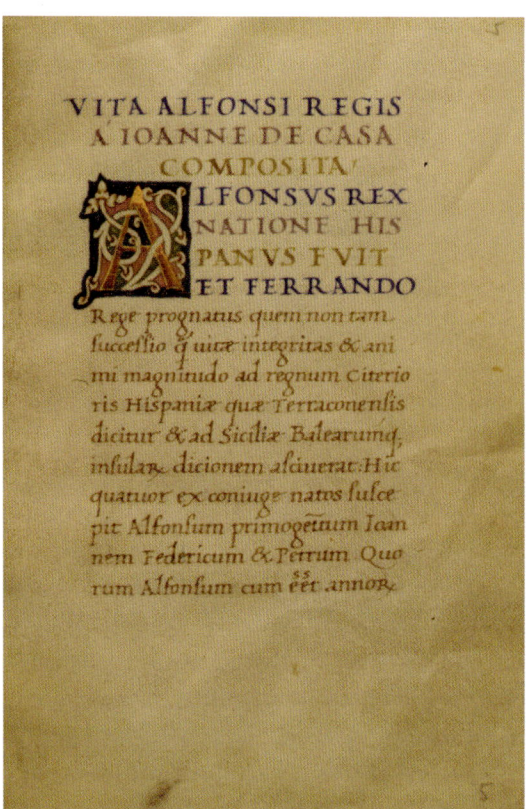

Figure 2.101 From Adobe Fonts.

Adobe Jenson | Robert Slimbach

The digital typeface Adobe Jenson, designed by Robert Slimbach in 1996, revives Jenson's original typeface with forms referencing calligraphic gestures. Consider how a specific hand movement and writing implement would create the modulated stroke evident in the tail of the J, the bowl of the d, b, and o, and the two distinct marks composing the e.

GESTURE IN AND OF LETTERFORMS

In art and design practices, particularly in painting and illustration, *mark-making* refers to the act of making a mark and the qualities of its particular surface manipulation. The way a writing implement moves across a surface is recorded in its consequent mark, becoming a representation of the gestural qualities of that action. Words which have been drawn or written by hand usually allude to their material means-of-making, featuring strokes or textures indicative of having been produced by writing utensils such as pencils, markers, or calligraphic pens. This is especially evident in modulated, thick-to-thin strokes of moving a marker to draw a letter, or in the intentional pooling of ink in a calligraphic line as drawn by a fountain pen.

Specific techniques of creating text or writing letters are subject to their own unique expertise, distinctions, and definitions. *Calligraphy* is concerned with the act of writing words and letters, often with a pen or ink in a refined or expressive manner. As an illustrative act, *lettering*

Figure 2.100 The Walters Art Museum, Baltimore.

The Handwriting of Bartolomeo Sanvito

A few notable Italian humanists with influential handwriting include Poggio Bracciolini, Coluccio Salutati, and Niccolò Niccoli. Here, the handwriting of famed Italian humanist scribe Bartolomeo Sanvito showcases an example of a humanistic script as demonstrated in the writing below the colored capitals.

calligraphic stroke qualities. For instance, when you next use the typefaces GT Ultra or Alegreya, look closely at their letterforms, most obviously their lowercase a's. These glyphs still feature echoes of these writing techniques imbued with the impact of gesture.

refers to drawing letters for a particular composition which are *not* a part of a larger system of repeated letters within a typeface. Lettering can be created using analog tools, digital methods, or a combination thereof—using scans of sketches, or by drawing letters on-screen with stylus and tablet. Through both their processes and definitions, lettering and calligraphy are intrinsically tied to gesture.

Artists and designers recognize that specificity and clarity of practice are important for building skills and techniques, as well as for communicating expectations to clients and audiences. As such, many creative practitioners consider lettering and calligraphy to be separate practices from typography. Because these practices all involve the visual composition and arrangement of letterforms (even *outside* of the letterform-repeating systems of a typeface), this book discusses lettering and calligraphy as a facet of typographic practice—while fully acknowledging that setting type, drawing letters, and writing text all require unique skill-sets with differing outcomes.

Handwritten or handmade qualities imply a connection to the hand or body which can create a personal affiliation, a reference to time and effort. This is especially evident in well-crafted, handwritten text which carries the skill of its writing and the commitment of its author—after all, there is no "undo" in inked calligraphy. Even when a friend hand-writes you a thank-you note, it becomes indicative of their endeavor, a physical representation of the time taken to acknowledge and express their gratitude. While a typed note may express the same textual sentiment, and might carry an earnest visual inflection, it differs from physical writing and the work it took to complete. If you've ever received a fake handwritten note which uses a deliberately deceiving typeface designed to look like ballpoint pen—or even worse, actually written out by machines—you understand the connection to handwriting and its potential for emotional impact. This is why mailers posturing to be handwritten are especially cruel (or especially effective?) as the recipient expects a personal note and is greeted instead with yet another insurance offer.

Thankfully, there is a difference between works which aim to *deceive* and works which draw on gestural references in order to create specific typographic tone or historical reference. Because of the connection between gesture, effort, and value, there is significant demand for typefaces which call on calligraphic forms and their consequent social meanings. There are many scenarios where these typefaces are most appropriate to use, especially where real inked or penned calligraphy would be impractical or impossible. While both digital typefaces and scribed or drawn letterforms rely on gestural mark-making to inform their meaning, they are inherently different. Their variance lies in their genesis and application—their respective histories, methods of making, material meanings, denotations, and connotations.

The necessary time, skill, and labor required to produce quality calligraphy and hand-lettering contributes to both its social and monetary value. Even in today's increasingly digital world, consider how often true handwritten calligraphy is still reserved for special and major life events. Great emotional significance remains in custom, hand-inked diplomas, wedding invitations, place cards, certificates, and announcements. In addition, custom-lettered logos, signage, art, advertisements, and murals carry bespoke and expressive qualities that may otherwise be unattainable through other means—all while referencing a particular care and craft.

Figure 2.102 *Manifest* by Loren Chestnut of Captivating Calligraphy. © Loren Chestnut, 2020. Reproduced with the permission of Loren Chestnut/Captivating Calligraphy.

Manifest | Captivating Calligraphy/Loren Chestnut

With a rich history across many cultures, calligraphy serves as a visual translation of corporeal skill. A variety of pens, paintbrushes, and markers can be used to write considered letters ranging from casual forms to impeccably measured scripts. Many forms of calligraphy require immense practice in order to continuously write delicate, repeated letterforms. Loren Chestnut, founder of *Captivating Calligraphy*, specializes in design and calligraphy. In her work *Manifest*, graceful skill of deliberate mark-making is evidenced through elegant handwritten letters, which are precise, yet personal. As a handwritten word, its intentional flourishes capture intricate gestures, imbuing this word with the care and consideration of its making. This corporeal connection continues to imbue handwritten calligraphy with admiration and acclaim.

Figures 2.103 and 2.104 *Change is Constant* and *Every Pair of Eyes* by Lisa Taniguchi. © Lisa Taniguchi, 2020.

Change is Constant and *Every Pair of Eyes* | Lisa Taniguchi

The lettering work of Lisa Taniguchi often features positive or pensive phrases. Influenced by personal growth and the shift caused by the Covid-19 pandemic, *Change is Constant* boldly reminds an audience of the inevitability of change. This lettering features reverse-contrast letterforms, which use visual stress in a part of a letter where it is not typically expected. While created digitally, these graceful, ribbon-like letterforms resemble letters drawn with a broad-edged pen. To facilitate empathy and connection, in *Every Pair of Eyes*, expressive lettering is paired with unique shapes to showcase the diversity of individuals sharing a common experience.

Figure 2.105 *Level the Playing Field* by Cymone Wilder. © Cymone Wilder, 2020. Reproduced with the permission of Cymone Wilder.

Level the Playing Field | Cymone Wilder

Designer and lettering artist Cymone Wilder, of the design practice *Simon and Moose*, created upbeat and optimistic lettering for the phrase "It's Time to Level the Playing Field" designed for the 2020 presidential campaign of Elizabeth Warren, a United States senator from Massachusetts. As part of a series of artist collaborations with women working in design and illustration, this phrase was featured on apparel and merchandise. Senator Warren's platform focused on structural changes in pursuit of economic and social equity; these energetic yet measured letterforms allude to a hand which feels confident and determined in its commitment to progress.

Figure 2.106 *I'm a Piece of Garbage* by Dirty Bandits, photo by Lucas Saugen. © Lucas Saugen, 2015. Reproduced with the permission of Annica Lydenberg and Lucas Saugen.

I'm a Piece of Garbage | Annica Lydenberg

Long before digital typefaces or mass-produced vinyl ads, businesses and retailers relied on sign-painters to produce lettering for public display. Today, this specialized craft is still taught, practiced, and embraced for a wide variety of applications. Sign-painted text (or type which emulates this style) embraces specific, skilled movements of brush strokes in order to create letterforms. Annica Lydenberg is the lettering artist, designer, and illustrator behind the design studio Dirty Bandits. In her series *I'm a Piece of Garbage* a number of discarded objects were reclaimed and adorned with hand-lettered, self-deprecating phrases. This juxtaposition creates a humorous take on insecurity, self-confidence, and reclamation. These carefully rendered, gestural letterforms imbue familiar mass-manufactured products with something both personal and jocular.

A CLOSER LOOK:
Gesture and contextual alternates

Designing a connected script typeface is challenging on multiple fronts. In order to create the illusion of cursive, each letter must flow seamlessly into the next, requiring significant planning and problem-solving to determine how, and at what point, these characters connect. If the typeface aims to emulate or reference handwriting, the identical, recurring letterforms of a digital typeface create an exact but unwelcome repetition, disrupting the fiction of imperfect hand-referenced text.

In real calligraphy or handwriting, letterforms vary as a result of natural gestures. Letters change depending on where in the word they are written, and effortless substitutions and accommodations occur. For instance, in writing a cursive word with two t's, the crossbar for these characters is added last to cross both letterforms at the same time. In a digital typeface, the individual crossbars in two t's in a script may awkwardly overlap one another as they exist side-by-side as identical glyphs. In some handwritten texts, the starting or ending letter is altered for spatial or decorative reasons, such as flourishes added to the respective tails or descenders of y's and g's at the ends of words. How, then, do some digital typefaces account for these obstacles?

Software made for designing type export fonts through specific file types, which allow the design and information of fonts to be stored, read, and used across a variety of programs: these include TrueType files (ttfs) and OpenType files (otfs). OpenType fonts have the ability to include programmable changes manifesting as OpenType features, by which designers can specify how and if substitutions or differing placements of glyphs can occur within certain instances, using particular lines of code to essentially specify *if this, then this*.

Consequently, OpenType features can facilitate elegant letterform combinations or natural substitutions to give the illusion of flow or more closely resemble handwriting. These include standard ligatures, discretionary ligatures, or contextual and stylistic alternates. *Ligatures* refer to special characters which join two letterforms for aesthetic or linguistic purposes. In Latin text set in English, some common, standard combinations include fi or fl, while discretionary ligatures, used more for decorative purposes, may include letter combinations such as Th or st. Using OpenType features, two adjacent t's may be replaced by a more finessed ligature designed to better accommodate the space. A lowercase y with a decorative flourish may be subbed in at the end of a word as a contextual alternative. OpenType features and substitutions allow for carefully planned but seemingly organic changes to occur in fonts as their letters are typed. These changes capture the gesture of real handwritten or calligraphic text.

Many script typefaces employ these features extensively, including significant numbers of custom ligatures and alternate glyphs to more thoughtfully connect letters through subtle functional or stylistic changes. If you've ever witnessed the letters of a font, especially a script, changing in real time when typed, this is likely what is taking place. As many script typefaces begin with handwritten letters (or a deep knowledge thereof) designers can make careful note of where changes can or should occur from original letterforms first created with pens, markers, ink, or paint on paper.

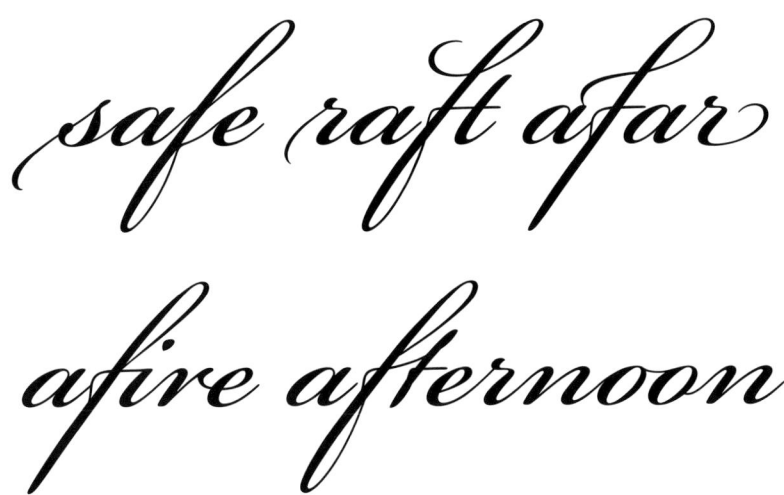

Figure 2.107 From Adobe Fonts.

Bickham Script | Richard Lipton
The Bickham Script family, designed by Richard Lipton, features an impressive range of contextual alternates. Using OpenType features, the characters in these words change relative to their surrounding letters—notably, the lowercase "f." Set here in Bickham Script Pro 3 Regular, the lowercase "r" also changes in relation to its placement at the beginning, middle, or end of a word.

Figure 2.108 Reproduced with the permission of Sabrina Lopez/Typesenses.

INTERVIEW

Sabrina Lopez | Typesenses

From page to screen, how are letterforms influenced by hand-drawn methods? Which factors impact how gestural references are evaluated and included in digital typefaces? Sabrina Lopez is an independent type designer. Her foundry, Typesenses, is based in Buenos Aires, in Argentina, where she "lives happily surrounded by her family." Her original typefaces—which range from playful sans serifs to impeccably detailed scripts—are created by "combining historical perspective, manual skills, and digital wizardry." With an education in graphic design and specializations in calligraphy, typeface design, and UX/UI, her diverse knowledge provides deep insight when interpreting handmade sketches for digital uses, which she describes as "both pillars of the creative process of any font."

Typesenses fonts have strong, vibrant voices and personalities; their letterforms "have played big roles as the protagonists of book jackets, magazine covers, stationery, packaging, brand identities, and ads worldwide." Teaching locally as well as internationally, Sabrina's work has been viewed and used globally—and she "loves traveling as her typefaces do." In this lightly edited interview, Sabrina generously shares insight into the gestural inspiration and methods of creating Typesenses typefaces.

What is the relationship between analog and digital methods in your work? Do all your digital typefaces begin with calligraphy or hand-drawn letterforms?

Yes. All my digital typefaces begin with calligraphy or pencil sketches. *All* of them. No matter if the final result would be a sans serif—I mean, the simplest forms. The first characters I draw—the ones which contain the main strokes that then will be repeated along all the alphabet—are made by hand. For me, this is the best way to materialize my ideas and to achieve more personal curves. A digital font family is an abstract product: it exists behind a screen until some user decides to materialize it in a design, in the case of it being printed or made in vinyl, fabric, wood, or something like that. It is possible that the user never brings those letterforms to the analog world. I like the idea that my letters are physical at some moment of their lives. That moment is their conception, at least. Then, they are converted to Bézier curves, algorithms, and codes, which is great—because that's the way they reach several users around the world at the same time.

The analog stage of my work is the creative one, when I connect with the sensitivity of the materials, papers, inks, and the movements of the curves with my own breathing.

It is a perfect environment for inspiration and for something completely new that is being conceived. It is the sensorial part. The digital stage allows me to systematize those forms, to be more precise, and of course, to increase the speed of workflow. Both methods have their own place, both are paramount, and each one dialogues with the other along the gestation of the work—at least of my work. Typefaces have calligraphic roots. Their curves relate to the movement of a hand using certain tools which determines their final shape, even in sans serif forms. It is possible that a designer has to come back to the paper and check those movements to see what the digital form will look like. Sometimes there is a curve that doesn't look well on screen—and they don't know why—and when they make that fast sketch on draft paper on their desk, they figure it out. Sometimes the ideas shake by changing the context, and good things happen.

That's so true! OpenType has allowed previously impossible features to appear in connected script typefaces. With so many options, how do you determine which gestural details, ligatures, or swashes to include in your work?

Let's start by saying that if I would like to create tons of alternates for one letter (as I would do it by hand) it is not possible with OpenType, and thank God. Not for considering myself super creative—but often when I start drawing, I can't stop, and this swash can be like *this* and also like *that* and so on. Sometimes it is difficult to decide what to keep. Trust me, for the very inspirational moments, it is good to have a limit. OT [Open-Type] features are awesome, but of course they are limited. To fit this limit is the first condition of selection. Combinations of strokes can be limitless, but stylistic sets, fortunately, are twenty.

There, I have to include beginning and terminal forms, as well as options for ascenders, descenders, and capitals. And then, of course, there is an alternative ascender that would look *great* with this other swash that goes below the baseline—and the typeface itself is asking loudly that they be combined. Because of this, the number of glyphs starts to increase.

This way, the first thing that determines this decision is the number of alternates that OT permits. Also, I have to save a few stylistic sets for the combination of some alternates that I've already done and I like. However, I don't limit myself while drawing by hand. I make a lot, I open the system, and then I close it by choosing what best matches with the entire landscape I want to achieve.

Ligatures are another story. There are some required ligatures—those that are mandatory for the typeface to connect or to avoid weird crashes—and on the other hand, the stylistic ones, which are decorative. The first [required ligatures] have a functional reason, but both are important. The stylistic ligatures [decoratively connecting letterforms] work like the stylistic sets [a chosen group of stylistic substitutions]. They are the result of creativity and selection of what is best for the whole landscape, while required ligatures need more attention and smart decisions from the beginning. It is not about opening the system in a creative and funny way: it requires focus on *how* the connectors will be, and *which* letters need different connections, *why*—and if they could be any other way. A bad decision now could result in extra work later. These ligatures could be almost infinite. You should be smart when designing the connectors, trying to have the least quantity of required ligatures as possible. It is also true that the more gestural your font will be, the more alternatives and ligatures you will design.

Your Typesenses typefaces are so detailed and elegant! It's clear that great care and knowledge goes into their design and construction. What do you find most joyful about lettering or type design? What is most challenging?
Thanks.

That which makes those typefaces detailed and high quality is what, to me, is the most joyful about type design: learning.

Each process of work is a new challenge, with new historical research, as well as the comprehension of a new group of letterforms. Sometimes I study the evolution of a typeface style, sometimes I learn a new calligraphy hand …

It is not the same trip to design a formal script than a more gestural one. They have the same basis, but each universe is different. To dive into a new universe of letterforms each time is the best part of my work! Also the most challenging.

That beginning when I ask myself—what is next, what universe will I explore now? How will I create new rules for that universe? What are the solid rules that I should not break? How can I put my voice in it?

In what contexts have your fonts been used? What do you hope they communicate?

My fonts are mostly for display use. I have found them in magazines, book jackets, stationery, packaging … conquering universes of fashion, gourmet food, coffee stores, winery, toys, weddings, and so on. Fortunately, they are all related to funny things. I enjoy that! I think that because they have this human gesture behind them, which makes them warm and playful, they fit perfectly in those contexts. And not casually—those are the uses I had in mind when I designed them.

Figures 2.109 and 2.110 Chonky, Dress, Limon, Blend, Fantasy, Wishes Script, Parfumerie Script by Typesenses. © Sabrina Lopez, 2020, 2018, 2017, 2015, 2014, 2013, 2011. Reproduced with the permission of Sabrina Lopez/Typesenses.

GESTURE OF MARK

In mark-making, the appearance of patterns, lines, and dots can be determined by both gestural methods and the materials they are created on. The physical properties of chalk will create different textures and affordances than paint, permanent marker, or ink, as each takes on a unique tone through pressure when applied onto a surface. As visual evidence of the speed or intent of physical gestures that made or caused them, marks can vary in their line quality and weight. Like the connection between sound and shape, the tone conveyed by a mark is a result of socially affiliated meanings with its overt or implied gesture, resulting in marks we may perceive as fast, tedious, or timid.

Because materials react to pressure and force, a mark made with a fast or firm gesture may result in a jagged line or exciting splatter. Lettering and calligraphy with these qualities may imply a kind of urgency, elation, energy, or authenticity (see "History and material meanings" earlier in this chapter), referring to something real, raw, and unfiltered. Because bodily connections are indicative of effort, a mark may intentionally reflect the labor of the artist or designer, adding important contextual or metaphorical information on how the work was produced. This is especially notable in marks made with the body itself rather than a writing implement, through evident fingerprints, scuffs, imprints, or impressions.

Figures 2.111 and 2.112 Monograms by Marion Guy. © Marion Guy, 2020. Reproduced with the permission of Marion Guy.

Stippling Monograms | Marion Guy

The work of artist and illustrator Marion Guy features detailed stippling—the process of using repeated small dots to form varying brightnesses, creating the illusion of depth on a surface. The precise mark-making in these monograms demonstrates the exactitude of the artist's process, the result of attentive and skilled hand-work. Because each dot is the result of a deliberate, planned placement, these methodical gestures carry meaning through both the impressive light and shadow portrayed in the drawings as well as the labor required to accurately render such details through each carefully made mark.

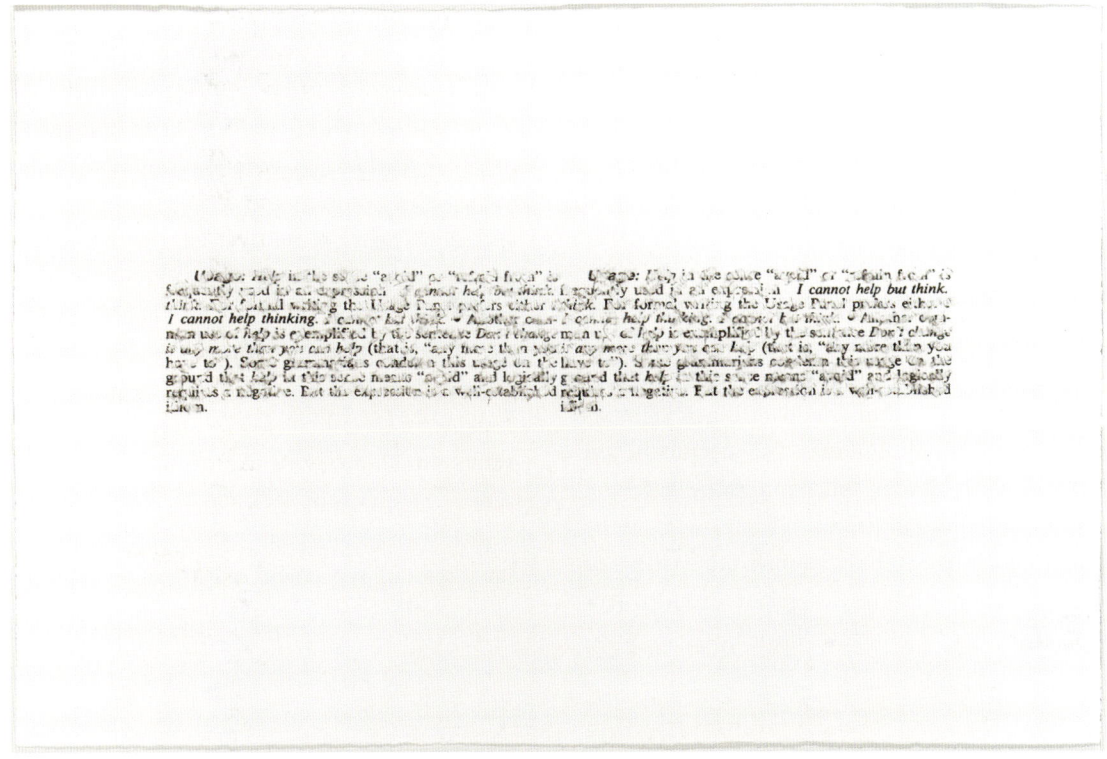

Figure 2.113 *Help, 1982*, 2015. © Bethany Collins. Dimitris Passas Collection, Athens Greece. Courtesy of the Artist and PATRON Gallery, Chicago.

Help, 1982 | Bethany Collins

Bethany Collins is a multidisciplinary artist whose practice explores the interaction of race, identity, and language through a variety of methods and materials. Linguistically, contronyms refer to words whose definitions carry opposite meanings. In *Help, 1982*, part of her *Contronym* series, opposing definitions or phrases remain visible and legible—while all other text has been obscured through a deliberate gesture. Societally, erasure refers to the deliberate exclusion of people and identities, purposefully silencing their stories and histories. In these works, erasure informs both method *and* meaning, manifesting as a literal, recorded gesture. Through the artist's act of rubbing spit into toner and graphite on Somerset paper (30 in. × 44 in. or approx. 76 cm × 101 cm), lines of text are removed and revealed, exposing and questioning binarisms of meaning.

Figure 2.114 *Wake Up And Live* by theboredkids. © Jamar Cave, 2017.

Wake Up And Live | Jamar Cave

An energetic gesture can imbue type with a similar emotion—demonstrated here by theboredkids' inspirational lettering by Barbados-born, United States-based graphic and lettering designer Jamar Cave. Here, gold ink is applied via a folded pen, a writing utensil with a metal nib featuring a long, broad edge which can facilitate wide, dynamic strokes. The intentional splatters and urgent marks of these letterforms create an invigorating message. In addition to its gesture of making, the variable baseline of *Wake Up And Live* infers a visual inflection of optimism.

GESTURE AND EXPRESSION

Though much of our world revolves around written text, so much of our communication is still nonverbal, relying on gestures and facial expressions to convey a particular meaning. A knowing look can communicate something very different from a warning glance; a grin differs significantly in its expression than a grimace. In the West, raising a particular finger on one hand—as a thumb's up—carries connotations of solidarity and agreement. (Raising a lone middle finger signifies something entirely different, and decidedly less kind.) These gestures and expressions have the ability to communicate specific meanings without anything having to be verbalized, written, or read. We know that the design and arrangement of typefaces creates visual inflection, but through what other means do typographers denote tone, reaction, or expression?

Research conducted by Dr. Paul Ekman, an American psychologist who studies the relationship between emotion and facial expressions, has revealed that while some facial expressions rely on cultural context to be understood, seven appear universal for humans across culture and language: anger, disgust, fear, surprise, happiness, sadness, and contempt. It comes as no surprise, then, that when we cannot fully articulate our meaning through written word alone, we make visual references to reactions, gestures, or facial expressions through the inclusion of short gifs, emojis, or emoticons. In tandem with type, these visual cues give tone to text similar to those of in-person communication.

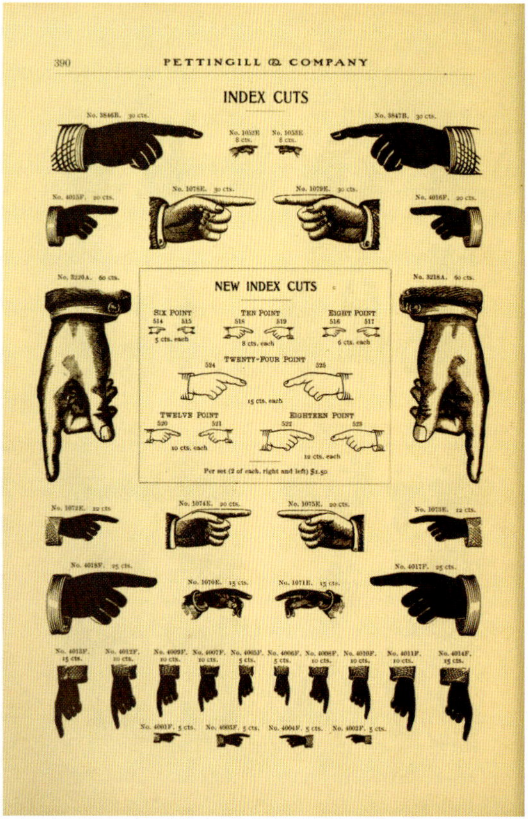

Figure 2.115 From archive.org.

The Manicule

☞ The manicule or index—sometimes called a digit, fist, or printer's fist, among other names—refers to a typographic mark in the form of a pointing finger on a hand. From approximately the twelfth to eighteenth centuries, this familiar, literal gesture was drawn in the margins of texts by both authors and readers as a way to specify attention and hierarchy. This symbol evolved from a hand-drawn addition to a more regular mark, appearing in contexts such as the 1865 wanted poster for John Wilkes Booth and accomplices after the assassination of Lincoln; the manicule points to the $100,000 reward. The manicule exists in select typefaces with its own set of unicode(s), referencing differing directions and features of hands. This page from the 1901 *Copper Alloy Type Book* produced by Pettingill & Company showcases their various options of indexes available to printers at that time.

Giving Type Meaning

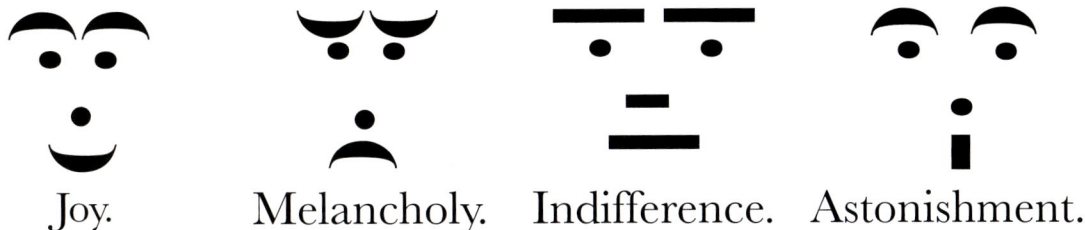

Figure 2.116 Digital recreation of *Puck*'s Typographical Art, 1881.

Typographical Art | *Puck* Magazine

While emojis are generally regarded as an invention of the 1980s, we can find evidence of their forebears 100 years prior in the 1880s. In the late nineteenth century, *Puck*, a humor magazine published in both German and English, featured witty articles and political cartoons. An article from March 30, 1881 featured *Typographical Art*, which proposed new ways to communicate emotions more clearly. The examples of joy, melancholy, indifference, and astonishment—shown here recreated by the author—were made by reconfiguring punctuation in the shape of recognizable facial expressions. Not long after, in 1887, American author and satirist Ambrose Bierce suggested sideways parentheses in the shape of a smile as punctuation for humor in his essay "For Brevity and Clarity." By imagining new punctuation to specify jokes or wit, he continued this pattern of further connecting written language to facial expressions.

Figure 2.117 Felicidad Bakery by invade design. © Felicidad Bakery, 2020. Reproduced with the permission of Felicidad Bakery.

Felicidad | invade design

Specializing in cookies and ready-to-bake cookie dough, Felicidad bakery sought an identity focusing on happiness. Focusing on the small, joyful moments in life, this cheerful branding by Colombia-based studio "invade design" cleverly recontextualizes letterforms to form a recognizable smiling face. Paired with a vibrant color scheme and energetic elements, this gestural typographic reference to a universally understood facial expression is both friendly and welcoming.

Emoticons, a shortening of the term "emotional icons," recontextualize existing letterforms and punctuation to create references to faces and gestures in many forms, styles, languages, or writing systems. Emojis may signify, among other things, happiness :) sadness :(distress :'(elation :D or love <3. Use of emoticons rose in tandem with an increase in digital communication, and are largely credited to American computer scientist Scott E. Fahlman in 1982, who suggested :-) or :-(to express intended tone for posts on an online message board. In contemporary digital communication, *emojis* do this more literally with small illustrations of faces, gestures, and objects; *gifs* provide even greater context by adding motion, visual analogies, and popular references. By combining or associating gestures with written text or typography, creators can further explore overt or nuanced expressions or reactions (see "Speculative typography" in Chapter 3).

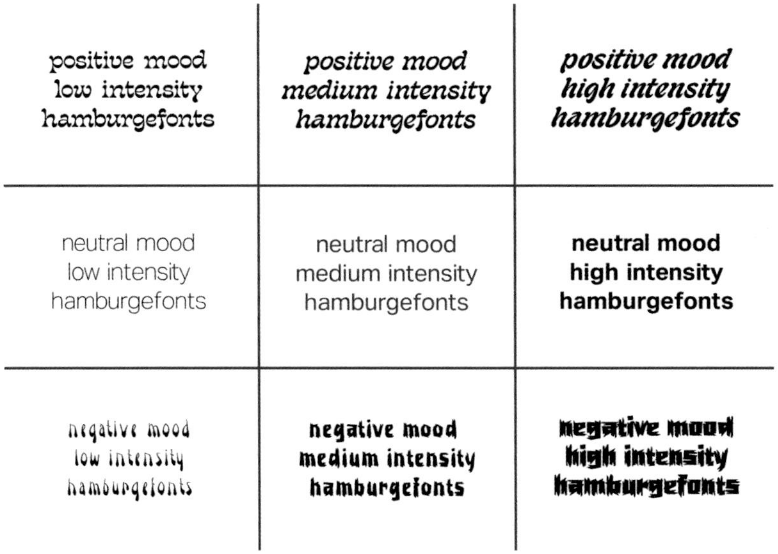

positive mood low intensity hamburgefonts	positive mood medium intensity hamburgefonts	*positive mood* *high intensity* *hamburgefonts*
neutral mood low intensity hamburgefonts	neutral mood medium intensity hamburgefonts	**neutral mood high intensity hamburgefonts**
negative mood low intensity hamburgefonts	negative mood medium intensity hamburgefonts	negative mood high intensity hamburgefonts

Figure 2.118 Facetype by Adam Lenzinger. © Adam Lenzinger, 2019.

Facetype | Adam Lenzinger

Exploring the intersections between facial expressions, emotion, type design, and communication, Adam Lenzinger's Facetype uses open-source artificial intelligence to map facial expressions to differing visual representations. These manifest in a variable font, where multiple weights and styles exist within a single file. Taking into consideration the social affiliations between shape and social meaning, each type-style corresponds to both the emotion and intensity of a particular facial expression. As an interactive work, these expressions are identified in real time through *face-api.js*, an open-source artificial intelligence which can track, recognize, and distinguish facial expressions. Within a matrix of options, happier expressions correspond to a more lyrical reverse-contrast font, which surprise bolds and italicizes. Sadness results in saggy, bottom-heavy letterforms, while anger yields thick, jagged shapes. Through these affiliations, Facetype thoughtfully showcases a direct connection between facial and typographic expression.

CORPOREALITY AND PERFORMANCE

In its most basic definition, *corporeality* is being of, or in relation to, the body, referencing things which are tangible or physical in their form. Because our lived experiences within our own bodies impact our emotional responses and perceptions, its role cannot be discounted in typographic communication as a method for making, or means of experience. Corporeality is important in literal meanings, such as something *made by hand*, or the physical ways in which works are accessed—or metaphorical meanings, like *matters of the heart*. References to corporeality are so innate to our understanding, it comes as no surprise that they are embedded in our typographic terms as a way to explain analogous visual concepts. Even in type anatomy, specific portions of letterforms are referenced by their respective body parts: a *shoulder*, *waist*, *leg*, *crotch*, or *eye*.

For humans, touch is essential for growth, development, and wellbeing. At its best, physical touch communicates warmth and connection—at its worst, it is the medium for sickness, physical violence, or harm. Therefore, corporeality is

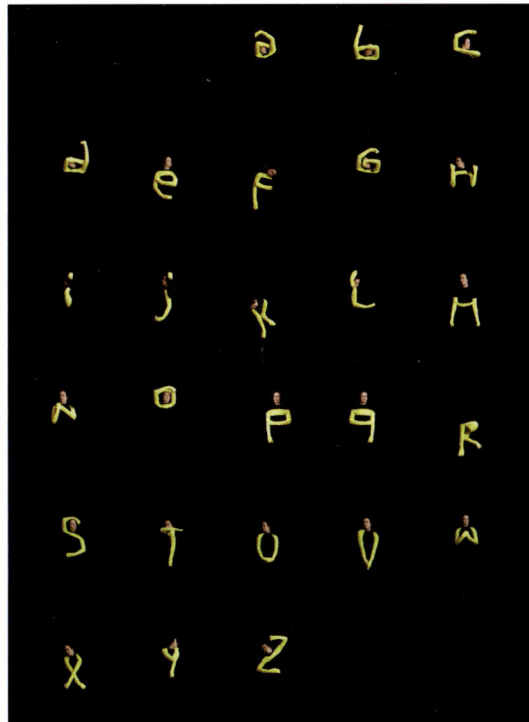 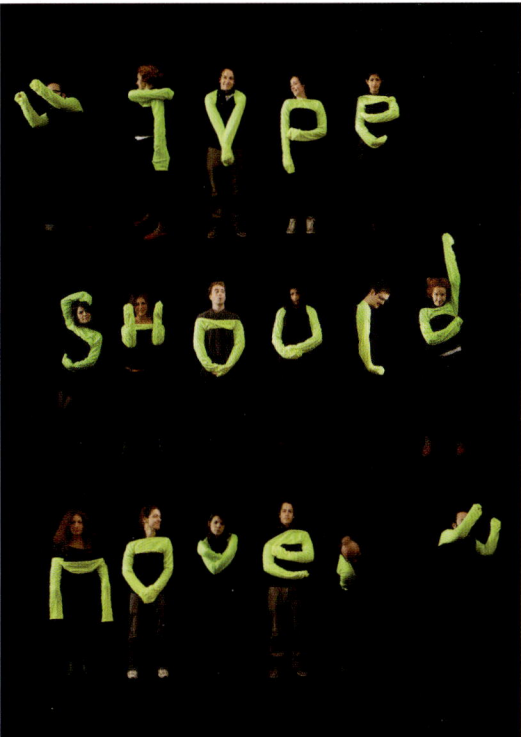

Figures 2.119 and 2.120 *Letterform for ephemeral messages* and *Thinking made visual* by Amandine Alessandra. © Amandine Alessandra, 2009. Reproduced with the permission of Amandine Alessandra.

Letterform for Ephemeral Messages | Amandine Alessandra

What does it mean to make letters with our bodies? Wearing bright-yellow boleros with long sleeves, designer and photographer Amandine Alessandra asked a group to pose as a series of numbers, letters, and punctuation for *Letterform for ephemeral messages*. Using specific body movements, this corporeal typography has been featured in a number of performances exploring the human body in relation to time and language—especially when viewed in real time. In one such public performance, the performers formed these bodily letters over the course of an hour, mimicking the digital clock at a train station, calling attention to the individual perception and value of time.

Figures 2.121 and 2.122 Semataphore (Alphabet) and Semataphore (Visual Test) by Laurent Mareschal. © artist/current rights owner, 2013. Reproduced with the permission of ADAGP (reproductions rights manager), Tami Notsani (photo credit).

Semataphore Alphabet & Visual Test | Laurent Mareschal

A semaphore refers to a method of communication via visual signals, often across large distances, such as between towers or ships; this method was most commonly used before the invention of the electrical telegraph. In semaphore flag signaling, flags are held in certain positions relative to the body to specify numbers or letters of an alphabet. Struck by this poetic visual, Laurent Mareschal's *Semataphore*—a play on the words semaphore and metaphor— explored how an alphabet could convey messages through body positions rooted in dance. Shown here as a respective alphabet (B&W photo print mounted on aluminum, 60 cm × 40 cm) and visual test (B&W photo print mounted on aluminum, 60 cm × 20 cm) in the form of an eye chart, this intention maps language onto the body, while giving typography a corporeal home.

Figures 2.123 and 2.124 *The Secret Eater* by E. M. Alysse Bowd, made in 2017. Photographer credit: Jordan Blackburn. Reproduced with the Permission of E. M. Alysse Bowd.

The Secret Eater | E. M. Alysse Bowd

In multidisciplinary artist E. M. Alysse Bowd's *The Secret Eater*, the artist performs an unexpected act of compassion and consumption by eating secrets of strangers. As an interactive and intimate performance, members of a public audience were invited to etch their secret—without ink—onto a small piece of paper. These secrets were clipped to a pulley system and carefully transferred to the mysterious individual at the end of the table: the Secret Eater herself. Then, the Secret Eater silently took the paper, dipped it in honey, and ate it—chewing and swallowing the confession, freeing the owner from their secret. This performance serves as a personal negotiation of vulnerability and discretion, an act of trust and transference between strangers. Here, the meaning of the written word, in the form of a scribed secret, is transformed by its corporeal conveyance.

inclusive of the gamut of experiences of having a physical body, including bodily processes, death, and decay. For centuries, art and design have used the human body as inspiration, as evidenced by the sheer number of sculptures and portraits celebrating or interrogating the triumphs and limitations of the human form. Because of the emotional connection to corporeal experiences, objects and artifacts dealing with the body have particular significance. Death masks of historical figures, or clothes of noteworthy individuals are fascinating—or morbid?—due to their analogously lived experiences through corporeal closeness. Works on, of, or from the body, become particularly visceral (see "History and material meanings" and "Personal space" earlier in this chapter).

Physical expressions—including body movements, vocalizations, actions, and reactions—are the basis for performance. In this context, these actions and events are intentional and often intended for a particular audience. They may be live, recorded, spontaneous, or planned. Performances may be lyrical, musical, dramatic—or works of art in and of themselves—called *performance art*, enabled through the single, participatory, or collective actions of an artist or participants.

Performance involving the body is a deeply human thing to do: across time, languages, and locations, the acts of storytelling or expressing through movement, sound, and action have been, and continue to be, valued cultural acts. Type made through a performance becomes an artifact of action, the evidence of an activity which marked its creation and informs its meaning. As *part* of a performance, typographic objects can be props. If during a performance, physical words or letters are thrown, broken, hugged, worn, or dissolved, they take on the consequent meanings and histories of those actions and interactions. If a bodily movement or performance creates a transitory message, typographic meaning may be influenced by its fleeting, precious, or disposable existence. Consider the enormous but ultimately brief life of performed sky-written messages. While notable for their effort of action and temporal text, they are inevitably dispersed by wind and weather (see "Time as medium" in Chapter 3).

Physical proximity to corporeal performance creates meaning, too. This is the difference between streaming a recorded theatrical performance versus seeing it live in the theater. In-person, the stakes are entirely different. This changes the ambience, architecture, and acoustics of the space, as well as the expectations and relationship between performer and audience. Planned or impromptu audience participation can change, inform, or shift the direction of a performance. While many performances involving typography exist as documentation, as videos, or still photos, the fact that they happened is important as an act itself. Their documentation serves as a way to continue to tell the story of a performance after the fact.

Figure 2.125 *Spin* (after Sol LeWitt) © 2021. Photo credit: Josh Hawkins for UNLV's Marjorie Barrick Museum of Art. Sign Spinner: Evan James.

Spin (After Sol LeWitt) | Yumi Janairo Roth

American Artist Sol LeWitt is best known for his contributions to minimalism and conceptual art, including his 1968 textual contribution *Sentences on Conceptual Art*, listing ideas relative to this movement. Yumi Janairo Roth's *Spin* recontextualizes this text through public performances, rather than in galleries or museums. In this performance, skilled and athletic sign-spinners spun lines from *Sentences on Conceptual Art*. By connecting sign-spinners and audiences in public places, this performance recontextualizes language, action, and the exchange of ideas regarding inclusivity and exclusivity of conceptual art.

3
Temporal Context

Time and History

All art and design is a product of the time in which it was created. The available resources, ideas, technologies, or politics of a particular era inevitably impact our language, aesthetics, and values—despite our best efforts to the contrary. Because visual communication can convey multiple meanings, its interpretations may align or contradict with its creator's intent. This becomes especially evident when a work's temporal context changes. Therefore, what something means is informed by both when something is *made* as well as when it is *viewed*.

In many instances, the history or evolution of specific visual language may be largely removed from its contemporary audience. Consider, for instance, the common ampersand. While most typographers know the origins of this beloved character, the majority of its users may not, even if they frequently employ its use and understand its visual and linguistic meaning. In very short summary, the ampersand began as a ligature of *et*, the Latin word for *and*. This typographic connection is clearer in ampersands with more a literal "et" ligature—but the origin of this character isn't at all obvious from the common, more abstract, double-counter ampersand (&) which graces our keyboards. While knowing the history of the ampersand certainly isn't a prerequisite to its use, it highlights how even familiar characters can have hidden histories.

As power structures, ideas, and viewers change, meanings and contexts are perpetually reconsidered and reimagined. Typographic communication is constantly evolving; new connotations and affiliations result from works being reclaimed, recontextualized, appropriated, or remixed. As such, a work's original meaning or intent may shift or be lost over time. *Unlike* the ampersand—whose initial meaning has carried throughout its history—the origins of italic type showcase distinct meanings in different temporal contexts.

Chapter 3's image: Travel_Motion via Getty Images.

A CLOSER LOOK:

Italics

For readers and writers of Latin text, italic type is ubiquitous. Throughout this book it has been frequently employed to highlight particular terms and titles, as well as to signify verbal and visual emphasis. Today, these are entirely familiar and otherwise unremarkable uses of italics—but this was not their original function or meaning.

The influence of the handwriting of Italian humanists extends beyond their contribution to the development of roman type. Niccolò Niccoli was an Italian humanist scholar best known for his written adaptations of classical texts. He deftly employed the use of humanistic scripts, but slanted them forward slightly in a quicker and more casual style which became known as *antica corsiva*. This style of handwriting became popular and served as the inspiration for the first italic typefaces, which became known as *italics* due to their origins and efforts to emulate Italian handwriting.

Fellow Italian humanist scholar and printer Aldus Manutius founded the Aldine Press in Venice in 1494; shortly after, he commissioned Francesco Griffo, a punch-cutter, to design and cut a typeface resembling this new style of handwriting, known as the *Aldine Italic*. The Aldine Press had begun printing books in a smaller octavo format, akin to modern paperbacks, which were easier to hold for readers on the go. Such examples included their printed edition of Virgil from 1501, which featured italic type. Why was this? These letterforms engaged with contemporary aesthetics and scholarly connotations of their time, appealing to their intended readers. Many scholars believe that this use of italics contributed to both spatial and financial economy, as condensed letterforms could fit more words onto fewer pages. Others disagree, and argue that it was not italics' lateral compression which saved space—or insist that in this application, text set in roman type would have occupied the same amount of space.

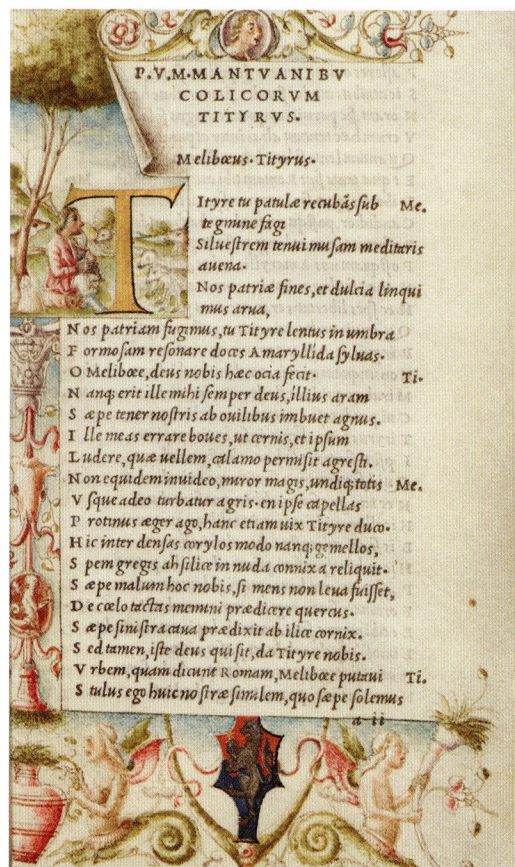

Figure 3.1 Virgil, Aldus Manutius; Aldine Press, 1501. Copyright of the University of Manchester.

In any instance, at their inception, roman letters and italic text were viewed as entirely different systems, and were not used seamlessly with each other, as they are today. The use of italics within roman text to indicate emphasis wasn't employed until later in the sixteenth century, when roman capital letters were redesigned for continuity within italic typefaces. Our contemporary use of italics for inflection and importance demonstrates how both use and meanings can change and evolve over time. What something communicates in the past or present does not guarantee its future use or interpretation.

TEMPORAL INFLUENCE: TECHNOLOGY AND SOCIETY

The typography of any particular era reflects the values, interests, and social shifts of that time. Consider the social influences—and consequent visual language—of type from the Victorian era. This time period was marked by the reign of Queen Victoria in the United Kingdom from 1837 to 1901, arriving on the heels of the Industrial Revolution, marking the birth of factories and mass production. This shift fundamentally transformed the materials and machinery used to produce objects and images—as well as the values of the society which rampantly coveted and consumed them.

The Industrial Revolution saw the rise of a middle class which could afford lavish-looking goods which had previously been reserved for the extremely wealthy. Aesthetics influenced by gothic art and architecture led to ornate objects which could be rapidly and industrially produced, often at the expense of skill and quality. Using methods such as stamping or embossing, businesses sought to emulate the look of handcrafted works via factory production, through objects like pressed glass, which offered a cheaper facsimile of laboriously made cut glass. In an act of *conspicuous consumption* (see "Power structures" in Chapter 1) the ability to own and display these ornate objects signaled a desired social status. By reflecting these societal values, decoration signified emblems of status and comfort, making copious ornamentation and filigree a common aesthetic of the Victorian era.

An overwhelming desire for goods led to increased competition in the marketplace, fueling the rise of advertising as a way to communicate the benefits of specific products to potential buyers. The invention of the high-speed steam press exponentially increased the production output of books and newspapers, while advancements in the realm of printing led to new, popular means of mass communication, such as the poster. In this era, large posters were pasted prominently in public spaces, including building walls, making them a common sight—the precursor to contemporary billboards and bus-stop ads. Because of their ubiquity and significant size, these new advertisements required big, riveting display typefaces to compete for a viewer's attention.

Commercial printers used specimen books to showcase available examples of typefaces—both decorative *and* subdued—in a variety of sizes. Frequently embellished borders and graphic motifs gave many advertisements a similar visual landscape of Victorian social goods. Wood type became popular among commercial printers, especially in large sizes, as it was easier and cheaper to form than metal type. Letterforms in the nineteenth century were subject to the same evolutions and trends that any long era endures, making "Victorian type" a vast category, with many styles and compositions varying by region and decade. However, Victorian print materials may be best known for their eccentric combinations of disparate typefaces, including visually rich Tuscans (which can include faces with bifurcated serifs and medial spurs), Egyptian type (also known as slab serifs), Didones, and fat faces—among others. Posters and packaging often reveled in visual excess, with prolific decoration in the form of floral ornaments and fanciful (though sometimes nearly illegible) letterforms.

The visuals we might perceive today as gaudy, saccharine, or visually overwhelming would have felt pleasantly contemporary to audiences of their time. While not all Victorian type was exceptionally decorative, the flourishes and fonts associated with this era did not spring from thin air: these temporally specific aesthetics were *directly* influenced by cultural values impacted by consumerism and the new affordances of prolific technological advancement.

The relationships between time, technology, and typographic outcomes aren't limited to the Industrial Revolution. In 1984, Apple launched the first Macintosh computer, which revolutionized the field of graphic design and

Figure 3.2 M. Westerman & Zn. Rijksmuseum, Amsterdam.

Feestviering bij de Onthulling van het Monument gewijd aan den volksgeest van 1830 en 1831 te Amsterdam op den 25, 26, 27 en 28 augustus 1856
This 1856 poster details a schedule of events celebrating the unveiling of a monument in Amsterdam, featuring a decorative border and a wide combination of typefaces in use.

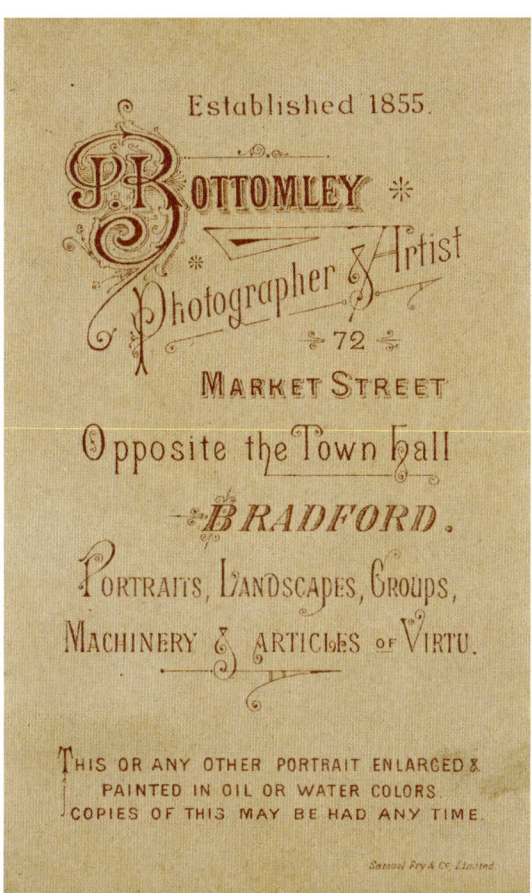

Figure 3.3 J. Bottomley Photographer & Artist; back of color photograph, *c.* 1890s. Wellcome Collection.

J. Bottomley Photography Studio
Studio information on the back of a photograph from the late nineteenth century showcases ornate text and letterforms full of flourishes.

introduced desktop publishing. These advances were influential both technically and conceptually, as evidenced in the pioneering New Wave digital designs of April Greiman in the 1980s and 1990s. Emigre, founded in 1984 by Rudy VanderLans and Zuzana Licko, was one of the first digital type foundries to make type on and for computers. These works and organizations are direct responses to technological shifts and their consequent design opportunities. As such, they paved the way for new digital formats to become standard ways of working.

Of course, technology is always shifting, and not all advancements last. With the exception of collectors and analog aficionados, most people aren't setting their type via a Linotype machine or saving their work to a floppy disk. For example, the development of the multimedia software platform Flash near the turn of the millennium led to an onslaught of innovative, interactive web experiences of text, image, and audio works. The possibilities afforded by Flash made over-the-top swift-moving website intros, in-browser games, and comical soundboards recognizable features of digital design in the early 2000s. As other more effective means emerged, Adobe (which acquired Flash in 2005) planned for its End of Life, a gradual phasing out of the software. This finally culminated in 2020, and Adobe blocked content from running in Flash Player in most places in early 2021. While creators had significant lead time of Flash's impending disappearance, many specific websites and videos of the 2000s are now permanently inaccessible, living only as blank screens with a final message conveying the mercurial nature of any technological advancement: "Adobe Flash Player is no longer supported."

Just as past media developments in the areas of film and photo (see "Kinetic and expressive type" in Chapter 2) sparked entirely new modes of creating, today's digital leaps in technology and communication continue to transform how typographic works are made, viewed, exhibited, and understood.

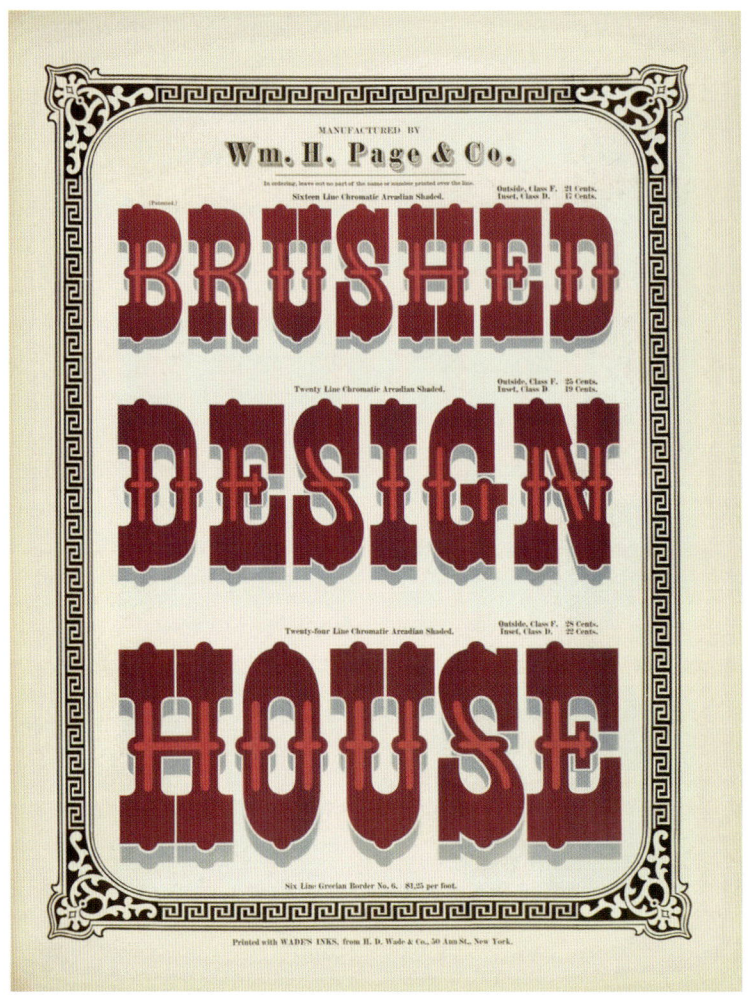

Figure 3.4 Electronic reproduction. New York, NY: Columbia University Libraries, 2013.

Specimens of chromatic wood type, borders, &c. manufactured by Wm. H. Page & Co. Greeneville, Conn.

Toward the end of the eighteenth century in Germany, Alois Senefelder invented *lithography*, a process by which writing and illustrations could be reproduced. Based on the principle that oil and water do not mix, a greasy pen would be used to create an image on stone which was then wet with water. Ink applied to the stone adhered to the drawing—but not the wet surface—allowing a reproduction of the image to be transferred onto paper. This revolutionary process was expanded further by the introduction of *chromolithography*, which relied on printing with individual colors via multiple stones onto a single print. These overlaps would visually blend to produce rich color images and served as the precursor to contemporary four-color offset lithography.

With new outcomes suddenly possible as a result of technological development, novel typefaces explored color, layering, and detail—as shown in this particularly vibrant specimen book of chromatic wood type and borders from William Hamilton Page & Co. in Grenville, Connecticut, from 1874. Inspired by the advances of chromolithography, this book features examples of chromatic type, which were designed to be printed via letterpress with multiple inks of varying colors; this particular example makes use of two. When one letter was printed on top of its counterpart with appropriate registration, their inks would overlap in specifically designed areas, creating an additional color.

Giving Type Meaning

 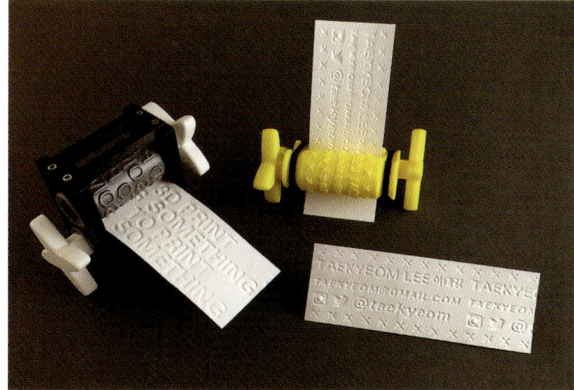

Figures 3.5 and 3.6 3D-printed type embosser by Taekyeom Lee. © Taekyeom Lee, 2017. 3D printed ceramic type A by Taekyeom Lee. © Taekyeom Lee, 2016. Reproduced with the permission of Taekyeom Lee.

3D-Printed Type | Taekyeom Lee

Until quite recently, 3D-printing was extremely cost-prohibitive and inaccessible for most creative practitioners. A rise in community maker-spaces, reliable materials, and affordable domestic printers has moved 3D-printing from a technological curiosity to an available and effective way of creating. The inventive and sculptural typographic work of artist and designer Taekyeom Lee is informed by computer-aided design (CAD) technologies and rapid prototyping methods. These typographic explorations are first designed digitally, before being 3D-printed from layers of extruded plastic or ceramic. Engaging with new means-of-making, they investigate how emerging technologies can bridge digital and physical environments and experiences. These works—shown here as a 3D-printed letterform and type embosser—simultaneously showcase the capabilities of technological advancements while interrogating their implications and opportunities for communication and interaction.

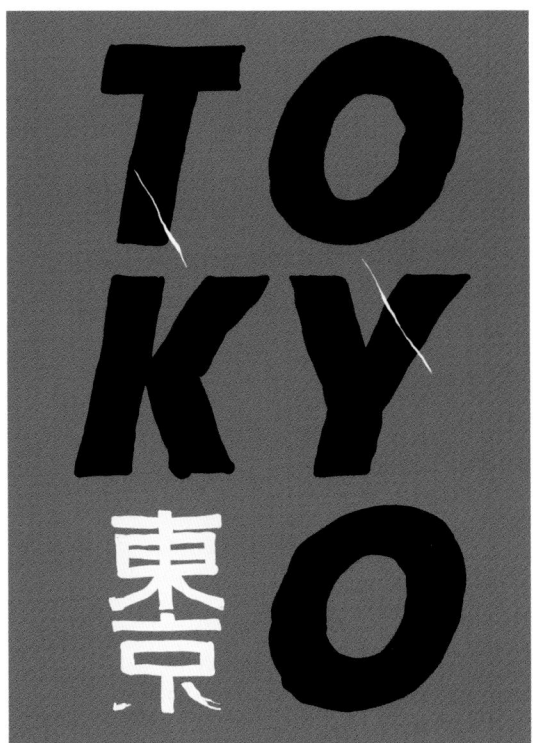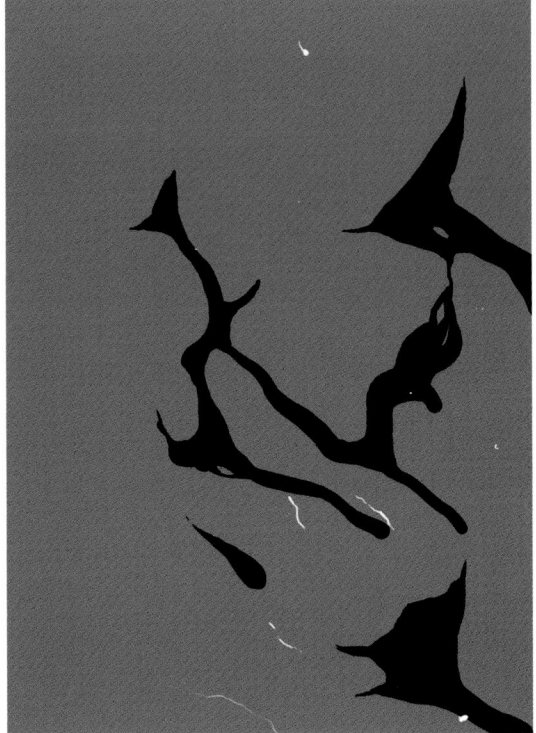

Figures 3.7–3.10 *Napoli Poster*, ShowUsYourType by Gabriel Pulpo. © Gabriel Pulpo, 2020. Reproduced with the permission of Gabriel Rivera Cruz. *Tokyo Poster*, ShowUsYourType by Aljoscha Höhborn. © Aljoscha Höhborn, 2013. Reproduced with the permission of Aljoscha Höhborn.

Show Us Your Type | Gabriel Pulpo, Aljoscha Höhborn

Gifs, short for Graphics Interchange Format, were developed in 1987 as a way to reduce the size of digital images and brief animations while still maintaining image quality. Their lossless format and manageable file sizes have made them perfect for sharing via blogs, websites, and text messages (see "Gesture and expression" in Chapter 2). This has made gifs incredibly popular in the current age of digital communication and social media. As a way of transmitting particular visual information, artists have transformed gifs into their own artistic medium—using this type of digital file for sharing data *and* conveying visual expression.

Founded in 2009, ShowUsYourType (a creative endeavor of designers Lisi Badia, Natalie Long, and Ana Guasch) combines an affinity for travel, typography, and design through a series of online and in-person exhibitions and collaborations. Designers from around the globe regularly submit posters highlighting the unique personality of a location by creatively portraying a city's name. Many of these digital posters live as short but lively gifs. These looping animations have the ability to visualize actions and transformations quickly and effectively, featuring expressive type in a concise digital format. Gabriel Pulpo's poster for Napoli transforms the vibrant cascade of the city's architecture to form its name; Aljoscha Höhborn's poster for Tokyo shows a typographic transition through the form of rain, embodying a moment on a drizzly night in the bustling metropolis.

TEMPORAL INFLUENCE: CURRENT EVENTS

Centuries of art and design have shown us that the works of artists and designers have always been influenced by what is happening *right now*: the events and scenarios shaping the present. Of course, current events only stay current for a short amount of time before they are absorbed into the past as part of a larger history. While this term might bring to mind images of 24-hour news cycles and instantly accessible information, current events don't have to make international headlines to warrant an emotional or artistic response. Works inspired by present happenings may respond to seismic global shifts like the Covid-19 pandemic, or events which are more local like the closing of a longtime factory or the passing of a city's beloved downtown window-washer.

Within the expanded field of art and design, designers are not just formatters of content, but creators of content. By making work in response to current political or social events, artists and designers craft opportunities to reflect and respond in meaningful ways—with works serving as reactions, commentary, or potential solutions. Typographically, these can manifest in a variety of expressive or utilitarian outcomes. Consider how lettering on protest signs can spark communal solidarity, while text-based get-out-the-vote campaigns work to disseminate information for political change. Cathartic or educational works, installations, exhibitions, or performances give artists and audiences alike new ways to process or understand events. Through their forms, narratives, and use, event-inspired typefaces can shape perceptions of historical, current, or even future happenings (see "History-inspired type" and "Into the future" in this chapter).

Works made in response to current events are framed and understood by their temporal context. Because of the immediacy or specificity of their reaction, they are explicitly linked to those specific moments—but can also seek to *influence* them. This is especially notable when the events and works in question pertain to protest or dissent.

A CLOSER LOOK:
Lorraine Art Schneider's *Primer*

In many parts of the world, the 1960s were a time of great change, marking significant political and historical shifts. In the United States, this decade saw advances in equality through the Civil Rights Movement, technological leaps in the Space Race, cultural upheaval with the introduction of the pill and the sexual revolution, and ongoing tensions with the Soviet Union as the Cold War continued. Simultaneously, the controversial Vietnam War raged on, which many Americans were strongly against.

One such American was Lorraine Art Schneider, an artist and mother who opposed the violence of the Vietnam War. In the mid-1960s, in response to these current events, she created a small etching for an exhibition at Pratt Institute—but submission requests stipulated that works could not exceed four square inches. Working within this requirement, she

Figure 3.11 *Primer* by Lorraine Art Schneider. © Another Mother for Peace, 1966. Reproduced with the permission of Elisa Kleven for Another Mother for Peace.

penned a direct, original, and irrefutable phrase in the tiny available space: "War is not healthy for children and other living things." Marked in bold, organic, childlike text, the message was earnest, straightforward, and resonant. She called this piece *Primer*.

When approached by a friend to use the work as the logo for a new peace organization, Schneider agreed, donating all profits from its use to the group, called Another Mother for Peace, founded in 1967. Seeking action to end the Vietnam War, Another Mother for Peace printed over 300,000 "mother's day" greeting cards featuring this design and sent them to members of congress, calling for an end to killing and commitment to peace. This brought the image international attention. Its direct message and captivating lettering very quickly became a masthead for the anti-war movement, and was frequently reproduced on apparel, posters, signs, banners, jewelry, and cards.

Here, an image of one of the original 200 etchings of *Primer* showcases the humble origins of this deeply influential, recognizable work. While Lorraine Art Schneider passed away in 1972, the legacy of her work lives on, stemming from a small but powerful reaction to current events—a mother's enduring hope for peace.

Figure 3.12 Ugly Gerry by Ben Doessel and James Lee, 2019.

Ugly Gerry | Ben Doessel and James Lee

In its most basic definition, a representative democracy seeks to represent the will of the people through their elected officials. However, this system only works when the respective populace is represented fairly and accurately. In the United States, *gerrymandering* refers to the act of redistricting electoral districts in order to give an advantage to a particular political party. This is deeply problematic, as gerrymandered areas do not represent the will of the people—they represent the will of those who form the districts. This unfairly keeps political parties in power even as demographics, ideas, and voter mindsets change. In addition, gerrymandered districts have intentionally been drawn to limit the political power of communities of color.

To raise awareness of this damaging practice and encourage constituents to take action against it, designers Ben Doessel and James Lee created a typeface called Ugly Gerry, whose letters are composed of real, convoluted, gerrymandered districts in the United States. These districts feature absurd shapes, highlighting the great lengths taken by political parties to remain in power. Designed in partnership with RepresentUs, a nonpartisan organization working to end corruption and secure fair elections, audiences are encouraged to use the typeface and to contact their representatives to take action. This typeface brings attention to current political events, exposing the fragility of democracy and the necessary steps required to protect it.

Figure 3.13 *Protest Banner Lending Library* by Aram Han Sifuentes, 2016–present. Installation at University Galleries at Illinois State University, photograph by Jessica Bingham.

Protest Banner Lending Library | Aram Han Sifuentes

The 2016 presidential election marked a stark change in the political landscape in the United States. For many Americans, it was a devastating moment, leaving people uncertain, scared, and angry. Protests surged around the country as acts of resistance and solidarity. To process these emotions and to participate in protests she could not attend, multidisciplinary artist and educator Aram Han Sifuentes turned to a lifelong practice of sewing to address pressing issues of social injustice. This was the beginning of the *Protest Banner Lending Library*—a library where sewn protest banners could be made, donated, checked out, and used by visitors. Repeated in multiple cities across the United States, these vibrant and powerful typographic banners included a variety of messages and topics, ranging from "Black Lives Matter," and "fight ignorance, not immigrants," to "water is life." These banners lauded phrases of inclusivity, equity, and determination, while their framework for use facilitated community and collective action.

Figures 3.14 and 3.15 *Blursday* by Ben Blount. © Ben Blount, 2020. *100 Years (Black Wall Street)* by Ben Blount. © Ben Blount, 2021. Reproduced with the permission of Ben Blount.

Blursday and *100 years (Black Wall Street)* | Ben Blount

The work of Detroit-born artist, designer, and letterpress printer Ben Blount frequently investigates concepts of identity, race, and narratives of the American experience—including current events. As a response to the uncertainty and strange passage of time during the Covid-19 pandemic, he created a print titled *Blursday*. Here, names of each day of the week are printed over one another in a flat gray, speaking to the unsettling monotony of 2020.

His work *100 years (Black Wall Street)* addresses the current event of a commemoration—the remembering of the 100-year anniversary of the Tulsa Race Massacre. In 1921, the thriving, affluent African American community of Greenwood (a district of Tulsa, Oklahoma) known as Black Wall Street, was attacked by a white mob who burned the neighborhood, looted homes and businesses, and murdered hundreds of people while displacing thousands of residents. This act of anti-Black violence was frequently and intentionally omitted from histories, making this bold print even more salient—a testament to the impact of this event and a call for its victims, survivors, and descendants to never be forgotten.

TYPOGRAPHIC TRENDS

As a verb, a *trend* speaks to the direction in which something moves. As a noun, it speaks to whatever is collectively perceived as popular or fashionable for a period of time. Just as social attitudes, influences, and aesthetic preferences change and evolve, so do typographic trends. Trends are often spoken of pejoratively due to their inherently fleeting nature, but just because something is fashionable doesn't make it unimportant. Practicing artists and designers should always be aware of popular approaches in typography, but should view them critically and thoughtfully, with future contexts of use in mind. Trendy aesthetics which feel very *now* will inevitably be very *then* at some point. If designing for longevity, it's wise to not make visual choices which feel so cutting-edge that they will appear dated the following week.

Not all trends are all-reaching. Niche pockets appear in subgroups and within particular cultural contexts, and not all popular design preferences become international styles. As such, while the feel of a certain time period may be defined by a recognizable aesthetic, this is rarely on account of a single typeface or method. Generally, because multiple trends occur concurrently, the "look" of a particular era is a wide collection of differing typefaces, patterns, ideas, and influences. Most trends peak in popularity before subsiding. While some recede into relative obscurity, others extend beyond their genesis to become an ongoing facet of a society's visual lexicon, or are rediscovered by new generations through revivals, resurgences, and recontextualizations.

A CLOSER LOOK:
Typographic trends

Mid-century modern scripts

As a genre, "Mid-century-modern" is broadly defined. Its exact span is nebulous, but tends to center on the 1950s following the Second World War. Objects, images, typefaces, and architecture were developed with a variety of visual outcomes and materials, encompassing the far-reaching general aesthetic of the mid-century in many parts of the world. Scandinavian influence was evident in sleek, tapered teakwood furniture, and overlapping "atomic" abstract shapes, bright colors, and parabola forms referenced scientific discovery and the pressing space-race. Mid-century typography manifests in many ways, but was often marked by a trend of playful typefaces and colorful compositions permeating with post-war optimism. As recovering economies boomed, this led to a plethora of ads showcasing shiny new cars, televisions, and refrigerators. Buoyant, aimable typography followed.

There are many recognizable typographic trends of the mid-century, especially in the United States, such as uneven baselines of sparkly, organic serifs or streamlined geometric, automotive scripts. Another such example is the frequent use of cursive typefaces emulating pen or brush handwriting. Casual vertical scripts and italic brush scripts frequently adorned headlines of magazine ads showcasing consumer goods. Bold, jouncing letters which emulated energetic handwriting or sign-painting were often paired with variations on fonts from serif typefaces like Century, Bodoni, or Clarendon, including Freeman Craw's Craw Clarendon family, released by American Type Founders *c.* 1955. These spirited typefaces embodied something both relieved and hopeful in their gesture and motion toward the future.

Here, two menu covers from 1953 showcase examples of quintessential mid-century scripts in use. For a gathering of the Wine and Food Society of New York at the Grand Ballroom of the Hotel Plaza, overlapping poised hands are paired with a vertical pen script, promising its attendees an effortlessly elegant occasion. On this Breakfast Room Service menu for The Shamrock, two distinct brush scripts and a typeface emulating sign-painting portray an intentionally bustling, jubilant approach to typography.

Figures 3.16 and 3.17 From The New York Public Library.

Y2K typography

From roughly the mid-1990s through just past the turn of the twenty-first century, new typography captured the spirit of the upcoming millennium; this general look is now colloquially referred to as the *Y2K aesthetic*, in honor of the infamous computer bug expected to disrupt systems as the year 1999 transitioned to 2000. Frequently featuring aerodynamic forms, stylized digital references, and allusions to speed and circuitry, many typefaces of this era reflect ideas about the past's perception of a potential future.

The confluence of a new millennium with increased digital capabilities and energized facets of popular culture led to a distinct visual language. Typography from this era was influenced by sleek materials and future contexts: layered renderings of chromed, reflective surfaces and extreme 3D-extrusions spoke to present and possible technological advances. Other flatter, angled rectilinear letterforms featured chamfered edges or thick curves, like the imagined bulkhead of a spaceship. Typefaces composed of elliptical shapes or merged pixels indicative of LCD displays spoke to digital connectivity and ever-growing possibilities of the World Wide Web. In addition, techno music and UK rave culture were deeply influential to this visual approach, often emulated on club flyers, websites, and album covers.

Visual representations of the future have historically been tied to advancements of the present. Illustrated scenarios imagining the year 2000 by French artist Jean-Marc Côté (among others) near the turn of the twentieth century feature fantastical automatic machines—composed of the recognizable propellers, gears, and mechanical advancements familiar at that time. The futuristic American cartoon *The Jetsons*, from the 1960s, features parabolic architecture and aesthetics undoubtedly influenced by mid-century buildings and the ongoing space-race. In the late twentieth century, Japan's technological developments of the 1980s were influential to notions of progress—which likely explains why late twentieth-century science fiction frequently makes aesthetic references to Japan as synonymous with ideas of the future. Consider the neon allusions to Tokyo and forms of consumer electronics as evidenced in the cyberpunk setting of Ridley Scott's iconic 1982 film *Blade Runner*, or the Japanese text from 1995's *Wipeout*, a racing game set in the future whose influential graphic identity by *The Designers Republic* became emblematic of Y2K design.

The design of both images *and* objects were influenced by this trend. The late designer and educator Steven Skov Holt is credited with coining the term "blobject"—a reference to rounded, fluid forms fashionable at the turn of the twenty-first century. While preceding decades' cars and domestic items frequently featured boxy forms, shifts in visual

Figure 3.18 From Adobe Fonts.

Figure 3.19 Cyberotica by Barry Deck. © Barry Deck, 1994. Reproduced with the permission of Barry Deck.

preference and technological advancements in computer-aided design ushered in more curvilinear shapes, such as the bulbous 1996 Ford Taurus or rounded iMac G3s of 1998. This trend inevitably extended to typefaces, which were met with thick, bubbly forms, rounded corners or smooth, forward features.

This collection of ideas and aesthetics manifested through a range of new typefaces such as Cyberotica, designed by Barry Deck in 1994, or the Shimano family (set here in Round Black) designed by Richard Lipton in 1995. Experimentation with forms in conjunction with an imagined future highlighted the hopeful possibility of the new millennium. This hope, however, was perhaps as short-lived as the Y2K aesthetic itself, disappearing in the wake of events at the turn of the century, including the dot-com bubble burst, 9/11, and their consequent cultural and political fallout.

Modern calligraphy

In the early 2010s, a new style of typeface and lettering style emerged and was met with immense popularity. These scripts, a contemporary take on traditional calligraphy, are often referred to as "modern calligraphy" or "bounce lettering," and feature lyrical, calligraphic cursive and bouncing baselines ranging from mild to extreme. Conjuring images of chalked coffee shop signage and personalized notes, their casual strokes and uneven cadence evoke something effortlessly but confidently handwritten. As these letterforms became widely used, their styles and variations expanded. Thin, breezy forms, textured brush scripts, and bubbly, high-contrast clusters contribute to the plethora of available options, ranging from limited letter-sets to expertly constructed fonts with ample contextual alternates for wider variation and customization (see "Gesture in and of letterforms" in Chapter 2).

The gesture of these letterforms implies a bold, energetic personality paired with a relaxed elegance, making them a go-to choice for wine labels, wedding invitations, bridesmaid accoutrement, domestic signage, and inspirational quotes, as shown in these stock images. Rising in tandem with both the stylistic and emotional concept of the "modern farmhouse"—which frames clean, rustic simplicity as a contemporary oasis—modern calligraphy's spin on traditional scripts lends a feeling of something refined, but not restricted. Both aspirational and unburdened, these scripts can present themselves both as a reflection of, and reprieve from, modern life.

Socially, and within a particular cultural context, these letterforms have become affiliated with particular notions of identity and are often referred to as "girly" or "feminine" frequently appearing on motherhood blogs and adorning women's and girls' apparel (see "Type and identity" in this chapter). In conjunction with the rise of social media personas and Instagram influencers, these typefaces may have reached their popularity in part because they embody the casual, assured, sassy poise associated with a curated online personality of the 2010s.

Figures 3.20 and 3.21 Asya_mix via iStock by Getty Images.

At the time of this book's writing—*greetings, future reader, from the early 2020s!*—current typographic trends have continued to shift in new directions. Tech start-ups and giant corporations have ditched previously campier logotypes for clean sans serifs aiming to be friendly yet accessible—perhaps as a way to seem personable and unthreatening, despite growing concerns of monopolies, data privacy, and online misinformation. A penchant for drippy, gloopy, highly experimental display typefaces has led to an onslaught of works which feel like unexpected amalgamations of trippy 1960s counterculture and early-2000s rave posters. Reverse-contrast fonts are once again appearing in common use. Wedding invitations and editorial features are awash with high-contrast serif letterforms featuring a wispy, Art Nouveau feel and *lots* of decorative ligatures.

This is, for better or for worse, a small facet of the current moment. Is this a result of nostalgia for the pre-digital age in the wake of a constant political upheaval and the stress of a devastating global pandemic? Are millennial designers longing to reclaim the aesthetic of their formative years, the early 2000s? While we can muse in the present about why these aesthetics capture collective appeal, future design historians will have the benefit of hindsight. Years from now, designers and scholars of visual culture will more aptly be able to analyze these forms and ideas, drawing parallels between societal shifts and typographic outcomes.

If all art and design is a product of its time, and temporal influences create temporary trends—can any type choice really be "timeless"? This concept is large and difficult to gauge with any accuracy. However, socially speaking, choices frequently touted as "timeless" typically refer to established typefaces which feel contemporary in nearly any timeframe. Historical typefaces like Baskerville, Bodoni, Didot, Futura, or Helvetica are frequently referenced in this capacity due to their enduring use across eras, demonstrating that typefaces from the past do not automatically or uniformly carry the social connotations of their time of design. Because specific decoration or embellishment is often linked to a particular trend or era, visual simplicity is often associated with the social concept of "timelessness"—but this is culturally, socially, and temporally subjective. In the future, typefaces which feel very "now" may be regarded as "classic." Of course, *how* these typefaces will be used is another story entirely.

Historical Type in Contemporary Use

First things first: while most people tend to use *historic* and *historical* interchangeably, there is a difference in their definitions. Typically, *historic* refers to something significant in history, while *historical* tends to refer to anything from history. Some examples of text, typography, or calligraphy use *are*, in fact, historic, made notable from their circumstance or context of use, like newspaper headlines from VE Day, the text of the Gutenberg Bible, or the signatures on the Declaration of Independence.

With these definitions in mind, what constitutes "historical type"? This term is a somewhat nebulous designation and necessitates a closer look at how we talk about time. Things which are *contemporary* are happening right now, but this term, too, is vague. It is a constantly shifting adjective—as what was considered contemporary in the past is not necessarily so in the present. The oxymoron "contemporary history" has generally referred to a time period from 1945—the end of the Second World War—to the present. "Contemporary art" may be defined using a similar range, but can also refer to art made more recently, and by living artists. As such, this ambiguity makes "historical" categorizations rather subjective. For clarity, this text uses "contemporary" to refer to the *general* present, referencing works, events, and styles in conversation with current visual culture and technology at the time of this of book's publication. Therefore, it uses *historical* in reference to anything before this. Within this text, *historical type in contemporary use* references type specifically from or inspired by a previous era as it is used in a present art and design practice.

Linguistically, we refer to different times in history through socially understood terms, each with specific connotations. Typographic works or typefaces which are *antique, antiquated, outdated, retro, passé,* or *vintage* all carry *very* different associations about a work's respective age and emotional appeal. Merriam-Webster specifies that something *antique* is from at least 100 years ago. Etsy, the online community of retailers selling handmade and vintage items, specifies that for anything to be considered "vintage" on its site, it must be at least twenty years old. "Retro" lacks a specific year-cutoff, but generally refers to a particular style originating from a previous period. Works which are *antiquated, passé,* or *outdated* refer to works of the past disparagingly, as no longer relevant—referencing a look which feels decidedly out of fashion (see "Typographic trends" in this chapter).

Socially and subjectively, each definition conjures different examples of type in use. Works described as *antique* may reference specific layouts or typefaces from the turn of the twentieth century. *Vintage* type may bring to mind a range of styles, from quivering 1940s horror-movie letterforms to thick, funky 1970s scripts. "Vintage" might even refer to a font in use across multiple time periods, like the enduring Cooper Black, designed by Oswald Bruce Cooper in the early 1920s (shown here in a revival) affiliated with both its contemporaneous print ads *and* 1980s camp shirts. *Retro* may simply describe any typographic throwback, encompassing both historical typefaces *and* contemporary works with identifiable aesthetics from another era.

Cooper Black

Figure 3.22 From Adobe Fonts.

A CLOSER LOOK:

Keep calm and carry on

There is a difference between works constructed or designed in a previous era and works which make visual reference to the past. While works and typefaces may *originate* from a previous time, the histories—and affiliated meanings—we associate with them are not always correct.

In the chaos of the Second World War, countries worked tirelessly to communicate instructions and calls-to-action to their respective citizens via propaganda posters. In the United States, the iconic War Advertising Council's *Loose Lips Sink Ships* poster reminded Americans not to share sensitive information related to the war effort—but mostly worked to prevent the spread of rumors which might hurt morale. In the United Kingdom, the Ministry of Information disseminated posters encouraging specific behavior while providing information on issues such as production, recruiting, and safety.

One such message produced by the Ministry of Information was a bright red poster with iconic, white sans serif text centered under a graphic of the crown of King George VI. Its succinct text read KEEP CALM AND CARRY ON—engendering clear notions of bravery and resilience, even under deeply tumultuous times. Viewed with nostalgia and pride, it has become a symbol of moral fortitude of everyday people during the Second World War, summoning images of unflappable Britons. While the poster's message—and its emotional response—is earnest, the historical circumstances surrounding its origins are significantly less riveting. Today, we imagine this poster as a common sight and refrain during the 1940s, but this simply wasn't the case. Intended to be used only as a last resort for dire circumstances, this massive campaign was printed, but never officially distributed to the public. How, then, has it gained such a following in the twenty-first century?

The Keep Calm and Carry On poster is a prime example of historic type gaining new meaning in contemporary use. While the original Keep Calm and Carry On poster is *from* 1939, its message and mythology are really *of* the 2010s. In 2000, the owners of Barter Books in Alnwick, Northumberland, discovered an original Keep Calm and Carry On poster in a box of old books purchased at auction, and posted it prominently in the bookstore. As it was immensely popular with patrons, the bookshop began to sell copies and other items featuring its message. Perhaps the resonance of its steadying text in the midst of the 2008 global financial crisis served to springboard the international affinity for this resolute phrase—as people sought steadfast messages of an earlier time to navigate an increasingly complex present.

Its popularity intensified, and inspired a number of custom online poster-builders including the useful *Keep Calm-o-Matic*, founded by Andrew Dancy in 2009. This website allows visitors to create custom versions of the iconic Keep Calm poster for a multitude of surfaces and products, giving audiences the option to customize a relatable sentiment into their own lives. Custom backgrounds, fonts, and sizes are available. Through these means, the phrase and relative typography of "Keep Calm And …" (or the cheeky antonym "I Can't Keep Calm I …")

became instantly translatable to any situation, including those intended for parody or satire. As a testament to its popularity and ubiquity, at the time of this book's writing, over 14 million images featuring variations on this phrase exist on the *Keep Calm-o-Matic* website.

What does this mean for the poster itself? The original 1939 poster and its twenty-first century counterpart exist as two things simultaneously: a historical artifact of ephemera marking a particular moment in time, and a contemporary message of determination fueled by nostalgic expectations of a presumed history. Its resurgence illustrates the transformative power of temporal contexts, as well as how easy it is to conflate present narratives with perceptions of the past. While the original Keep Calm and Carry On poster was *not* historically shared in the way it has been collectively imagined, perhaps there is some poetic justice in a once-shelved campaign finding new life in the digital age, reaching a far greater audience than it could have in its own time.

Figure 3.23 The Ministry of Information's 1939 Keep Calm and Carry On Poster, courtesy of http://www.wartimeposters.co.uk/.

Figure 3.24 Keep Calm and Design Type image. © Keep Calm Network Ltd, and courtesy of keepcalms.com.

REVIVALS AND REFERENCES

With so many new typefaces presently available, why do designers frequently make use of typefaces and compositions from or referencing the past? Visually referring to a specific time, place, or style through typography creates a point of reference—providing additional information used to construct meaning. Choosing a historical typeface or aesthetic reference can be used for purposes of historical accuracy, rediscovery, or recontextualization.

Throughout history, visual choices from the past have been brought back into contemporary use through revivals across art, design, and architecture. Typographically, a *revival* refers to the act of revisiting a previously designed typeface through re-design. Typically done with older or otherwise obscure letterforms, a typeface revival has the ability to shepherd forgotten typefaces into present use. After all, many examples of type existing in wood or metal were designed and used *centuries* before computers or digital font files. Some revivals are faithful reproductions of their historical predecessors, while others seek to be transformative in nature, using the original structure of identifiable letterforms from the past for adapting or remixing. Revivals differ somewhat from other design or preservation efforts through digital means, such as transforming historical handwriting or calligraphic forms into a typable font. These acts are not true typeface "revivals"—as they are not reviving *typefaces*, per se—but are new and important interpretations of historical letterforms.

While typeface revivals and visual references to the past have been deeply popular in the age of digital design, they are not unique to the relative present. Throughout history, revivals and references have been frequently employed as trends and typefaces develop, disappear, and are later rediscovered or reinterpreted for a new audience. In some instances, applications of historical letterforms are so successful that the *new* use of a particular aesthetic eclipses its historical origins and original use.

A CLOSER LOOK:
Sex, drugs, and Art Nouveau?

When is this Dutch "Delftsche Slaolie" poster from?

To an unsuspecting audience, it looks positively trippy, featuring recognizable visual representations frequently affiliated with the West in the 1960s and its respective cultural touchstones: sex, drugs, and rock and roll. While Jan Toorop's advertisement for Delft Salad Oil features aesthetics often associated with the free-flowing trends of the 1960s, it's actually from 1894. How, then, did these visual choices come to be associated with a time period some sixty years later?

This social connection speaks to the success of an aesthetic revival. In 1897, a group of Austrian artists, architects, and designers rebelled against the prevailing artistic organization of the Vienna Künstlerhaus to form their own group, in what became known as the Vienna Secession. This group, which included

Figure 3.25 Jan Toorop. Rijksmuseum, Amsterdam.

Josef Hoffman, Gustav Klimt, Koloman Moser, and Alfred Roller—among many others—sought to push back against the conservative, traditionalist academy which championed historical approaches and rejected new material and aesthetic advances.

Disseminated through a publication and various exhibitions, this Art Nouveau-related movement took contemporary visual choices even further en route to Modernism, and frequently featured graphic patterns, high-contrast compositions, and bold, experimental letterforms. These visual developments spoke to cultural and aesthetic pushback, shown here in the work of Alfred Roller, whose 1903 poster for the 16th exhibition of the Viennese Secession (printed by Albert Berger, Vienna) employed thick, emotive lettering, blending rectilinear forms with softer curves.

Decades later, in the mid-twentieth century, historical letterforms were revisited as visual inspiration. When new political and social movements in the 1960s sparked cultural pushback against conventional norms and traditional approaches, many design choices did too. Such is the case of American designer Wes Wilson, who was highly inspired by Art Nouveau and their affiliated movements, like the Vienna Secession. Commissioned to create promotional posters in the mid-1960s for concerts featuring bands such as Jefferson Airplane, The Grateful Dead, and The Byrds, his notably vibrant works revived and recontextualized lettering similar to Alfred Roller's. In this use, relatively stable letterforms were reimagined as something free and unconstrained—resulting in fluid or flaming baselines, exaggerated emphasis, implied motion, and messaging which required close attention. Paired with dazzling color use, this aesthetic became known as *psychedelic*, a broad term encompassing visual choices including sinuous patterns, lush colors, and disorienting compositions referencing the perception-altering visual effects of hallucinogenic drugs. While many of his iconic, visually vibrating posters advertised concerts for headlining bands at the Fillmore Auditorium in San Francisco, his iconic style also appeared on other applications—such as this poster titled *Open Up and See* for the opening of new offices in Los Angeles for the J. Walter Thompson Co. in 1967.

Figure 3.26 2022. © Photo Austrian Archives/Scala Florence.

The influence of Art Nouveau typography and its affiliated contemporary movements, like Germany's *Jugendstil*, are evident in a plethora of posters from the 1960s and 1970s, through references and recontextualizations. This aesthetic trend associated then-contemporary music and counterculture with a vibrant, youthful aesthetic, resulting in an avalanche of psychedelic works and new typographic interpretations from a range of designers in the same era, such as Bonnie MacLean, Victor Moscoso, Rick Griffin, Alton Kelley, and Stanley Mouse. Because of its ubiquity and popularity, the wide-reach of psychedelic design has become linked with these revisited letterforms and aesthetics—often without an audience knowing they were revived at all.

While psychedelic works are a distinct movement from those of Art Nouveau or the Vienna Secession, it's easy to mistake many works originating from the 1880s to the 1910s as products of the 1960s or 1970s due to their aesthetic and typographic similarities. This may be particularly true in places like the United States, where original Art Nouveau architecture and influence is less apparent in the built environment as a reminder of its long history.

Figure 3.27 *Open Up and See* by Wes Wilson. © Wes Wilson Estate, 1967. Reproduced with the permission of the Wes Wilson Estate.

An *anachronism* is something which is out of context of its original time. Because history builds and evolves, references from the past frequently appear in the present, often out of their original temporal context—but are still largely understood. This is especially apparent in idioms or common phrases. For instance, in English, "a broken record" refers to someone repeating themselves, while a close resemblance may be described as a "carbon copy." Even though their origins come from technology (vinyl records) or scenarios (using carbon paper to make a duplicate) to which most speakers do not find themselves currently or frequently encountering, they remain a part of contemporary speech. While these phrases are clearly from another era, they don't pause conversation with their use,

making that which is anachronistic a matter of notable *discontinuity*, or that which feels out of place. In this way, anachronistic placements have the ability to create abrupt shifts or meaningful contrast. This can be done accidentally, like using a Futura-headlined newspaper in a film set in the 1880s, or intentionally, such as employing hand-painted, antique letterforms on the signage for a museum or historical residence, differentiating its visual language from that of its contemporary surroundings.

Historical typefaces—and their respective methods of use—are frequently employed for the sake of world-building and period references. Creative directors often require accurate textual applications for film or theatrical productions in order to imitate the look of an earlier era. In these instances, period-specific typefaces (or similar letterform styles) featured through on-set signage or print materials help suspend disbelief, aiding in the fidelity and believability of a particular narrative. Examples of anachronistic type in films have been well covered by keen-eyed designers and typographers. To most casual viewers, however, the minutiae of historical type specificity is often lost or overlooked in the spirit of similarity to past references rather than exactitude.

This is why type choices *generally* referencing the past can be so effective (and are so often used) to capture the feel of an era—or at least, what we socially expect that feeling to be. Many movies set in the American Wild West feature contemporary variations of type commonly used in the nineteenth century on their promotional materials. These include condensed Egyptian typefaces as well as *French Clarendons* or *French Antiques* (shown here via the headline of an 1880s circus exhibition broadside), whose frequently tall forms and extended platform serifs have become socially synonymous with the text of WANTED posters. Textures emulating printing with wood type further reference particular time periods and their respective technology (see "Material meaning" in Chapter 2). Some of these typefaces used in contemporary practice are period appropriate, like Clarendon (*c.* 1845) while others simply reference analogous styles, like Rockwell, a slab-serif released by Monotype Corporation in 1934. While not used exclusively during this time or location, these typographic tropes have become visual shorthands for a particular place and era, and can be spotted on contemporary advertising materials for films such as *The Magnificent Seven* (2016), *The Hateful Eight* (2015), and *True Grit* (2010), which seek to reference this time and feel.

Using typefaces or aesthetics from the past can also be used for purposes of *nostalgia*, referring to a reveling in, or longing for, a particular era or experience of the past. Because everyone's past and perceptions thereof are unique, nostalgia-inducing typography is incredibly subjective, and not all historical typography facilitates this particular emotional response. In recent years, a number of popular products have featured special "throwback" packaging featuring vintage typography, reverting to earlier designs from the recent past. Nostalgia can be an effective means of communicating by facilitating a strong emotional response, especially regarding a familiar or idealized notion of the past.

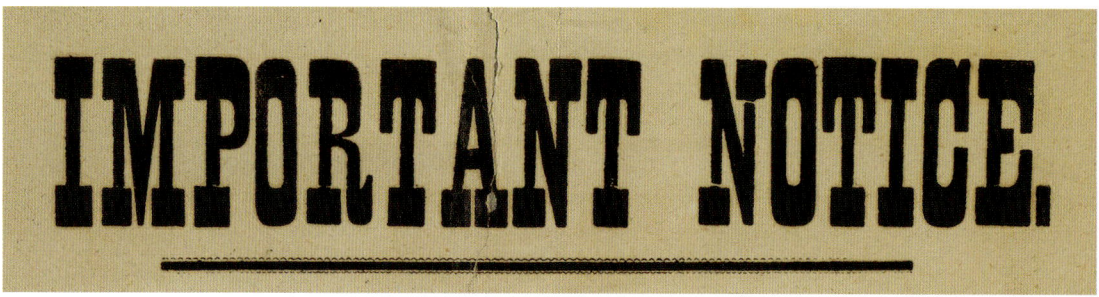

Figure 3.28 Circus exhibition broadside. J. Edwards, machine printer, &c. of 11 Abbey Street in Accrington, *c.* 1880. Wellcome Collection.

ITC Benguiat

Figure 3.29 From Adobe Fonts.

ITC Benguiat | Ed Benguiat

ITC Benguiat (set here in Bold Condensed) was designed by Ed Benguiat and released in 1978 via the International Typeface Corporation. This typeface frequently adorned the covers of horror and sci-fi novels of the 1980s, making it an appropriate choice for Netflix's hit program *Stranger Things* (2016), a sci-fi horror set in the 1980s—which features ITC Benguiat in its title as both a historical and conceptual reference. Paired with ample nostalgia, the popularity of the series brought this specific context of use back into public conversation through articles, blog posts, and even its own online custom title-generator. Through contemporary use, type of the past can reappear through *resurgences*, wherein an existing typeface regains prominence after falling out of trend—without necessarily having been redesigned.

TEMPORAL RECONTEXTUALIZATIONS

Since its publication in 1597, Shakespeare's classic romantic tragedy *Romeo and Juliet* has been performed at countless theaters—and through a variety of temporal recontextualizations. This sets the familiar story in a different or contemporary setting outside of its original Elizabethan context. Shifting the time period in which the play is portrayed (while leaving the dialogue largely intact) transforms how the historic text is understood, giving audiences a novel way to access or interpret the centuries-old love story.

In typographic communication, temporal recontextualization works similarly. We know that using historical typefaces, compositions, or methods of making can create a historical reference, harking back to a particular era. However, when artists and designers *change* the expected context or content of historical type, its meaning is transformed as well. This contextual shift allows viewers to interpret historical references in a new capacity, using the tone of the past to convey a specific meaning when presented in a different time or manner. However, these meanings are contingent on an audience's knowledge of a work's historical reference or original context. Without familiarity of *when* an original work is from or *how* it was intended to be seen, an audience will fail to recognize that a recontextualization has taken place.

Through these methods, artists and designers can reimagine or critique the original intent of a historical style or composition. This may be through setting contemporary messages in historical typefaces, altering the physical or visual context of recognizable typography from the past, or reclaiming past letterforms (physically or digitally) for a new use (see "Recontextualization" in Chapter 1).

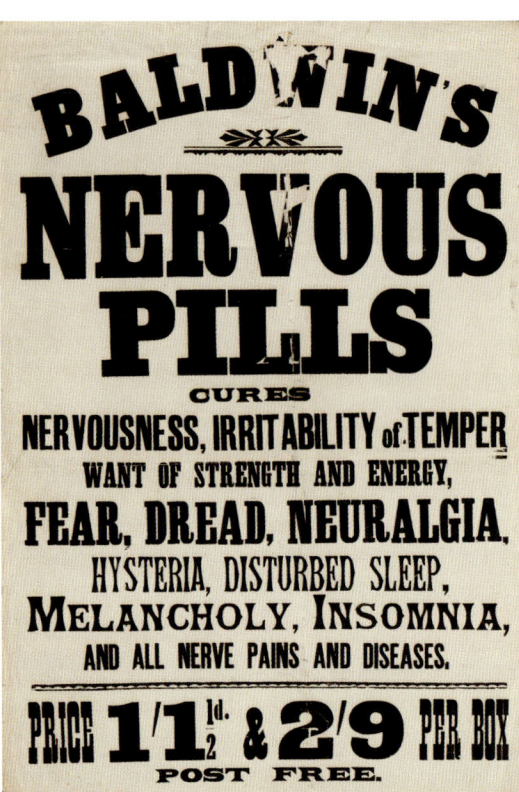

Figure 3.30 Baldwin's Nervous Pills. G. Baldwin (firm) *c.* 1900. Wellcome Collection.

Baldwin's Nervous Pills

This letterpress poster, from England *c.* 1900, uses a plethora of typefaces to proclaim the effectiveness of Baldwin's Nervous Pills. Like many advertisements of the era, it fantastically overstates its ability to alleviate a host of ailments and illnesses, including "hysteria," a catch-all pejorative diagnosis often encompassing the behavioral, mental, emotional, sexual, or reproductive health of women.

Figure 3.31 *Ladies!* triptych by Jennifer Farrell. © Jennifer Farrell, 2020. Reproduced with the permission of Starshaped Press.

Ladies! Triptych | Jennifer Farrell

Based in Chicago, Starshaped Press exclusively uses antique wood and metal type in a variety of design applications, including the design and production of detailed business cards, books, invitations, and posters. Designer Jennifer Farrell's *Ladies!* Triptych uses historical recontextualization to highlight everyday sexism faced by women in the United States. Written in an intentionally sarcastic manner, these works satirize the familiar, exaggerated persuasive text and over-the-top visual inflection of nineteenth-century advertising posters to call attention to persistent inequalities. In addition to its visual historical reference, the fact that it was printed from real, vintage wood and metal type imbues the work with deeper meaning through its material history and narrative origins.

Figure 3.32 Library of Congress, Prints & Photographs Division, LC-USZC4-7905.

World War I Propaganda Poster | United States Food Administration

This First World War propaganda poster was designed by Crawford Young and produced by the W. F. Powers Company on behalf of the United States Food Administration. As part of a larger series, these posters worked to persuade the public to cut down on food waste and adjust their diets accordingly—including eating less meat and wheat—in order to help feed the Allied forces.

Figures 3.33 and 3.34 *Where* and *Neighbor* by Ericka Walker. © Ericka Walker, 2015. Reproduced with the permission of the artist.

Where and *Neighbor* | Ericka Walker

In her works *Where* and *Neighbor*, artist and printmaker Ericka Walker revisits and recontextualizes historical typography from American First World War propaganda posters. As a critical investigation, new perspectives are derived from familiar, historical messages. These phrases may immediately evoke a sense of pride or nostalgia, but their meanings are subtly subverted by their new proximity to contemporary weaponry and desolate landscapes. These striking shifts pit resolute messages against realities of the United States military industrial complex, highlighting the challenges of opposing identities, ideals, and narratives.

HISTORY-INSPIRED TYPE

The SS *Edmund Fitzgerald* was a Great Lakes freighter which sank on Lake Superior in November of 1975, claiming the lives of all twenty-nine men on board. Canadian singer-songwriter Gordon Lightfoot was moved by this disaster and penned a new ballad—*The Wreck of the Edmund Fitzgerald*—narrating a semi-factual timeline of the tragedy. Released in 1976, this became a hit song in the United States, bringing national attention to what otherwise may have been an overlooked regional catastrophe. As a new work inspired by a historic event, this creative response influenced perceptions of both the song *and* the event itself. By carrying an account of the past into the future, audiences can discover or engage with historical narratives in new ways.

Typographic works responding to history can engage audiences in this manner, too. Historical references, revivals, or recontextualizations all depend on the information and influence of previous eras in order to create particular social or emotional associations. In addition, many creative works are created in response to, or in conversation with, historical events, objects, or movements themselves. In these instances, actions and artifacts of the past serve as essential components for both the genesis and consequent understanding of these works.

When specific historical inspiration is communicated to an audience, typefaces and typographic applications have the opportunity to contribute and influence present knowledge and interpretations of past events. In this context, history-inspired type and typography can become a narrative agent. By highlighting specific facets of history, these works can draw attention to actions, individuals, and movements that might otherwise be unknown. Because works inspired by history are created through the authorship of their respective designers, these works serve as interpretations, rather than direct representations, making these perspectives subjective. Such subjectivity facilitates works which can be dramatic, interrogative, critical, commemorative, disruptive, or celebratory—among many other things—as influenced by their creator's intent.

In the same way that historical *material* meanings can imbue physical typography with affiliated meaning, so too can the respective use of history-inspired type in a contemporary context. This can be obvious, inconspicuous, or accidental. For instance, if hand-sewn lettering from a women's suffrage sash is adapted into a digital typeface, its origins are embedded in its design and consequent use. If conspicuously used in museum assets for an exhibition on voting rights, this creates a direct and obvious historical reference. If used *inadvertently* on an unrelated concert poster, it may still communicate an effective message with its intended visual inflection, but it subtly and simultaneously imparts this narrative of the past into the present, however unintentional.

Works which make *historical references* and those which are *history-inspired* are not mutually exclusive, and both hold significance in their design and use. History-inspired type can take many forms, such as practical revivals informed by historical typefaces, or new works inspired by the past in order to create visual analogies or comparisons. While it is impossible to know the history and origins of all modes of typographic communication, a general knowledge of when something is from, who made it, and how it developed can contribute important context to its contemporary use and consequent meaning.

Figures 3.35 and 3.36 Martin by Tré Seals. © Tré Seals, 2016. Reproduced with the permission of Vocal Type Co.

Martin | Tré Seals

Tré Seals is a typeface designer and the founder of Vocal Type Co., a foundry seeking to diversify the design industry through one of its most essential visual components—typography. At the time of this book's writing, recent surveys have revealed that the majority of American designers are white. This can create a homogeneous workforce and repeated aesthetic which neither reflects nor represents the rich plethora of cultures and identities in the United States. Established in 2016, Vocal Type Co. counters this by specializing in typefaces promoting diverse voices and cultural histories. Each typeface is inspired by a historical event from communities of underserved genders, ethnicities, and races.

In 1968, the sanitation workers of Memphis, Tennessee, most of whom were Black, went on strike following the death of two men as a result of a malfunctioning garbage truck. They protested poor treatment of employees, and called for fair pay, safe working conditions, and union recognition—which were ultimately received as a result of this action and solidarity. Dr. Martin Luther King Jr. joined in support for the striking workers, who carried signs with a powerful axiom of equality: "I AM A MAN." When Dr. King was tragically assassinated not long after, on April 4, 1968, new signs were printed, stating "HONOR KING: END RACISM!" Vocal Type Co.'s typeface Martin was influenced by these typographic posters carried by hundreds of people in a display of persistence, community, and resilience. Inspired by this history, Martin carries the narrative of this event and its impact. Amplifying the voices of its participants through its contemporary use, Martin is a typeface which is visually, historically, and conceptually bold.

Figure 3.37 Marseille typeface. Designed by Louise Fili, Andy Anzollitto, and Nick Misani 2018. Permission by Tipofili LLC.

Marseille | Louise Fili, Andy Anzollitto, and Nick Misani

As an international style in the 1920s and 1930s, Art Deco is often characterized by tall, elegant, and sharply refined forms, often featuring geometric ornamentation and aesthetic influence from African and Asian sources. Marseille is an Art Deco-inspired typeface based on letterforms originally created by designer Louise Fili for the cover design of *The Lover* (an autobiographical novel by Marguerite Duras which takes place in the 1930s) published in 1984. Designed in 2018 by Louise Fili, Andy Anzollitto, and Nick Misani, Marseille's visual inflection is informed by its historical reference to a particular style and time period. Ideal for applications requiring sophistication, its stylish letterforms conjure a celebration of modernity and sleek poise.

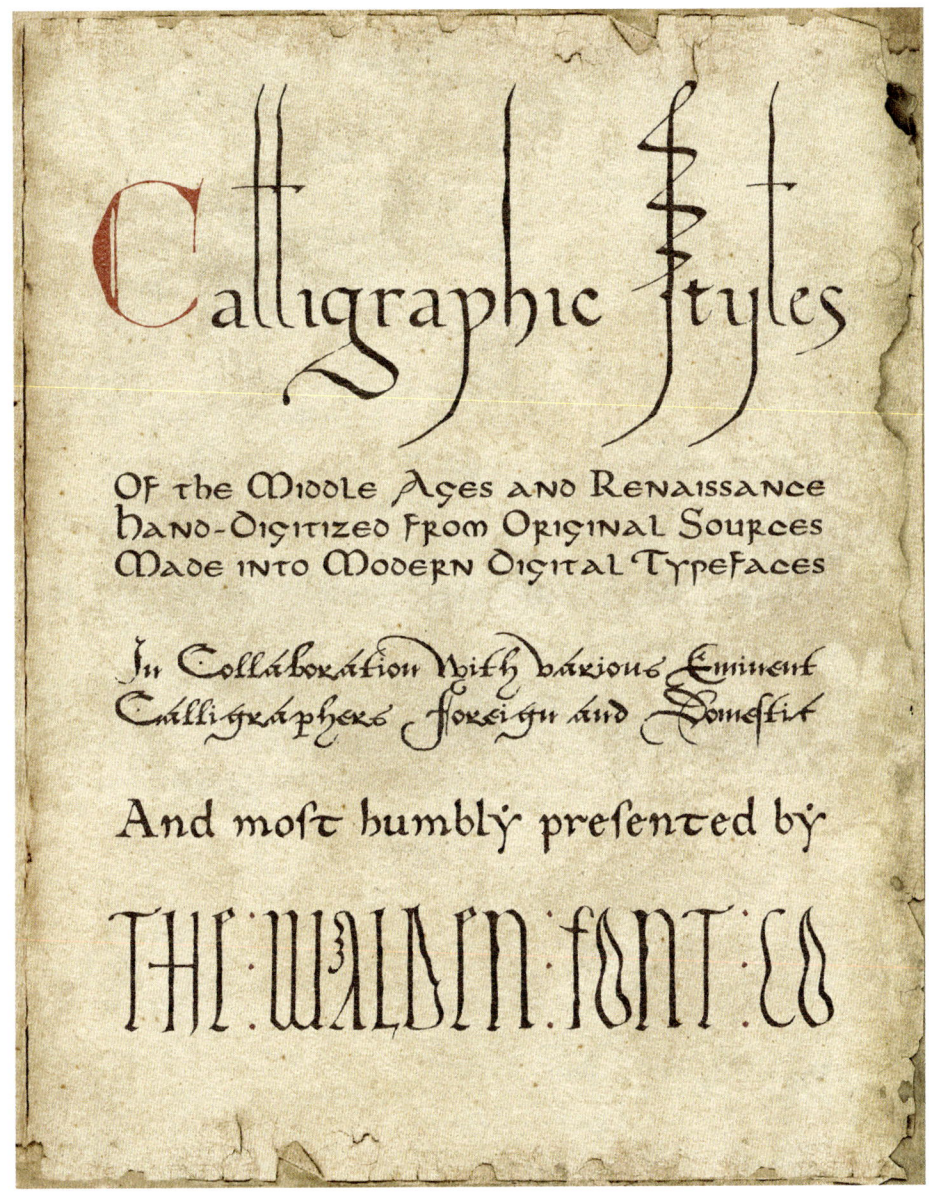

Figure 3.38 "Sample of digital typefaces that reproduce medieval penmanship" by Oliver Weiss. © 2022 Walden Type Co. Reproduced with permission.

Walden Type Co. | Oliver Weiss

Contemporary typefaces inspired by history can revisit previous eras or shine light on forgotten—or otherwise unacknowledged—modes of visual communication. By using historical letterforms as source material, past ideas, styles, and approaches can be brought into present use. Spanning centuries of letterform development, ranging from hand-scribed letters to fonts from American Second World War Posters, the Walden Type Co., headed by designer Oliver Weiss, proudly "resurrects old typefaces." Here, examples of medieval penmanship have been reproduced as digital typefaces; careful attention to detail conveys their original author's gestural movements. From top to bottom, individual fonts featured are: WF Astaroth, WF Uncial, WF Bastarda, WF 10th Century Bookhand, and WF Orgeuil.

Figure 3.39 *Peace is Possible* by Remedios Rapoport. © Remedios Rapoport, 2002. Reproduced with the permission of Remedios Rapoport.

Peace is Possible | Remedios Rapoport

Remedios Rapoport's positive and vibrant works are inspired by historical signage and lettering—but also engage with a specific cultural history of craft. These works often employ *trompe l'oeil*—a French phrase meaning "deceive the eye"—a painting technique which creates photorealistic depth and detail. This is a part of *Filete Porteño*, a traditional painting style originating from Buenos Aires, Argentina, which the artist learned from skilled masters of this craft. This distinct style originated at the turn of the twentieth century, when Italian immigrants began painting decorative elements on the sides of wagons in the factories where they were produced. Examples of *Filete Porteño* tend to feature symmetrical and highly stylized architectural flourishes surrounding ornamental phrases. In *Peace Is Possible*, Rapoport makes strategic use of these techniques and visual references. This precision and luminance creates a reverent medium for hopeful messages promoting social change.

Figure 3.40 Forged from Fortitude by Young & Laramore. © Hotel Tango Distillery, 2019. Reproduced with the permission of Hotel Tango Distillery.

Hotel Tango Distillery Identity | Young & Laramore
Tasked with designing an identity for a distillery founded by a combat-disabled veteran of the United States Marine Corps, the designers at Young & Laramore sought to communicate values of discipline and diligence. The history-inspired graphic identity for Hotel Tango Distillery references typography of vintage United States Military Meals Ready-to-Eat (MREs), creating a conceptual analogy. Clear, no-nonsense sans serifs and a distinct historical and social reference highlight an intentional connection between its founder's military precision and the distillery's carefully crafted spirits. This extensive and consistent design work includes additional assets inspired by the typography of US military accoutrement—including this Forged from Fortitude poster.

Figure 3.41 Science (2017) by Anna Weber. © Anna Weber. Reproduced with the permission of Anna Weber.

INTERVIEW

Anna Weber | Astoria Design Studio

How is contemporary sign-painting informed by the past? From bustling city streets to country intersections, signs exist everywhere—giving patrons and passers-by information about a particular business or location. Anna Weber is a designer and sign-painter at Astoria Design Studio, based in Astoria, Oregon; she specializes in both the design and production of logos and signage. In this brief, lightly edited interview, Anna shares how both history and spatial contexts inspire her work.

Glass gilding, sign-painting, and sign fabrication require very specific skills of design and production. How did you get into this line of work?

I learned from my dad, Noel Weber, who is a traditionally trained sign-painter. Growing up, I would go to his sign shop after school and help out where I could. This sent me on a visual arts path—but I didn't decide to make sign-painting a career until my late twenties.

Your works often reference vintage letterforms; how do you determine what kind of letters are most appropriate for specific signs or logos, and what sort of research informs them?

It depends on the type of business, the architecture of the building, its locality, and also the clients' personal taste. Additionally, I always try to push for goldleaf on glass which works especially well in Astoria, where it is gray and cloudy for most of the year. Anything that reflects light really pops in this coastal climate. I like to find historic photos of previous businesses that existed in a building. There is a lot of history in Astoria, Oregon, and it's fun to research past establishments that existed in a space and investigate what kinds of signage they had.

What are some favorite projects you've worked on?

I really love the projects that I've done where clients give us their full trust. I also love the jobs that I've done for long-term clients who I've been able to work with over the years, sometimes helping them change their logo to fit the aesthetic of a new location. I also really enjoy big collaborative projects that I've worked on with my family. We work pretty well together, and I like spending time with them.

That sounds wonderful! A commitment to excellence in craft is particularly notable in your work. What do you hope these qualities communicate?

My hope is that the signage I create for businesses conveys a message of permanence, as if it has always been there and always will be.

I also want my work to feel inviting for people who see it as they enter a space. I hope to continue contributing to the historic charm of my coastal town through its signage.

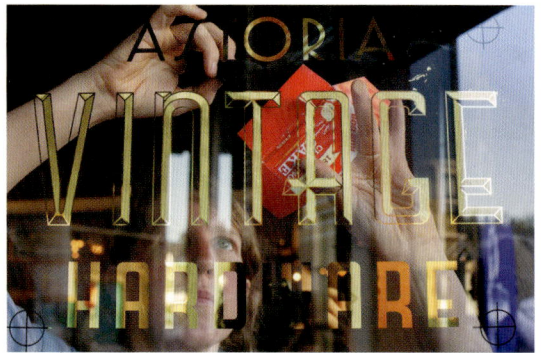

Figures 3.42 and 3.43 Astoria Vintage Hardware (2017), and Reclamation Marketplace (2019) by Anna Weber. © Anna Weber. Reproduced with the permission of Anna Weber.

Voices in Design

Mid-century American designers Charles and Ray Eames were a married couple whose multidisciplinary practice has remained deeply influential to the American design landscape. In a 1956 interview with Arlene Francis on an NBC television show called *Home*, they were introduced alongside their work. Ray is introduced as "very interesting and able" and is directed to "tell us how she helps Charles design these chairs" pertaining to "her husband's work." This phrasing relegates her as an assistant rather than a collaborator, downplaying her contributions. While Charles does clarify that they design "together," the language in this segment speaks to how ingrained traditional gender roles were at that time, limiting both recognition and participation.

Consider that even with the benefit of press, privilege, and time, Charles and Ray Eames are *still* often misrepresented today as "The Eames Brothers" even by the most well-intentioned creative practitioners.

An important consideration to make regarding type informed, inspired by, or in conversation with history are the circumstances of when and by whom it was made, valued, and shared. If "history is written by the victors," present and past power structures have informed which works have been seen, documented, and championed. Throughout much of history, the voices of select individuals and collectives (largely white, Western, and male), have been prioritized, creating a design canon which has historically sidelined or excluded nearly everyone else. Because of societal expectations, marginalization, and discrimination, the significant achievements of many groups—notably, though not exclusively, women and people of color—have been historically underrepresented throughout art and design history.

Art and design are wide and continually growing disciplines. It should be acknowledged that design does not have a singular history, and both its practice and participants benefit from as many perspectives as possible. No design education or text (including this one) can be truly comprehensive, as highlighting specific narratives and projects will inevitably sacrifice others. However, when encountering *any* history, critical analysis is necessary in evaluating who has been historically included or excluded from the design canon, and how future actions and initiatives can create more thorough and thoughtful representation.

For instance: Have you heard of Elizabeth Friedländer, one of the first female type designers? Are you aware of the work of accomplished type designer Matthew Carter (Verdana, Georgia, Snell Roundhand), but not of artist and type designer Carol Twombly, whose impressive works in type design include Adobe Caslon, Charlemagne, and Chaparral? Are you familiar with the text-based paintings from 1960s pop-art painter Roy Lichtenstein, but not the vibrant and powerful works of the interdisciplinary AFRICOBRA movement, whose work promoted and celebrated Black visual culture and experiences?

Why is this? Historical exclusions are often intentional in the interest of maintaining the preferred narrative of an existing power structure, as those in power generally wish to remain in power. However, these exclusions are not limited to the past. Over time, original and intentional omissions can become overlooked and systemic within institutions and organizations, as people teach what they have been taught or repeat what they've heard. Without critical reflection, it can be easy to prioritize the same events, approaches, or individuals without second thought. Clearly, not all omissions are malicious—but they are omissions nonetheless. With this in mind, any assertion of a "complete" history should be viewed with skepticism.

Visual communication with text and type is a global endeavor. As such, the many voices contributing to contemporary design and typography should be highlighted and celebrated. *Everyone* has the capacity to communicate meaningfully and intentionally through typography. Biases and exclusion in design relative to race, ethnicity, culture, sex, gender, socioeconomic status, sexuality, age, background, or educational experience should be confronted in contemporary educational settings, professional organizations, publications, and archives. Though this effort has increased in recent years—thanks to the organized efforts of activists and advocates—there is still a long way to go.

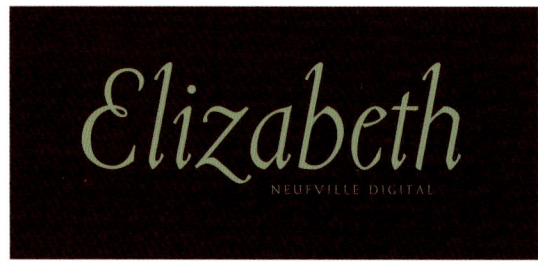 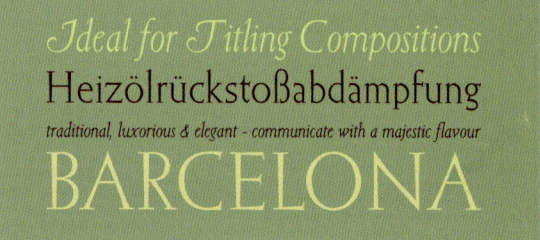

Figures 3.44 and 3.45 Elizabeth ND type specimen. © Bauer Types. Reproduced with the permission of Bauer Types.

Elizabeth ND | Bauer Types

Elizabeth Friedländer was born Elisabeth Friedländer to Jewish parents in Germany in 1903. After studying calligraphy and typography under Emil Rudolf Weiss in Berlin, she was commissioned by the Bauer Type Foundry to design a typeface in 1927—an uncommon venture for women at that time. Because of the rise of Nazism, her originally titled typeface Friedländer-Antiqua (featuring a recognizably Jewish surname) was renamed Elizabeth, and was produced in the late 1930s, after she had left the country. After the Second World War, Friedländer worked as a book and graphic designer, notably for Penguin Books. Elizabeth is frequently cited as one of the first typefaces designed by a woman; in 2005, a digital version was designed by Andreu Balius, giving contemporary audiences new access to this pioneering, elegant typeface.

Chaparral

Figure 3.46 From Adobe Fonts.

Chaparral | Carol Twombly

Carol Twombly's Chaparral was released by Adobe in 2000. This slab-serif typeface features humanist details and sophisticated proportions. Its approachable glyphs and impressive selection of weights and styles make it a refreshing choice for a wide variety of applications.

When we assess the current and future design canon, it's important to ask: When we consider the works which we laud and use, who was involved, but not recognized or credited? Who was or continues to be intentionally excluded from participation, and why? Which voices are acknowledged and repeated, and which have yet to be heard? Through what actions or initiatives might the typographic community become more intentionally inclusive—instead of more exclusive and insular?

Figure 3.47 Revolutionary, Wadsworth Jarrell. © Wadsworth Jarrell, 1972. Reproduced with the permission of Kavi Gupta Gallery.

Revolutionary | Wadsworth Jarrell

AFRICOBRA (African Commune of Bad Relevant Artists) was founded in Chicago in 1968 by artists Jeff Donaldson, Wadsworth Jarrell, Jae Jarrell, Gerald Williams, and Barbara Jones-Hogu; their mission and visual style was informed by African art, dance, and music, as well as African American heritage and experience. This philosophy rejected limitations of the Western art canon and embraced action and aesthetics informed by Black people and culture. The artists of AFRICOBRA frequently used pattern, bright "coolade colors," and text-based approaches in their work, including Wadsworth Jarrell's 1972 work *Revolutionary*, which features an abstract representation of Angela Davis—a well-known civil rights leader and political activist. Surrounded by rhythmic, vibrant text based on a line from one of her speeches, these radiating and empowering words frequently focus on the letter B, alluding to words like "Black," "Boss," or "Beautiful." This 33 in. × 26 in. (83 cm × 66 cm) screenprint was reproduced from an original painting selected to be made into accessible and affordable editioned prints "for the people."

Figure 3.48 Salbabida Sans V2 (2021) by Jo Malinis. © Jo Malinis. Reproduced with the permission of Jo Malinis.

INTERVIEW

Jo Malinis | Type63

How might designers connect, share knowledge, and celebrate culture through their creative communities? What role do digital platforms and directories play in supporting the many voices of the typographic community?

Jo Malinis is a graphic designer, illustrator, and type designer based in the Philippines; her creative works include an impressive range of typefaces and brand identities. She has worked as a designer at Plus63 Design Co. under Hydra Design Group, and is presently an instructor at the University of the Philippines Diliman College of Fine Arts. In addition to a bustling design and teaching practice, Jo is the founder of Type63, an online platform to recognize the works and voices of Filipino type designers. Founded in 2020, this platform showcases a variety of creative work and lists its contributors in a digital archive, named after the country code of the Philippines, +63. In this interview, lightly edited for clarity and length, she discusses how Type63 came to be—and why this initiative is so important.

Could you tell me a little about Type63? What inspired you to found this platform?

I'll start by reading its description: "Type63 is an initiative that aims to showcase and celebrate Filipino type design, ranging from custom type for projects to fully realized typefaces and typographic layouts." We feature different types of work from different types of people—as long as they're Filipino. You can be from the city or from the provinces, or from any region—even from outside the country! As long as you are a Filipino, we love to showcase your work.

The inspiration behind it was born out of frustration. The Philippine typographic scene has actually been here for a long, long time, and it's rooted mostly in culture and expression. But *type design* is actually new—or at least has just begun to become mainstream, for lack of a better word—because there is very little or no type education in the country. We don't really talk about how typefaces are made or what fonts are; we just talk about typography in the broad sense. There were very few people here in the country that I personally knew who were making typefaces, and they had nowhere to turn to for these things locally. I would always look for inspiration outside of the country, or join type programs online, etc. That frustration of having to keep looking outside drove me to start Type63. I'm not saying looking outside is a bad thing—but it's something I had to reflect on and see if I could do something about it.

Archives and directories have become increasingly important—not just for highlighting what creative works are being made, but who is making them, and where they are being designed. What impact do you hope Type63 has for type designers locally, in the Philippines, as well as globally?

Locally, my main goal is for people to understand that we exist and to recognize the skills we have. Because I was not the only person who kept looking outside of the country, I realized you need that type of empowerment for the designers here in the Philippines. You need to make them understand that "hey—we can also do these things" and that we also exist. In addition, an impact that I want to have is for us to put a name to things that we probably recognize, but don't know who made them. An example would be a typeface called HK Grotesk, by Hanken Design Co. A lot of people were using it here locally, and they thought it was a typeface made by someone from the United States—but it's actually a foundry in Batangas, Philippines, which is one of the provinces here in Luzon.

When we featured it on Type63, most of the comments were like "Oh my gosh, I've been using this for so long, I didn't know a Filipino made it!" or "I had no idea this was a locally made typeface!"

It's not just about Filipino pride; it's also about understanding that we can make these things. If one person was able to do this, who's stopping you from making your own?

Globally, I just hope people see who we are and understand the value of the perspective that we bring. There are similarities in our approaches to type, but there are also differences—and both of these are things that we can learn from.

Absolutely! Have connections made through this platform impacted your own creative practice? Has it influenced how you teach design? If so, in what ways?

Yes, definitely! I am an extrovert, and I like talking to different people. Because of Type63, I was able to open and join in conversations with people that I would never have met in my lifetime because the Philippines is a huge country. We are an archipelago, so it's hard to connect to people from a different region because sometimes you have to take a plane to meet them. However, through Type63, I've been exposed to more and more people and have got into conversations with them. That's been amazing for me. It's not just about finding new friends in the design scene, but also understanding what they're trying to bring to the community and understanding their perspectives. It has impacted how I view type in general.

In terms of teaching, design education in the Philippines is very Westernized, and we are very influenced by the Global North. The history, the art history, the design history that we teach is mostly focused on those things, and for the longest time we haven't taught local design history. When I was in college, I didn't really know who the graphic designers of the country were, and I only knew about them when I started working. And that's kind of sad—because there are a lot of designers here in the country whose work and inspiration we should be talking about. For my own practice, I've always tried to integrate local history and design examples from within the country to try to get my students to understand that these things exist, and we can learn stuff from them. Looking *inside* has impacted my own design teaching.

How have your students responded to this shift?

A lot of students were surprised by the breadth of design here in the country. I think a lot of them didn't think that these things were done here, or that these things existed in the first place. It was something new to them, but I don't know if the shift was as evident for them as it was for me, who experienced the old way of teaching. Integrating these new practices has been an interesting transition—to switch your mindset like that. It's been interesting for me and my co-teachers who are trying to integrate that type of perspective in our own practices.

What do you think is essential in a creative community?

For me, it's always been about inclusion, transparency, and the willingness to share.

I think by having different voices talk about the same thing you get a lot of different perspectives.

It's always beneficial and very important to understand how to approach one thing from different angles.

Especially because most of us have only been exposed to a certain type of point of view, that means we devise what good or bad design is based on that singular point of view—and I think that's so limiting! There's *nothing* exciting about that, and so I think it's really important to get more people into the mix. Whether or not you agree with them is also important. Understanding and formulating your own stand and opinions based on what you think is bad or good *because* you have a big mix of people to base your opinion on is better than having one person tell you "this is good and bad design." I think that's essential.

Transparency is also important in the age of the internet with a lot of things being referenced. There are a lot of websites you can go to and reference from, and so transparency in citing your sources is very important to me—especially if you're referencing a certain culture or community that you are taking your inspiration from. I think it's very important to be transparent about those sources and to educate people through your own designs and your own audience. Let them know where you are getting your sources from. Try to make them understand that these already exist, and these are the people who I have been inspired by.

What's next for Type63?

This is a question I also ask myself. I am not sure what's next for Type63. The difficult thing about it is that I'm the only one who is managing it,

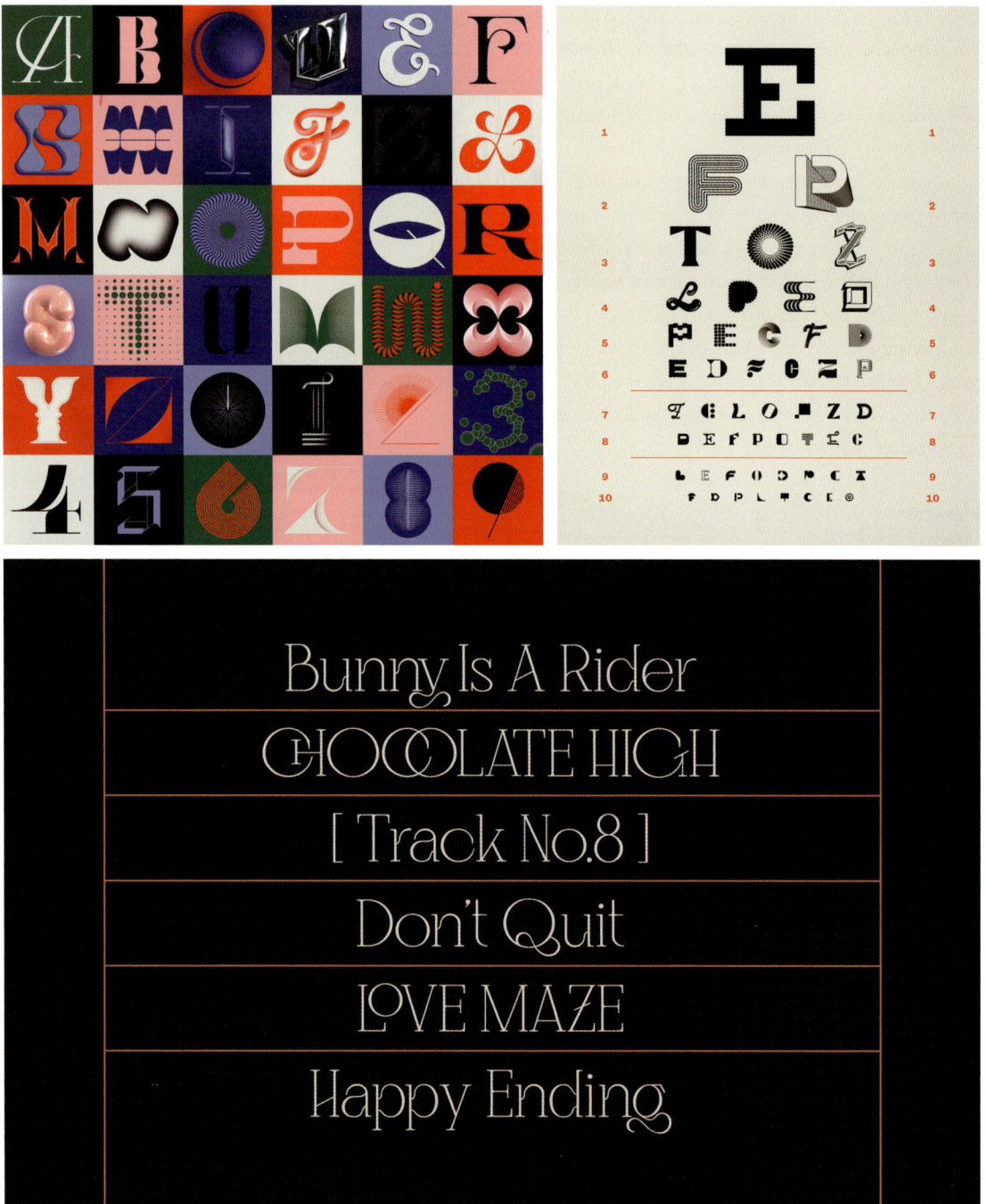

Figures 3.49–3.51 36 Days of Type (2020), Eye Snellen Chart (2018), and Hook (2020) by Jo Malinis. © Jo Malinis. Reproduced with the permission of Jo Malinis.

but there are a lot of people helping me with different aspects of it. In the future, I want to get more people to help out with Type63 and have more people to join a core team who can help me figure things out. It's just been so busy—but hopefully, the goal is to get more people involved. The other more concrete goal is launching a website so people can go to one URL and directory. Instagram has been great, and has been very accessible to a lot of people, but having one website would be better, so that's next. (At the time of this book's writing, Type63's Instagram handle is @type63_)

Another thing is for us to keep talking to different designers and people in order to bring their own opinions out to the community. We've had a series for Type63 called *Type Talks Tuesdays* where I interview a type designer and talk about their work and ask them questions—much like the ones you're asking me right now—and share their answers with the community. I've already done three episodes, and they're available on Instagram and on YouTube. I had to stop because of so many other commitments, but my goal is to get that running again later this year, because so many people love that segment of Type63, and so many people learned from it.

Is there anything you want to discuss that I haven't asked about?

I think it might be good to mention that here in the Philippines, this exploration of type and understanding of type is very new. Sometimes you look at other countries who have established their own type communities, type practices, type education, and feel like "Oh, I wish we were even close to that point in talking about type and experiencing type," but I do think it's very exciting to be at *this* stage—where everyone is trying to figure out what Filipino type is, and *if* we even have to define what Filipino type is. It's an exciting moment for all of us. It's important to note that we are at this stage. We don't necessarily have all of the answers ready at this moment, and that in itself is okay. This is an exciting time to be in, especially now that so many things are online. There are so many new voices. It's so fun to be a part of it.

TYPE AND IDENTITY

While the author of this text is not (and cannot claim to be) a historian, the wide subject of history should be acknowledged as an evolving field. History is—and should be—critically reevaluated as new information becomes available. Because meaning can be influenced by both when something is made *and* when something is viewed, we tend to view historical works through a contemporary lens, bringing present values and knowledge to our visual evaluations. Creative works are a product of their time, and can portray outdated cultural ideas and depictions, including harmful prejudices and stereotypes in regards to identity—including, but not limited to race, ethnicity, gender, or sexuality—from their time of creation or publication. When we encounter historical works, it's important to contextualize them as such, while acknowledging that racism, sexism, xenophobia, homophobia (among many other discriminatory prejudices) are not acceptable.

Visual inflection is created through type choice and placement. It is informed by connotations from formal qualities and social meanings engendered from contexts of use. With this knowledge, we choose, make, and use specific letterforms in an attempt to create deliberate meaning relative to the intent of our message. Type choice can communicate an endless array of messages—including those which reinforce *stereotypes*, which flatten an identity or idea into a single, oversimplified concept, often negatively. It is important, then, to evaluate not just what letterforms communicate, but what they *perpetuate*.

In recent years, much has been written and discussed on how letterforms have historically or continue to contribute to prejudice. This includes typefaces or lettering styles that take truncated or stylized formal qualities of specific writing systems, mimicking them in Latin letterforms. Especially notable in typefaces often referred to as "wonton" "chop suey" or "chopstick(s)," these typefaces rely on a Western audience's perception or imagination of what calligraphic Chinese characters look like, rather than offering a realistic portrayal. This erases both subtlety and authenticity, making their visual inflection reliant on flippant visual imitation. When used as a stand-in for a particular culture to highlight that which is "Asian," "ethnic," or "foreign" they become cliché stereotypes—not translations—and can contribute to the othering of cultures and people. It should be acknowledged that typefaces attempting to communicate cultural references develop and manifest in multiple ways, and are not solely limited to these specific examples or the typographic applications referred to here.

The meanings of these typefaces and lettering styles are not static. They are informed—at least in part—by who they were designed *by*, who they were designed *for*, and *where* their application is used. In Alicia Yin Cheng's book *This is What Democracy Looked Like: A Visual History of the Printed Ballot*, she gives context to such applications by highlighting the use of "chopsticks"-esque lettering on an 1876 ballot for a congressional candidate whose campaign focused on an anti-Chinese platform. In his article *Stereo Types* for *Print Magazine* in 2009, design historian Paul Shaw notes that "chop suey" typefaces developed in the United States in the mid-to-late nineteenth century were frequently employed by Chinese-American restaurateurs in the decades following, shown here on mid-century signage. This served as a visual indicator to advertise their cuisine, relying on the quick, socially understood affiliation of these typefaces, rather than their visual accuracy.

The "English Speaking Foreign Alphabets" section of *Photo-Lettering's One Line Manual of Styles: Index to Alphabet Thesaurus Vol. 3, 2, 1* from 1971 features a range of typefaces claiming success in "establishing a national identity"—including typefaces mimicking Chinese, Japanese, Hebrew, Arabic, and South Asian writing systems, among others. Further, it states "If you can't speak a foreign language you can at least get the thrill of writing one (in good old English.)"—signaling that the designers of these letterforms were most likely *not* of the cultures they sought to represent. While these typefaces might have been viewed as clever visual solutions at that time, today they feel insensitive or unoriginal, at best.

With the ever-expanding options for visual language and available typefaces supporting numerous writing systems, there are ways to reference culture visually without resorting to

Figure 3.52 Library of Congress, Prints & Photographs Division, photograph by John Margolies, LC-DIG-mrg-07705 (digital file from original color transparency).

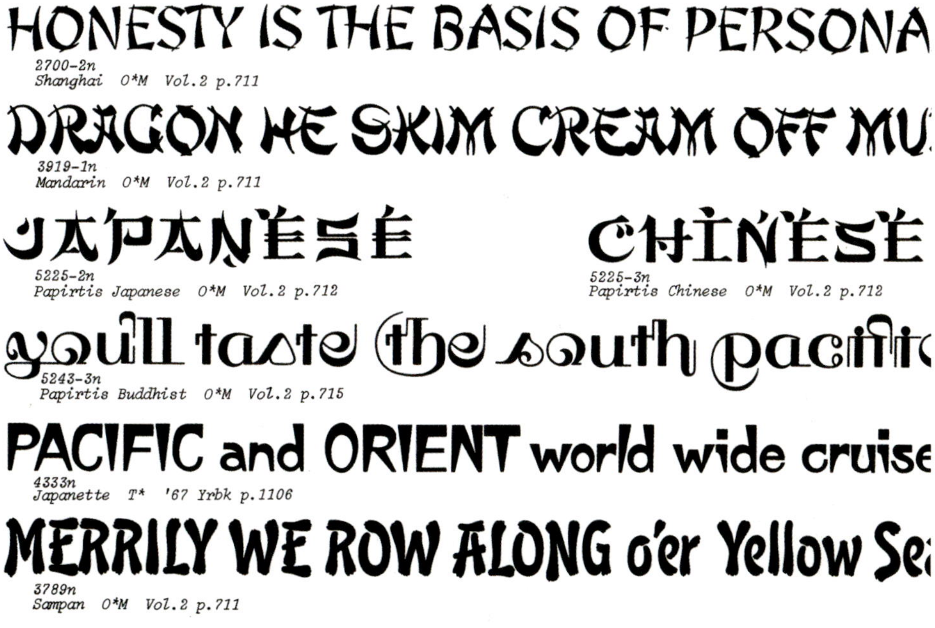

HONESTY IS THE BASIS OF PERSONA
2700-2n
Shanghai   O*M   Vol.2 p.711

DRAGON HE SKIM CREAM OFF MU
3919-1n
Mandarin   O*M   Vol.2 p.711

JAPANESE
5225-2n
Papirtis Japanese   O*M   Vol.2 p.712

CHINESE
5225-3n
Papirtis Chinese   O*M   Vol.2 p.712

you'll taste the south pacific
5243-3n
Papirtis Buddhist   O*M   Vol.2 p.715

PACIFIC and ORIENT world wide cruise
4333n
Japanette   T*   '67 Yrbk p.1106

MERRILY WE ROW ALONG o'er Yellow Sea
3789n
Sampan   O*M   Vol.2 p.711

Figure 3.53 *Photo-Lettering's One Line Manual of Styles*, Copyright © 1960, 1961, 1962, 1963, 1964, 1965, 1971, Photo-Lettering, Inc. Published by Van Nostrand Reinhold Company, a Division of Litton Educational Publishing Inc. Reproduced with the permission of Wiley.

cliché or outdated fonts. In all instances, designers should thoughtfully reflect on their type choices and consider if their use contributes to othering or negative stereotyping. If the typeface used is culturally reductive or otherwise imitative, pause, and make a different visual choice.

How does typography perpetuate stereotypes surrounding gender? First and foremost: *gender* and *sex* refer to different concepts. Gender refers to one's identity—how one understands and experiences one's own being—while *sex* refers to physical anatomy. One's gender may match one's sex assigned at birth, or it may not. Gender *expression* refers to how someone expresses their gender, which can take many forms and approaches. The *gender binary* refers to a model which views *masculine* and *feminine* as "either-or" opposing concepts, and does not fully encapsulate the full range of gender identities involved in existing.

The connections between gender identity and aesthetics are socially constructed *and* perpetuated through use. These associations are woven into contemporary design discourse, as formal qualities socially perceived as "masculine" or "feminine" are frequently applied to language, images, and objects. However, these descriptions are not always helpful or inclusive—especially when they perpetuate or reinforce the gender binary by excluding other identities, or by relegating who "should" use or enjoy specific typography or visual choices.

In *Visualising Gender Norms in Design: Meet the Mega Hurricane Mixer and the Drill Dolphia* by Karin Ehrnberger, Minna Räsänen, and Sara Ilstedt, published in the Vol. 6(3) of the *International Journal of Design* in 2012, the relationships between gender and visual choices are explored through formal and social qualities of objects in what they refer to as "product language." Here, they showcase how objects have frequently employed affiliations between the gender binary and aesthetics to communicate specific qualities. Hard lines, angular structures and that which is strong or rugged is associated with that which is "masculine," while softer lines and curvilinear features representing elegance or poise have been traditionally affiliated with that which is "feminine." To highlight these frequently used, but often "invisible" design tropes, the designers swapped the expected "product language" of a power drill and immersion blender, respectively, interrogating the connection between visual language and societal values pertaining to the gender binary.

How does this manifest typographically? The social affiliations between gender, form, and expression may accurately apply and appeal to *some* people—but they certainly do not apply to all people in all instances. While there is nothing wrong with designing for a specific audience in mind, *continually* applying these aesthetics typographically in binary uses described as "for men" and "for women" reinforces the incorrect notion that there are only two genders—while simultaneously truncating the full, diverse gamut of how gender is expressed. This exposes the problem of assuming that one solution represents the identity of an entire group of people, as evidenced in the outdated advice once commonly shared by industrial designers, in which designing for women was distilled to "shrink it and pink it."

Designing for (or in response to) identity is complex, and creative practitioners have questioned whether type should have any gendered descriptions at all. Identifying where cliché type choices are used—as well as more thoughtfully choosing and naming them—can call attention

Figure 3.54 Alder New York Breakout Control Kit Product Photo by David Krause. © Alder Boutique LLC, 2022. Reproduced with the permission of Alder Boutique LLC.

Breakout Control Kit Product | Alder New York

In recent history, skincare and beauty products have been strategically marketed at women, emphasizing youth, glamour, and style through editorial, cute, or bubbly typography perceived as "feminine." Because these products are *for everyone*, companies have begun to communicate this to their potential audiences through both the individuals featured in their ad campaigns and specific typographic choices. Alder New York is a "queer and woman-owned independent skincare brand" which creates products for all ages, genders, and ethnicities. Rather than rely on traditional visual approaches of "masculine" or "feminine," their product packaging employs clean, direct typography, intentionally subverting cliché expectations and representations of the gender binary.

to *how* stereotypes are perpetuated. Designers should evaluate if using a "gendered" typeface—or referring to one as such—is more trite than true in articulating a particular message or reaching a specific audience.

Time as Medium

If you traveled by car in the United States between 1926 and 1963, it's likely you would have happened across a curious site by the side of the highway: a series of horizontal advertising signs, often featuring white type on a bright red background. Otherwise indiscernible on their own, each sign featured a few words—a single line of a rhyming poem, placed approximately 100 paces from its predecessor. This was the famed roadside advertising method to promote *Burma-Shave*, a brushless shaving cream from the US-based Burma-Vita Company. This iconic campaign featured a multi-line poem, often referred to as a *jingle*, spread out across a stretch of highway. Its specific configuration meant the poem could only be discovered over a distance while traveling by car. These stanzas frequently featured a joke about shaving or safety, and always concluded with the sharp Burma-Shave wordmark. Consider these Burma-Shave signs from 1959, featuring a warning about highway safety: "THE ONE WHO/DRIVES WHEN/HE'S BEEN DRINKING/DEPENDS ON YOU/ TO DO HIS THINKING/BURMA-SHAVE"

With messages revealed over hundreds of feet, this popular series of physical signs made strategic use of *spatial* context in order to be read. However, through narrative sequence, anticipation, and expectation, the build-up and consequent reveal of their viewing order across a landscape relied on another medium in order to be understood: time.

When something is made and viewed influences its consequent interpretation, but time can serve as its own medium, too. Works which are *time-based*—such as motion graphics, kinetic type, or animation—require a linear structure of consecutive moments. Time is an essential component of installations with short life-spans, works which are revealed, or pieces which change or evolve during a specified period. As a means-of-making, time is essential for outcomes which intrinsically rely on *duration* for development. Additionally, works may be designed to be viewed in or at a unique or limiting time—making their temporal context less general (the present) and more specific (before the Winter Olympics, during an exhibition's existence, in the dark) in order to facilitate a particular interaction or experience.

Time is a complicated medium to discuss; it is simultaneously fleeting, everlasting, and all-encompassing. In our day-to-day experiences, the perception of time is both subjective and situationally dependent. Stressfully awaiting news of a medical diagnosis can feel like an eternity, while a vacation almost always seems too short, no matter how much time has actually passed. These variations in perception can be shaped strategically to convey particular meanings. Writers, filmmakers, and animators all engage with specific methods to set intentional *narrative pacing*, the literal or perceived pace by which a story is told or revealed. Narrative pacing influences emotional impact. Works which begin *in medias*

Figure 3.55 Division of Work and Industry, National Museum of American History, Smithsonian Institution.

res drop a viewer directly into the middle of the action or plot, fostering immediate urgency and suspense as a viewer or reader grapples with the available information. This differs from endings which rely on a tense *cliffhanger*, a plot device which purposefully leaves a narrative undetermined, creating a longing for resolution.

In design and typography, creative practitioners can't manipulate time itself, but can *use* time and visual space to facilitate specific interactions and perceptions. Here, narrative pacing is shaped by visual choices. In publication design, a single word placed on a book's page can create an intentional pause or focus for the reader. In kinetic typography, a slow fade-in might set a leisurely or even foreboding pace, a foil to the immediate flash of quick-moving text. For type in motion—which inherently relies on time as medium—adjusting line length, speed of movement, and methods of transition are essential conduits of meaning.

Offer today! Limited time only! This won't last! Things which are fleeting are often perceived as precious or precarious—creating a call for

Figures 3.56–3.59 "Shop Vac" by Jarrett Heather. © Jarrett Heather, 2010. Reproduced with the permission of Jarrett Heather.

"Shop Vac" | Jarrett Heather

Singer-songwriter Jonathan Coulton's catchy song "Shop Vac" subversively speaks to contemporary suburban malaise. In a corresponding lyric video, artist, musician, and software designer Jarrett Heather makes exquisite use of kinetic type, featuring visual analogies, recontextualizations, and social connotations to create a humorous and engaging animation. Here, fast-paced transitions of type in motion create a recognizable action or object using the song's lyrics. In these still clips, the ear of the lowercase g wags like a dog's tail, and type flips and moves across a green field akin to the movement of a riding lawnmower. Recognizable logos are frequently reimagined as relevant phrases, and the chorus repeats through a series of words expanding across a familiar instructional booklet. These "scenes" build and blend, creating intentional pacing. This use of motion across *time*—all 3 minutes and 26 seconds of the video—creates compositions and analogies to effectively communicate its narrative.

Figure 3.60 *On Edge* by Kiana Honarmand. © Kiana Honarmand, 2018. Reproduced with the permission of Kiana Honarmand.

On Edge | Kiana Honarmand

Iranian artist and designer Kiana Honarmand's work frequently engages with Persian calligraphy to discuss cultural identity and sociopolitical issues, including the violation of women's rights in Iran and Western perceptions of the Middle East. In her work *On Edge*, the time at which the work is viewed is essential. This large (7 ft^2 or 2.1 m^2) installation engages with panels featuring calligraphic letterforms and a light source. An inner light casts shadows onto nearby walls in intricate typographic patterns which can be obscured by, or projected onto, exhibition viewers. The full scope of this work can only be viewed at a specific time—when the light is on, in a darkened space—prompting discussions on language, censorship, or translation.

Figure 3.61 *Time Changes Everything* by Daku. © Daku, 2016. Project Name: St+art Delhi 2016. Project in partnership with Asian Paints. Project Location: Lodhi Art District, New Delhi. Photo by Pranav Gohil. Reproduced with the permission of St+art India Foundation.

Time Changes Everything | Daku

Indian street artist Daku creates powerful typographic interventions in public places, frequently engaging building signage, billboards, and installations. In Daku's work *Time Changes Everything*, designed for St+Art India, flat, cut phrases are meticulously designed and attached perpendicularly to a building's facade in New Delhi. Because of their placement, the shadows of these large words appear and move as a result of the sun, much like the indicator on a sundial. This installation relies on the passing of time in order to be seen and understood. Words appear in the morning and shift throughout the day before disappearing at night. This transition poetically alerts an audience that the concepts listed—light, space, ideas, identity, and life—are all inevitably altered by time.

Figure 3.62 *Seeing The Good Is A Superpower* by Xack Fischer & Peregrine Church. © Rainworks, 2021. Reproduced with the permission of Rainworks.

Rainworks Typography | Peregrine Church and Xack Fischer

How might hidden messages spark discovery? How could an image only be viewed in specific conditions—or in specific weather? This is what Peregrine Church and Xack Fischer, the creatives behind Rainworks, were curious to find out. Made using a custom-developed hydrophobic coating, a *rainwork* refers to a message or image created on a surface which is invisible when dry, but visible when wet. These messages, which have been created all over the world, are both enduring and fleeting. Because they are hidden during dry weather and only appear in rain, *specificity of time* is an essential factor to their viewing. In addition, the Rainworks team created their own font for improved production: attached counters and rounded corners allow for easy stencil-removal. Here, this rainwork appears on a wet surface, spreading a message of positivity.

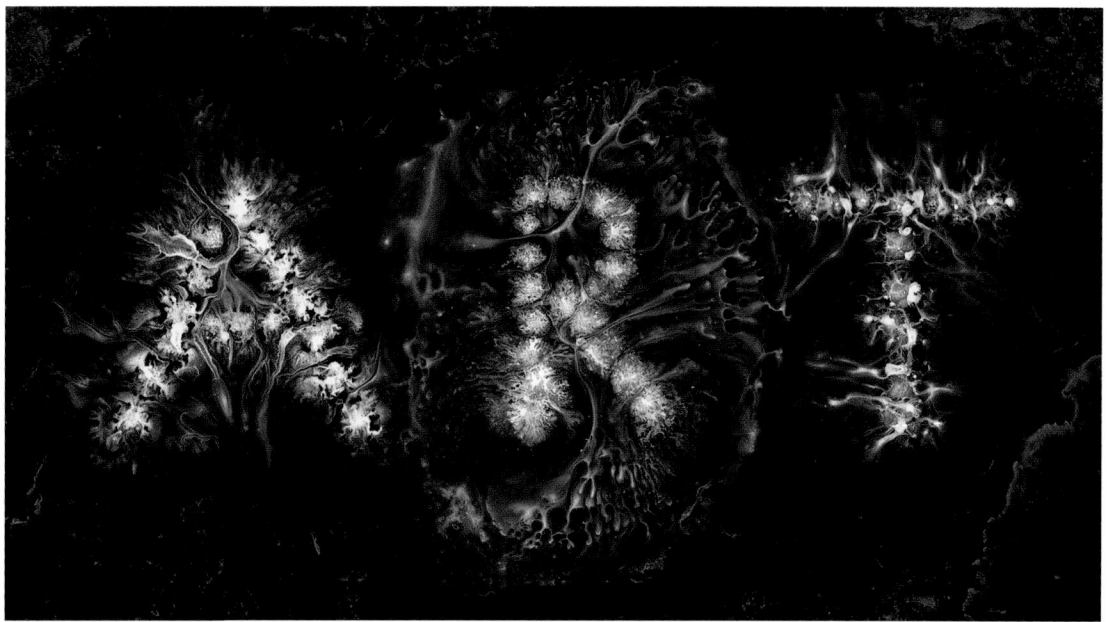

Figure 3.63 *Liquid Calligraphy* by © Rus Khasanov, 2018. Reproduced with the permission of Rus Khasanov.

Liquid Calligraphy | Ruslan Khasanov

In *Liquid Calligraphy*, an experiential typography series by artist and designer Ruslan Khasanov, time is essential to both process and outcome. Working on a controlled wet surface, drawn letterforms spring to life as ink spreads, moves, and branches, creating unique patterns and kinetic features. These fluid forms change and evolve in real time before vanishing—making a work which is both created by, and indicative of, something delicate disappearing.

Figures 3.64 and 3.65 *A million Times 120* by Humans since 1982. © Humans since 1982, 2016. Reproduced with the permission of Humans since 1982.

A million Times | Humans since 1982

Humans since 1982 is a Stockholm-based art and design studio; much of their work explores visual and kinetic representations of passing time. In their ongoing *A million Times* series, individual clock hands move in intricately choreographed abstract patterns. These pause to form numbers, showcasing the current time in the style of a digital clock. Shown here in *A million Times 120*, these entrancing works use the passing of minutes and seconds as their own medium, transforming time-telling from something utilitarian into something poetic and evocative.

action within a limited timeframe. The prestige and spectacle of a solar eclipse, coronation, or even an annual holiday is bolstered by relative infrequency. Typographic works can make use of this emotional urgency as well, creating opportunities for experiences which are temporally specific—requiring works to be viewed at particular times or in defined circumstances. Because of their limited viewing windows, works which are reliant on time as medium can create rare interactions or unique opportunities for discovery.

A CLOSER LOOK:
Ghost signs

Some works rely on the passage of time as an integral part of their genesis. The growth of a typographic topiary or the development of glyphs from bacteria on a petri dish may require hours, days, or months in order for letterforms to appear. Conversely, the passage of time can be integral to works whose very existence is made possible by their advanced age, decay, or disappearance. Consider that an *heirloom* is only defined by its passage from one generation to the next, and that which is *antique* requires a long-past date of production.

For much of the nineteenth century, and into the twentieth, businesses frequently advertised their locations and wares by painting directly onto the side of buildings. Exposed to the elements over decades, many of these signs and advertisements for long-defunct products and businesses have faded—becoming a mere shadow of their original form. This passage of time has transformed them into something new: *ghost signs*.

A *ghost sign* refers to the faded remnants of a painted sign on an architectural facade. One ghost sign can be composed of many texts and advertisements painted on top of each other; these are only revealed as paint weathers, becoming a visual cacophony. As layers of pigment fade and deteriorate, ghost signs often expose a visual record of the passage of time, showcasing many facets of history on a single surface in a testament to advertisements, objects, and people of the past. Shown here, multiple advertisements painted on the side of a former tobacco warehouse form this ghost sign in Lexington, Kentucky while nearby, an ad for Uneeda Biscuits (introduced in 1899 by the National Biscuit Company) continues to fade.

The fascination with ghost signs stems not only from their place-based history and vintage typography, but from their relationship with time itself. While these signs give contemporary audiences a glimpse into the past, their intrigue relies on their strange dichotomy as something simultaneously enduring *and* disappearing. Their history makes them valuable; their fragility makes them precious. Ghost signs therefore occupy a precarious position. Leaving them alone means admitting an inevitable demise, while restoring them inherently alters their faded status as "ghosts." As buildings are razed, painted, or further erected, obscuring them from sight, ghost signs will inevitably fade and disappear from public space. As this happens, we may find their context relegated to *virtual space* instead, where they may live on in digital images, archives, or street-views long past their demolition or destruction.

Figures 3.66 and 3.67 Photos by Mia Cinelli, 2022.

Into the Future

Despite our inability to predict the future, artists and designers frequently make use of design and typography in an attempt to subvert or influence its outcome. In the same way that contemporary practices react and respond to current events (see "Temporal influence: Current events" in this chapter), artists and designers have undertaken projects and proposals in hopes of changing behavior *in the present* in order to best achieve (or avoid) particular futures. With these intentions in mind, what practical or conceptual frameworks best achieve this?

In 2009, US-based designers and educators Bruce and Stephanie Tharp published an article on the well-known design blog *Core77* called *The 4 Fields of Industrial Design: (No, not furniture, trans, consumer electronics, & toys)* in which they proposed sorting the wide discipline of industrial design into four non-exclusive categories by their driving forces: commercial design, responsible design, experimental design, and discursive design. As a discipline, design is frequently—albeit narrowly—specified by its "utility" and ability to "solve problems." In both its definition and practice, *discursive design* pushes against this expectation and engages with design as a means to catalyze conversation, reflection, or debate. Though frequently used to describe artifacts, *discursive design* can include objects, images, or scenarios which seek to communicate ideas, using design as a means to investigate, question, propose, or discover.

Within typography, conceptual frameworks such as discursive design provide new avenues to discuss challenges and opportunities shaping the future; their visual inquiries provide viewers with a new way to engage or consider these ideas in the production of knowledge. Letterforms may visualize undesirable scenarios—much to the discomfort of their audiences—or embody educational or philosophical approaches in their visual representations. When accessed through

Figure 3.68 *Coastlines* by Eino Korkala and Daniel Coull. © Eino Korkala and Daniel Coull, 2021. Reproduced with the permission of Eino Korkala and Daniel Coull.

Climate Crisis Font | Eino Korkala and Daniel Coull

Global climate change is undeniable, but a larger question remains: is it unavoidable? Designed by Eino Korkala and Daniel Coull for the widely circulated Finnish newspaper *Helsingin Sanomat*, the Climate Crisis Font visualizes the devastating effects of climate change in an alarmingly disappearing typeface. Informed by the National Snow and Ice Data Center's data on Arctic sea ice from 1979 to 2019, the respective weights of this font family follow this trend of change, predicting global warming's impact on Arctic sea ice through 2050. Shown through the passage of time, these letterforms become nearly unrecognizable in displaying a tangible urgency: we are running out of time to act to deter catastrophic climate change. To further disseminate this message, punctuate journalism on global warming, and encourage respective action, this typeface has been made available for free download and use.

Giving Type Meaning

Figures 3.69–3.72 *It Ain't Ok Mama* by Selman Design. © Selman Design 2020. Reproduced with the permission of Selman Design.

It Ain't Okay Mama | Selman Design

Moved by concern for future generations, Johnny Selman (of Selman Design, an NYC-based creative studio) considered what could be done to communicate the urgency of combating climate change. Combining talent in both music and design, Selman worked with a team to create a visual representation of his original song called "Mama," which details the harms caused to both earth's environment and inhabitants as a result of global warming. In this interactive web experiment made for Earth Day 2020, users can engage with typography of the song's refrain plagued by imagery of destructive climate change: fire, floods, drought, disease, and war. By digitally connecting with this experimental text, visitors can reverse these plights—and consider what actions can be taken to avert these future disasters. Visitors to the website are encouraged to donate to the Natural Resources Defense Council, a nonprofit organization working to combat climate change.

exhibitions, publications, or use, they may bring otherwise complex or overlooked topics into contemporary discourse. If what we say today may influence what happens tomorrow, discussing possible futures through typography can serve as a form of activism—an impetus for impact and action.

LANGUAGE, FORM, AND MEANING

What might typography look like in the future? While there is no certain way to predict what is yet to come, we can anticipate that the future of typography hinges on its understanding as a visual representation of language and culture (see "Cultural context" in Chapter 1). Your capacity to comprehend this book is contingent on your ability to connect the relationship between form and meaning relative to language. As you read, ample contrast of brightness and visual perception of figure-ground relationships allow you to discern familiar, individual letters or characters. Proximity allows you to formulate recognizable words, and their *syntax*, or the order in which they are arranged, creates perceptible phrases. When these connections are visually disrupted, they obscure the relationship between letterform, language, and meaning—as demonstrated in this jumbled, visual puzzle (and the author's attempt at its solution) from an early twentieth century Bovril ad.

However, *how* meaning is communicated is dependent on the visual representation of the language you are reading. All languages rely on *morphemes*, the smallest understood linguistic units of meaning. A *grapheme* refers to the basic visual unit of written language—such as a number or letter. Generally speaking, some writing systems are *alphabetic*, whose letter combinations denote affiliated sounds and consequent syllables with socially agreed-upon meanings. These form morphemes as words or parts of words, producing recognizable arrangements. In English, the individual morphemes "*play*" or "*ed*" used together allow us to understand *played* (as a single word) as occurring in the past tense. Other writing systems are *logographic*, in which characters are *logograms*, representing a single word or morpheme. For examples such as logographic Chinese characters, their combinations tend to represent pronunciation and meaning; only a few of these characters are *pictographic* in nature, in which a glyph bears a visual resemblance to the object or action represented.

As a small part of a much larger field of study, these categories and definitions are by no means exhaustive, but their differentiations are important. Crafting *linguistic* meaning from written text is dependent on connecting what a character represents on its own or in combination with others. In English, a solo letter "a" is an indefinite article, giving general reference to nouns. In combination with other letterforms, it allows us to form words and phrases. However, the *character* of a lowercase a is different from its unique (and infinite) visual representations as a *glyph*. Typographic meaning builds on this, and is informed by *how* glyphs are visually portrayed with *what* they linguistically communicate—bridging interpretation of both look and language. What happens, then, when characters have specific, intended meanings which are inaccessible to an audience?

Evaluating the connections (or lack thereof) between letterforms, language, and meanings of the past catalyzes considerations for future developments in typography. How do changes to language impact changes to letterforms?

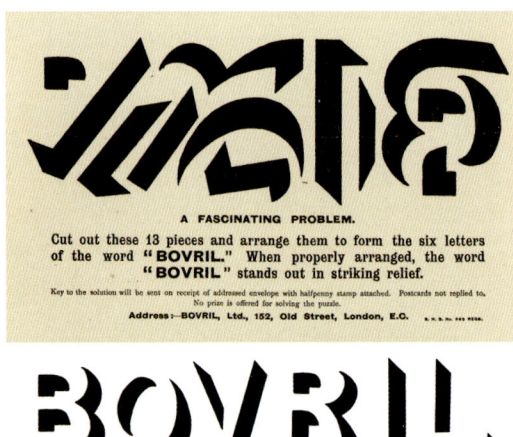

Figure 3.73 Bovril advertisement. Wellcome Collection.

Figure 3.74 From archive.org.

Linear A

Linear A is the name given to the writing system used by the Minoans from approximately 1800–1450 BCE; examples of its use have been found on Crete as well as the Aegean Islands. The Mycenaean Greeks later borrowed elements of this system to form Linear B, representing an early Greek dialect. While Linear B can be deciphered because of its relationship to a discernible language, the *meaning* of Linear A has eluded scholars because the *language* the characters refer to is unknown.

This illustrates how visual representations of writing systems rely on cultural, linguistic, and temporal contexts in order to be understood. Without knowledge of *what* these characters allude to, their intended meanings are lost. (Consider how the Rosetta Stone, on which a decree from 196 BCE was inscribed in three scripts—Greek, Demotic, and hieroglyphics—was key in deciphering Ancient Egyptian hieroglyphs in the early nineteenth century.) This digital interpretation of Linear A (inscribed on the interior of a cup) is based on an illustration from *Scripta Minoa: The Written Documents of Minoan Crete, With Special Reference to the Archives of Knossos* by Arthur J. Evans, from 1909. This particular inscription clearly meant something to someone—but what?

How far can a glyph be transformed before it is no longer recognizable as a specific character? Both contemporary and historical experimental typography have pushed boundaries of how letterforms are visually represented. This challenges expectations for legibility, readability, and communication.

What happens, then, when a *lack* of recognition is both intentional *and* essential to a letterform's very definition? *Asemic writing* refers to a wordless form of writing in which strokes or forms are written, but not in linguistically identifiable writing systems. Instead, asemic writing relies on a level of familiarity of pattern,

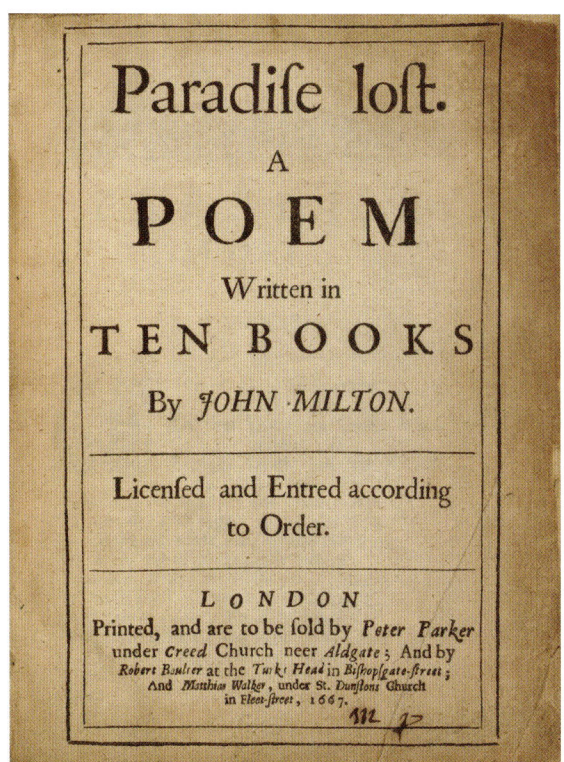
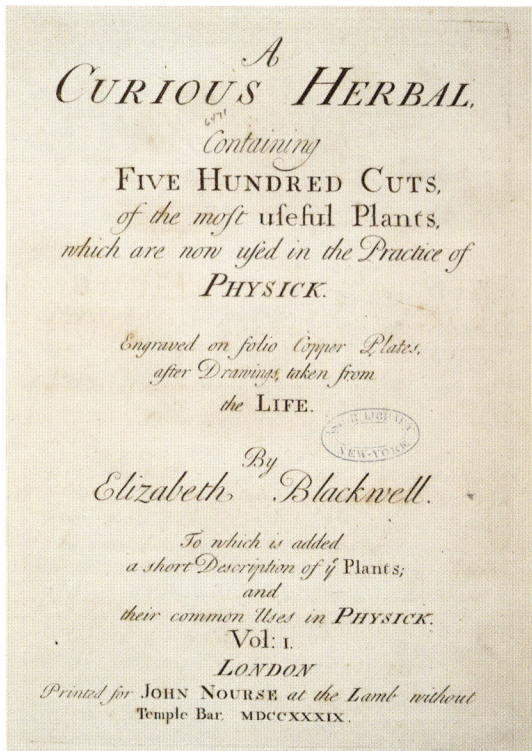

Figures 3.75 and 3.76 From The New York Public Library.

The Long S

Have you ever encountered a strange, discontinuous letter in historical text? A frequent point of confusion for contemporary readers is the "long s"—an archaic character used to denote an "s" which differed from the "short s" that we use and recognize today. Used at the beginning or in the middle of words, the "long s" resembles a lowercase f with its crossbar extending to the left (ſ) or a gracefully curved ʃ, extending below the baseline when italicized. The still-used German ligature *eszett* (ß) or "sharp s," typically represents a double-s. This is derived from the "long s" character, whose form can be seen on its left-hand side.

Though this character developed from a calligraphic tradition, it fell out of fashion near the turn of the nineteenth century, lessening both labor of typesetters and confusion of an expanding literate audience. The *meaning* of this character as a kind of "s" relies entirely on previous knowledge about what this glyph represents. As such, literate audiences at that time would have been able to discern its sound/syllabic meaning without problem. However, because this character has not been commonly used for 200+ years, its use befuddles most readers today. In these situations, contemporary viewers attempt to make meaning through similar form—the lowercase f—as a familiar frame of reference. Shown here in a 1667 printing of *Paradise Lost* by John Milton, its title can easily be misread as *Paradife Loft*. In a 1739 title page from a printed book of illustrations of plants with medicinal purposes by Scottish illustrator and engraver Elizabeth Blackwell, a number of different "s" characters, including the "long s," are used.

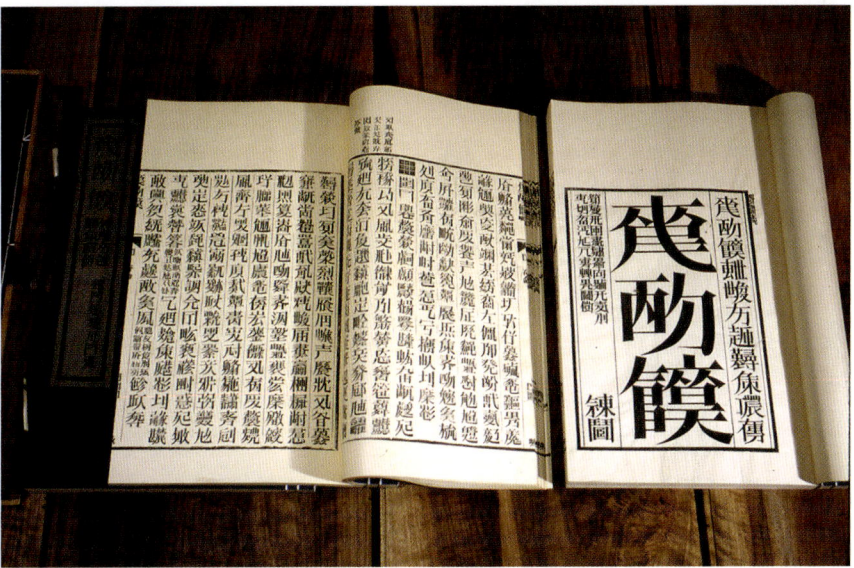

Figures 3.77 and 3.78 Xu Bing, *Book from the Sky* (1987–1991), installation view at Blanton Museum of Art, Texas, 2016. © Xu Bing Studio. Xu Bing, *Book from the Sky* (1987–1991), Mixed media installation/handprinted books and scrolls printed from blocks inscribed with "false" characters. © Xu Bing Studio.

Book from the Sky | Xu Bing

Over the course of four years, Chinese artist Xu Bing hand-carved thousands of characters in movable type, printing them onto a series of scrolls and books to compose an impressive installation titled *Book from the Sky*. While these characters may appear to be Chinese, they are *not*. Instead, these original characters are intentionally designed to be visually familiar yet entirely illegible. These letterforms—fashioned in a style from the Song Dynasty, used during the Ming Dynasty—are formally designed and arranged to subvert expectations of text and written communication. Both intriguing and inaccessible, this work poignantly challenges audience assumptions about what text is, what language means, and how we communicate.

 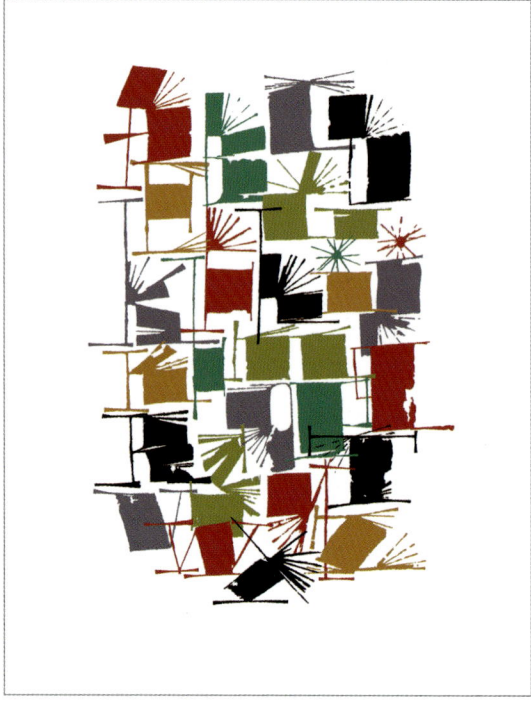

Figures 3.79 and 3.80 *Alphabet from Twenty-six of 26* by Susan Skarsgard. © Susan Skarsgard, 2010. Reproduced with the permission of Susan Skarsgard.

26 of 26: An Edition of Twenty-Six Alphabets | Susan Skarsgard

Experimenting with letterform fidelity allows for new experiences in form, meaning, and understanding in typography. In a thoughtful investigation of letters as essential components of language, artist and designer Susan Skarsgard reimagined and abstracted letterforms for her 2009 work *26 of 26: An Edition of Twenty-Six Alphabets*. This collection of twenty-six images—featuring unique alphabets, each in an edition of twenty-six—was crafted through a variety of mark-making and printmaking techniques. These works explore how letters are made as well as how their novel forms influence consequent interpretation.

placement, and figure-ground relationships in order to recognize its visual arrangement as a form of writing. Much like abstract art, asemic writing is nonrepresentational. While examples of asemic writing are created with intention, their understanding relies heavily on audience interpretations to make meaning from otherwise indiscernible marks—or engages with ambiguity as the point itself. Asemic texts can be drawn, written, or regularly assembled, such as repeated abstract glyphs within a typeface. While asemic writing may be free from traditional associations of letterforms pertaining to *language*, it does not mean that these forms are meaning-less.

SPECULATIVE TYPOGRAPHY

Humans have been imagining unknowable futures for centuries, theorizing both feasible and fantastical solutions. The field of *speculative design* visualizes "*what's next*" by asking "*what if?*" Speculative design—both an area and term largely popularized by designers Anthony Dunne and Fiona Raby—imagines or exposes potential futures through design. As a field of inquiry, it has frequently been associated with architecture or industrial design, whose immediate familiarity and tangibility produces easy-to-imagine contexts of use, but its frameworks apply to typefaces and type in use, too. While it may seem like a relatively new notion, the idea of speculative design is supported by a rich history in typography, as designers have worked to propose or interrogate the future in their typographic work.

Notably, in 1962, American advertising professional Martin K. Speckter made note of the common yet awkward use of an exclamation point and question mark together for shocking queries. As a more streamlined alternative, he proposed and designed the interrobang, a punctuation mark used to end incredulous or rhetorical questions, such as: "You left the front door open‽" or "He told her what‽" While this punctuation did not become widely recognized, it was included as a key option on several typewriters produced by Remington Rand in 1968, and is still included in some digital typefaces today. Similarly, French writer Hervé Bazin proposed new punctuation marks in his essay *Plumons L'Oiseau* from 1966. These include marks for certitude (an exclamation point with a crossbar), love (two facing question marks in the form of a heart), and acclimation (two exclamation points sharing a single dot).

While proposed, not all speculative designs enter mainstream use—and not all share such aspirations. Some examples exist solely as discursive concepts, while others seek to reflect on the potential evolution of language, type, and expression over time. Works of speculative design rely on interpretation within a temporal context in order to create meaning; when viewers encounter speculative work in the present, they can assess, evaluate, or imagine an otherwise obscure future through the lens of their current knowledge and situation. Because meaning is made relative to its relationship with time, speculative design and typography can only propose a future in relation to the known present, ultimately asking: what kind of society do we want to live in, and what do we want to do about it *now*?

Arial Sarcastic

Figure 3.81 Arial Sarcastic by Glenn McAnally/the Sarcastic Font Movement, formerly of http://glennmcanally.com/sarcastic/index.htm.

Arial Sarcastic | Glenn McAnally

In order to understand sarcasm, listeners require the ability to understand the difference between the stated and intended meaning of a phrase or reaction, largely influenced by *vocal* inflection. This makes sarcasm particularly difficult to translate through written word alone. In 2004, a curious website appeared online under the authorship of Glenn McAnally: *The Sarcastic Font Movement*. To alleviate confusion of meaning and provide greater clarity in written information, this sardonic website both proposed and distributed Arial Sarcastic. Transposing expectations of italic emphasis, this irreverent version of Arial slants leftwards rather than rightward to serve as a visual indicator of sarcasm. To spread the word, the site encouraged visitors to download and use the font before unceremoniously disappearing from the web—though its legacy and humor lives on.

Figures 3.82 and 3.83 *Signs of Change* by Radical Norms. © Radical Norms, 2020. Reproduced with the permission of Koby Barhad.

Signs of Change | Radical Norms

What might a city's future infrastructure look like? This is the query posed by Radical Norms, a design research company based in Toronto, Canada, led by Daniel Daam-Rossi, Angelika Seeschaaf-Veres, and Koby Barhad. Created during DesignTO 2020, Canada's largest annual design festival, Radical Norms asked visitors to imagine and suggest a sign of the future. Presented through familiar, recontextualized traffic signs, text and image collide to propose ideas and experiences of the world to come—where spaces and interactions have adapted to new laws, technologies, and values. *Signs of Change* asks what *should* be by visualizing what *could* be—probing the consequences of plausible or preferable futures.

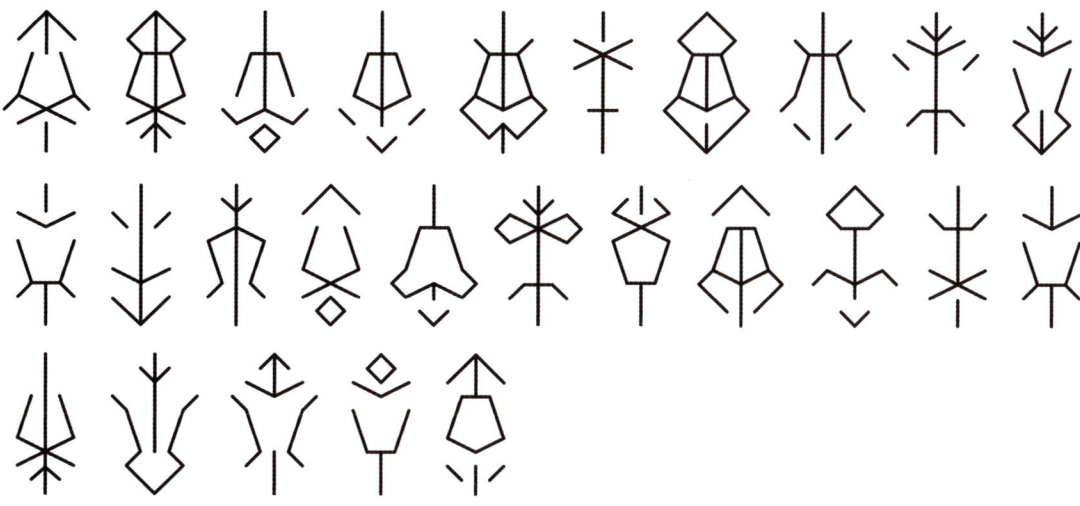

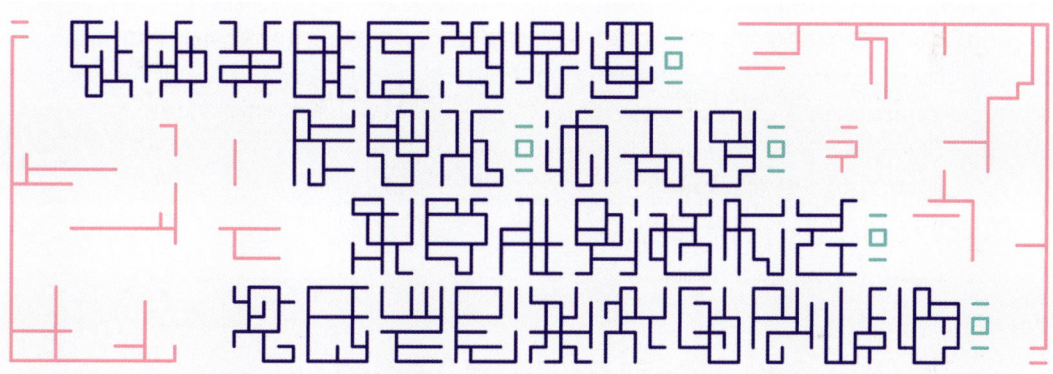

Figures 3.84 and 3.85 *Edie Alphabet* by Barry Spencer. © Barry Spencer, 2015. *Clara Cryptic Artwork #2* by Barry Spencer. © Barry Spencer, 2016. Reproduced with the permission of Barry Spencer.

Speculative Type | Barry Spencer

How do we currently make meaning from recognizable letterforms, and how might this change in the future? Barry Spencer is an Australian educator and speculative type designer whose playful and provocative works imagine future visual communication through inventive type design. Inspired by a section of roofing at the Edge Theater in Melbourne, Australia, his typeface Edie features vertically set architecturally gridded symmetrical forms. Their design and arrangement suggest new ways of reading and writing, while only subtly hinting at the Latin letterforms from which they are derived. Designed to be purposefully cryptic, his typeface Clara subverts expectations for what Latin letterforms *should* look like entirely. These unfamiliar characters intentionally probe the relationship between recognition, legibility, and communication. Their inherent meaning lies in the challenge of their translation; at the time of this book's writing, Clara's letterforms have yet to be deciphered by viewers.

What's Next?

How do you use typography in your own work or creative practice? Whether it's for practical or expressive purposes, the efficacy of communication is essential. How we design, choose, and use type has lasting impact, both personal and political. Because meaning is contextually bound, it's important to consider not just the social, spatial, and temporal context of the works *created*, but the information *provided*.

In all art and design practices, there is a negotiation between subtle hints and obvious declarations in an attempt to convey what a creative work means. Over-explanation can ruin poetics and self-discovery—the basis of the writing adage "show, don't tell"—while too little information can erroneously or intentionally obscure communication. While typographic applications communicate on their own, gallery wall text, expository artist statements, brief histories, colophons (descriptive inscriptions in publications), or even instructions can all supplement existing visual language to bolster understanding. This is especially true when an original context changes—such as works viewed via documentation—where access to *additional context* is crucial to determining what a work seeks to communicate.

What something is, how it is perceived, and what it means often, but do not always, align.

Subjectivity of interpretation can never be avoided, but anyone communicating visually can more thoughtfully consider how they make, contextualize, and present their work. By knowing and utilizing various frameworks for contextual meaning, designers can make visual and typographic choices in a more informed way, allowing us to ask *and* answer: What do you see—and what does it say?

RESOURCES FOR EDUCATORS AND STUDENTS

Chapter 1: Social Context

Creative brief: Recontextualization

Choose an existing typographic application, such as a sign or package, whose context and visual inflection catalyzes a specific, recognizable meaning. By making *one* change to its text, size, material, or spatial context, create a new social meaning through recontextualization. How does this shift change the meaning of this message?

Writing prompt: Power structures

What existing power structures do you know and recognize, and how do they visually represent themselves? Compare and contrast the typographic choices of three organizations, politicians, or institutions currently in or attempting to gain power. Why do you feel these type choices were made? In what contexts are these works presented? How do you think they are meant to be perceived—and how do you personally perceive them? Why?

Discussion questions

- Keeping both intercultural and intracultural contexts in mind, how do the cultural values of your specific location influence local or regional visual communication?
- How can visual inflection be used in persuasion?
- How might visual metaphors create clarity of textual information? Are there scenarios where they should be avoided?

Chapter 2: Spatial Context

Creative brief: Expressive typography conversation

Identify a short conversation between two or more people from a TV show, podcast, interview, or movie. Transcribe this conversation and set the type in an expressive manner, reflecting the tone of voice of the speakers, the pace of conversation, the volume used, and the inflection of words spoken. This may take the form of a printed book, website, or animated video. Consider the typeface chosen, the visual space occupied by text, and how pauses, sounds, actions are represented through kerning, tracking, size relationships, and intentional use of Gestalt principles.

Writing prompt: Type walk

Take a quick walk around an area with public buildings, documenting the typography you encounter architecturally, in windows, and on signs. In a written response, consider and answer: What is the history of the area or particular building? What is the typeface and its history? Why might it have been chosen for this purpose? What materials are type made from, and why? Socially, what meanings do these materials, histories, or locations impart? Did any of these messages convey an unintentional message? If so, what could have improved their efficacy?

Discussion questions

- Typographical, what material meaning could catalyze two very different meanings based on its differing connotations?
- What typographic items or messages do you choose to display in your personal space? What do you hope they communicate to others?
- How do digital methods and virtual space inform your own creative practice?

Chapter 3: Temporal Context

Creative brief: Future influence

Considering ideal or unpleasant futures, design a text-based image/artifact or typeface intended to influence current actions in order to achieve—or avoid—a specific future. Carefully consider how context will best inform the perception of these works. Who is your intended audience, and what action do you hope it prompts? Where, and through what medium, will they encounter this work?

Writing prompt: History-inspired

Identify a typographic work which was inspired by history. In a written response, identify the historic event, when it took place, and who was involved. Then, analyze: Why might the author have chosen this event? How does their new work create a new point of view or understanding?

Discussion questions

- What typographic trends do you observe happening now? What technological or societal influences do you think informed their social meaning and popularity?
- How does your identity influence the ways in which you make and interpret typographic works?
- What archives, online resources, or texts do you typically use for inspiration or information?
- What works/creatives are present, and which are missing? What factors may have influenced this?

SELECT BIBLIOGRAPHY

Social Context

Avella, Natalie. *Graphic Japan: From Woodblock and Zen to Manga and Kawaii*. Mies: RotoVision, 2004.

Barrett, Terry. *Making Art: Form and Meaning*. London: McGraw Hill Education, 2011.

Berer, Josh. Email message to author, May 26, 2021.

Bourdieu, Pierre. *Distinction: A Social Critique of the Judgement of Taste*. Cambridge, MA: Harvard University Press, 1984.

Bourdieu, Pierre. "The Forms of Capital" Essay. In *Handbook of Theory and Research for the Sociology of Education*, edited by J. G. Richardson, 241–58. Westport, CT: Greenwood, 1986.

Brownlee, John. *Errol Morris: How Typography Shapes Our Perception of Truth*. Fast Company, May 18, 2015. www.fastcompany.com

Cila, Nazli. *Metaphors We Design by: The Use of Metaphors in Product Design*. Ph.D. Dissertation, Technical University of Delft, 2013.

Cornell, Alex. "Gap Redesign Contest." Web log. ISO50 (blog), October 6, 2010. http://blog.iso50.com

Department of Islamic Art. "Calligraphy in Islamic Art." The Metropolitan Museum of Art, October 2001. https://www.metmuseum.org

Duncombe, Stephen. *Notes from Underground: Zines and the Politics of Alternative Culture*. London: Verso, 1997.

Euse, Erica. "Why That Tribal Tattoo Won't Work in a Woke World." *i-D Magazine*, August 10, 2017. https://i-d.vice.com

Freeland, Cynthia A. *But is it Art? An Introduction to Art Theory*. Oxford: Oxford University Press, 2001.

Gap. "Thanks for everyone's input on the new logo!" Facebook, October 6, 2010. https://www.facebook.com/gap

Geoghegan, Tom. "Lessons to Be Learnt from the Gap Logo Debacle." BBC News, October 12, 2010. https://www.bbc.com

Ghosh, Mainak. *Visual Semantics for Visual Communication (Contd. 11)*. YouTube, 2017.

Grazian, David. *Mix It Up: Popular Culture, Mass Media, and Society*. New York: W. W. Norton, 2010.

Hume, David, and John W. Lenz. *Of the Standard of Taste, and Other Essays*. Indianapolis: Bobbs-Merrill, 1965.

Inbar, Shira. *Homa Delvaray Gives Poster Design a New Dimension*. AIGA Eye on Design, July 27, 2020, https://eyeondesign.aiga.org

Kinsella, Sharon. "Cuties in Japan" Essay. In *Women, Media and Consumption in Japan*, edited by Brian Moeran and Lise Skov, 220–54. Honolulu, HI: University of Hawaii Press, 1995.

Lee, Laura. *Around the World in 80 Cliches: Overused Expressions from across the Globe*. New York: Wellfleet Press, 2016.

Lidwell, William, Kritina Holden, and Jill Butler. *Universal Principles of Design: 125 Ways to Enhance Usability, Influence Perception, Increase Appeal, Make Better Design Decisions, and Teach through Design*. 2nd ed. Beverly, MA: Rockport, 2010.

Loewy, Raymond. "The Maya State and Consumer Acceptance." SAE Technical Paper Series, January 1, 1950.

Lovitt, Carl R., and Dixie Goswami, eds. *Exploring the Rhetoric of International Professional Communication: An Agenda for Teachers and Researchers*. Abingdon: Taylor & Francis, 2020.

Mars, Roman. "Episode 288: Guerilla Public Service Redux." 99% Invisible. Podcast audio, December 12, 2017. https://99percentinvisible.org

Morris, Errol. "Hear, All Ye People; Hearken, O Earth (Part 1)." *New York Times*, August 9, 2012.

"Prayer Niche (Mihrab)." Cleveland Museum of Art, n.d. https://clevelandart.org

Rjeily, Rana Abou. *Cultural Connectives*. West New York, NJ: Mark Batty Publisher, 2011.

Shen, Juliet. "Lushootseed Indigenous Font Design." Public Lecture, San Francisco Public Library, 2018.

Shen, Juliet. "Native American Fonts and Tribal Sovereignty." Book Club of California Quarterly, July 2018.

Streitmatter, Rodger. "Vice Versa: America's First Lesbian Magazine." *American Periodicals* 8 (1998).

Tuwim, Julian. *Pegaz dęba*. Krakow: Czytelnik, 1950.

Verba, Joan Marie. *Boldly Writing: A Trek Fan and Fanfiction History 1967–1987*. Scotts Valley, CA: Createspace Independent Publishing, 2003.

Veytsman, Boris. "The Fonts We Choose." *TUGboat* 33, no. 3 (2012).

Worley, Matthew. "Punk, Politics and British (Fan)Zines, 1976–84: 'While the World Was Dying, Did You Wonder Why?'." *History Workshop Journal* 79, no. 1 (2015): 76–106.

Spatial Context

"A History of Monument Lettering and Design." Monument Lettering Center, n.d. https://www.monumentletteringcenter.com

"About the Right to Access Swedish Nature." Visit Sweden, n.d. https://visitsweden.com

Adebiaye, Frank. Video call with author, October 13, 2021.

Albert, Alphaeus Homer. *Washington Historical Buttons: Washington Inaugural Buttons, and Other Buttons Bearing the Portrait of Washington or Alluding to Him and His Administration*. Princeton, NJ: Princeton University Press, 1949.

Barton, Bruce, and James Craig. *Thirty Centuries of Graphic Design: An Illustrated Survey*. London: Watson-Guptill Publications, 1987.

Bech Dyg, Kasper. *Laurie Anderson Interview: A Virtual Reality of Stories*. YouTube. Louisiana Channel, Louisiana Museum of Modern Art, 2017.

Blitz, Matt. "City Says 'Defund the Police' Message at BLM Plaza Was Erased due to Road Work." dcist. WAMU 88.5, American University Radio, August 17, 2020. https://dcist.com

Bringhurst, Robert. *The Elements of Typographic Style*. Vancouver, BC: Hartley & Marks Publishers, 2004.

Cheng, Karen. *Designing Type*. New Haven, CT: Yale University Press, 2005.

Couzy, Michiel, and Ruben Koops. "Meerderheid Raad: Weg Met Letters I Amsterdam." Het Parool. October 10, 2018.

Cunningham, Daniel, and Steffi Cheng. "Motion Type Project." Neocha Culture & Creativity in Asia, April 23, 2018. https://neocha.com

Danesi, Marcel. "Visual Rhetoric and Semiotic." In *Oxford Research Encyclopedia of Communication*. Oxford University Press, May 24, 2017.

Dixon, Keetra Dean, and J. K. Keller. Public lecture, Rocky Mountain College of Art + Design, VASD Program, 2016.

Edwards, Kristen. "Black Lives Matter Mural Painted in Downtown Lexington" Lex18, September 14, 2020. https://www.lex18.com

Eisenstein, Elizabeth L. *The Printing Revolution in Early Modern Europe*. Cambridge: Cambridge University Press, 2012.

"Electioneering Prohibitions." National Conference of State Legislatures, April 1, 2021. https://www.ncsl.org

Ellroy, James, and Edward Ruscha. *Ed Ruscha: Fifty Years of Painting*. London: Hayward Publishing, 2009.

Francesca, Gavin, and Tiffany Field. *Touch*. London: MIT Press, 2003.

Francesca, Gavin, and Lawrence Weiner. OSL series: In conversation. OSL Contemporary, October 1, 2019. https://oslcontemporary.com

Gale, Robert L. *An Ambrose Bierce Companion*. Westport, CT: Greenwood Press, 2001.

Gibson, Chantal. Video call with author, September 30, 2021.

Gibson, Jeffrey. Public Lecture, Cranbrook Academy of Art, January 19, 2016.

Gibson, Jeffrey. *Jeffrey Gibson, Visual Artist | 2019 MacArthur Fellow*. YouTube, 2019.

Glaister, Geoffrey Ashall. *Encyclopedia of the Book*. New Castle, DE: Oak Knoll Press, 1996.

Goffman, Erving. *The Presentation of Self in Everyday Life*. New York: Anchor Books, 1959.

Graphic Means. [Film]. Dir. Briar Levit. Relayer Films, 2017.

Greene, Roland, and Stephen Cushman, eds. *The Princeton Handbook of Poetic Terms*. Princeton, NJ: Princeton University Press, 2016.

"Guillaume Apollinaire." Poetry Foundation, n.d. https://www.poetryfoundation.org

Hall, Sean. *This Means This, This Means That: A User's Guide to Semiotics*. London: Laurence King Publishing, 2012.

Heller, Steven, and Seymour Chwast. *Graphic Style: From Victorian to Hipster*. New York: Abrams, 2018.

Higgins, Dick. *Pattern Poetry: Guide to an Unknown Literature*. Albany, NY: SUNY Press, 1987.

Hilder, Jamie. *Designed Words for a Designed World: The International Concrete Poetry Movement, 1955–1971*. Kingston, ON: McGill-Queen's University Press, 2016.

Hoefler, Jonathan. "Tools for Teaching: Typographic Illusions." Web log. Hoefler&Co. (blog), November 5, 2019. https://www.typography.com

Houston, Keith. *Shady Characters: The Secret Life of Punctuation, Symbols, and Other Typographical Marks*. New York: W. W. Norton, 2013.

"Interview with Lawrence Weiner: The Materialist." Sedition, November 9, 2015. https://www.seditionart.com

Lehman, David W., Kieran O'Connor, Balázs Kovács, and George E. Newman. "Authenticity." Academy of Management Annals. Academy of Management, January 2019.

Lieberman, Jethro Koller. *Fifty Years a Typesetter: Adventures in Printing Together with Some Meditations on Theory and Craft*. United States: Press at James Pond, 2003.

Lombardo, Giorgia. "Can You Control a Typeface Using Only Your Facial Expressions?" Medium. DeMagSign, June 18, 2020. https://medium.com

Lubalin, Herb, Aaron Burns, Ed Rondthaler, Jack Anson Finke, and Mark Johnson, eds. "U&lc: Upper and Lower Case." *International Journal of Typographics* 1, no. 2 (1974): 8.

Martz, Jason. National Park Service, Gettysburg National Military Park. Email message to author, January 18, 2022.

McDonald, Fiona. *The Popular History of Graffiti: From the Ancient World to the Present*. New York: Skyhorse, 2013.

Pohl, Frances, ed. *Mirella Bentivoglio – Pages*. Claremont, CA: Pomona College Museum of Art, 2015.

Rundle, David. "Poggio Bracciolini's International Reputation and the Significance of Bryn Mawr, Ms. 48." Essay. In *Poggio Bracciolini and the Re(dis)covery of Antiquity: Textual and Material Traditions*, edited by Roberta Ricci with assistance from Eric L. Pumroy, 41–70. Florence: Firenze University Press, 2020.

Segerstråle, Ullica, and Peter Molnár, eds. "Universal Facial Expressions of Emotion: An Old Controversy and New Findings." Nonverbal Communication. Routledge, February 19, 2018.

Senft, T. M. "emoticon." *Encyclopedia Britannica*, February 27, 2022. https://www.britannica.com

Sherman, William H. "Toward a History of the Manicule." Center for Editing Lives and Letters. http://www.livesandletters.ac.uk/, March 2005.

Skarbek, Mary. Email message to author, November 3, 2021.

"State Laws Prohibiting Electioneering Activities Within a Certain Distance of the Polling Place." National Association of Secretaries of State, October 2020. https://www.nass.org

Svaren, Jaqueline. *Written Letters: 33 Alphabets for Calligraphers*. Porter's Landing, Freeport, ME: The Bond Wheelwright Company, 1975.

Walters, John L. *Fifty Typefaces That Changed the World: Design Museum Fifty*. London: Octopus, 2013.

Yassine, Leen. "Artist behind 'you are beautiful' wants people to 'be yourself, and that's enough.'" *Chicago Sun-Times*, December 11, 2020. https://chicago.suntimes.com

Temporal Context

"1921 Tulsa Race Massacre." Tulsa Historical Society and Museum, n.d. https://www.tulsahistory.org

Adobe Systems Incorporated. Chaparral ® Pro Release Notes, 2001.

Ambrose, Gavin, Paul Harris, and Sallyanne Theodosiou. *The Fundamentals of Typography*. 3rd ed. London: Bloomsbury Visual Arts, 2020.

"America Meets Charles and Ray Eames." Home, Hosted by Arlene Francis. NBC, 1956.

American Civil Liberties Union. "Civil Rights Groups Challenge South Carolina's New Redistricting Map," n.d. https://www.aclu.org

Anders, Charlie Jane. "When Did Japan Stop Being the Future?" Gizmodo, June 18, 2009. https://gizmodo.com

"Association of Visual Artists Vienna Secession," Secession.at, n.d. https://www.secession.at

Balius, Andreu. "Elizabeth ND: A Typeface Designed for Bauer Types." https://www.andreubalius.com

Bazin, Hervé. *Plumons l'oiseau: divertissement*. France: B. Grasset, 1966.

Brivati, Brian, Julia Buxton, and Anthony Seldon, eds. *The Contemporary History Handbook*. Manchester, UK: Manchester University Press, 1996.

Burnhill, Peter. *Type Spaces: In-House Norms in the Typography of Aldus Manutius*. London: Hyphen Press, 2003.

Carter, Harry. *A View of Early Typography: Up to about 1600*. London: Oxford University Press, 1969.

Cheng, Alicia Yin. *This is What Democracy Looked Like: A Visual History of the Printed Ballot*. Princeton, NJ: Princeton Architectural Press, 2020.

Church, Peregrine, and Xack Fischer. Email message to author, August 11, 2021.

Davies, Martin. *Aldus Manutius: Printer and Publisher of Renaissance Venice*. Tempe, AZ: Arizona Center for Medieval and Renaissance Studies, 1999.

Dougherty, Carissa Kowalski. "The Coloring of Jazz: Race and Record Cover Design in American Jazz, 1950 to 1970." *Design Issues* 23, no. 1 (2007): 47–60.

Douglas, Aaron, and Renée Ater. *Aaron Douglas: African American Modernist*. New Haven, CT: Yale University Press, 2007.

Eastman, Mark. "Type in the Future Tense." *Communication Arts*, January/February 2000.

Ehrnberger, Karin, Minna Räsänen, and Sara Ilstedt. "Visualising Gender Norms in Design: Meet the Mega Hurricane Mixer and the Drill Dolphia." *International Journal of Design* 6, no. 3 (2012): 85–98.

Ericson, Colleen A. "Susan Skarsgard Explores the Shape of the Alphabet." mlive, May 3, 2009. https://www.mlive.com

Estes, Steve. "'I AM A MAN!': Race, Masculinity, and the 1968 Memphis Sanitation Strike." *Labour History* 41, no. 2 (2010): 153–70.

Etsy. "Vintage Items on Etsy," November 16, 2018. https://www.etsy.com

Ewen, Stuart. *All Consuming Images: The Politics of Style in Contemporary Culture*. Oxford: Basic Books, 1988.

Flynn, Laurie J. "Adobe Buys Macromedia for $3.4 Billion." *New York Times*, April 19, 2005. https://www.nytimes.com

Food News Notes for Public Libraries. Washington, DC: US Government Printing Office, 1917.

Gazette Washington Bureau. "Mothers Seek End to War, Shower Cards on Fulbright." *Arkansas Gazette*, May 16, 1967.

Genovese, Alfredo. *Filete porteño*. Buenos Aires: Comisión para la Preservación del Patrimonio Histórico Cultural de la Ciudad Autónoma de Buenos Aires, 2007.

Genzlinger, Neil. "Bonnie MacLean, Psychedelic Poster Artist, Is Dead at 80." *New York Times*, February 20, 2020. https://www.nytimes.com

Gordan, Phyllis Walter Goodhart (trans.); Poggius Bracciolini and Niccolò Niccolis. *Two Renaissance Book Hunters: The Letters of Poggius Bracciolini to Nicolaus de Niccolis; Translated from the Latin and Annotated*. New York: Columbia University Press, 1991.

Haley, Allan. "Italics." www.fonts.com/, n.d.

Haley, Allan, Richard Poulin, Jason Tselentis, Tony Seddon, Gerry Leonidas, Ina Saltz, Kathryn Henderson, and Tyler Alterman. *Typography, Referenced: A Comprehensive Visual Guide to the Language, History, and Practice of Typography*. Beverly, MA: Rockport, 2012.

Harley, Trevor A. *The Psychology of Language: From Data to Theory*. London: Psychology Press, 1995.

Harris, Sylvia. "Searching for a Black Aesthetic in American Graphic Design." Essay. In *The Education of a Graphic Designer*, edited by Stephen Heller, 125–9. New York: Allworth Press, 1998.

Hasic, Albinko. "See the 'Loose Lips Sink Ships' Propaganda Posters of World War II." *Time*, December 8, 2016. https://time.com

Holt, Steven Skov, and Mara Holt Skov. *Blobjects and Beyond: The New Fluidity in Design*. San Francisco, CA: Chronicle Books, 2005.

Jarrell, Wadsworth. *AFRICOBRA: Experimental Art toward a School of Thought*. Durham, NC: Duke University Press, 2020.

Jaspert, W. Pincus., Berry, William Turner, Johnson, Alfred Forbes. *The Encyclopaedia of Type Faces*. London: Blandford Press, 1970.

Keep Calm and Carry On. Kansas City, MO: Andrews McMeel Publishing, 2010.

Kleven, Elisa. Email message to author, November 23, 2021.

Lawson, Alexander S. *Anatomy of a Typeface*. Jaffrey, NH: Godine, 1990.

Lowry, Martin. *The World of Aldus Manutius: Business and Scholarship in Renaissance Venice*. Kiribati: B. Blackwell, 1979.

Madge, Bruce. "Elizabeth Blackwell-the Forgotten Herbalist?" *Health Information and Libraries Journal* 18, no. 3 (2001): 144–52.

Margolin, Victor. "American Jazz Album Covers in the 1950s and 1960s." In Proceedings of the 9th Conference of the International Committee for Design History and Design Studies. São Paulo: Editora Edgard Blücher, 2014.

Meggs, Philip B., and Alston W. Purvis. *Meggs' History of Graphic Design*. 6th ed. Nashville, TN: John Wiley & Sons, 2016.

Meletis, Dimitrios. "'Is Your Font Racist?' Metapragmatic Online Discourses on the Use of Typographic Mimicry and Its Appropriateness." *Social Semiotics*, 2021. https://doi.org/10.1080/10350330.2021.1989296

Merriam-Webster.com Dictionary, s.v. "antique." https://www.merriam-webster.com

Millington, Roy. *Stephenson Blake: The Last of the Old English Typefounders*. New Castle, DE: Oak Knoll Press, 2002.

Muller, Jens. *The History of Graphic Design: 1 1890–1959*. Edited by Julius Wiedemann. Cologne: Taschen, 2021.

Murrell, Denise. "African Influences in Modern Art." Metmuseum.org, April 2008. https://www.metmuseum.org

Myers, Walter Dean. *Jazz*. Pine Plains, NY: Live Oak Media, 2018.

Nash, Paul W. "The Abandoning of the Long s in Britain in 1800." Humanities Commons, 2001.

New Specimen Book and Price List of Types, Rules, Borders and Other Printing Material. San Francisco: Hawks and Shattuck, 1889.

New York Times. "Martin K. Speckter, 73, Creator of Interrobang." February 16, 1988. https://www.nytimes.com

Oklahoma Commission. "Tulsa Race Riot: A Report by the Oklahoma Commission to Study the Tulsa Race Riot of 1921." Tulsa, Oklahoma, 2001. https://www.okhistory.org

Patton, Sharon F. *African-American Art*. Oxford: Oxford University Press, 1998.

Popova, Yulia. *How Many Female Type Designers Do You Know? I Know Many and Talked to Some!* Eindhoven, Netherlands: Onomatopee, 2020.

Raizman, David Seth. *History of Modern Design*. Upper Saddle River, NJ: Prentice Hall, 2004.

Rowsome, Frank. *The Verse by the Side of the Road: The Story of the Burma-Shave Signs and Jingles*. New York, NY: Penguin Publishing Group, 1979.

Salgarella, Ester. *Aegean Linear Script(s): Rethinking the Relationship Between Linear A and Linear B*. Cambridge: Cambridge University Press, 2020.

Sandler, Stuart. *Filmotype: The Complete Illustrated History: by the Letter*. United States: Font Diner, Incorporated, 2009.

Schneider, Lorraine Art, Stanley Schneider, Virginia Rubin, and Barbara Avedon. *Lorraine Art Schneider, 1925–1972: An Illustrated Catalogue of Her Graphic Work (1963–71)*. Los Angeles, CA: Plantin Press, 1974.

Seddon, Tony. *The Evolution of Type: A Graphic Guide to 100 Landmark Typefaces: Examining Letters from Metal Type to Open Type*. Richmond Hill, ON: Firefly Books, 2015.

Selman, Johnny. Video call with author, August 23, 2021.

Senefelder, Alois. *The Invention of Lithography*. New York and London: Fuchs & Lang Manufacturing Company, 1911.

Seuret, Mathias, Saskia Limbach, Nikolaus Weichselbaumer, Andreas Maier, and Vincent Christlein. "Dataset of Pages from Early Printed Books with Multiple Font Groups." Proceedings of the 5th International Workshop on Historical Document Imaging and Processing. ACM, September 20, 2019.

Shaw, Ian, and Paul T. Nicholson. *The Princeton Dictionary of Ancient Egypt.* Princeton, NJ: Princeton University Press, 2008.

Shaw, Paul. "Stereo Types." *PRINT Magazine*, June 17, 2009. https://www.printmag.com

Stephenson, Blake and Company Ltd., Sir Charles Reed & Sons, *Specimens of Point Line Type: Borders Ornaments Brass Rules &c. &c.* Toronto: Stephenson, Blake & Co., 1908.

Tharp, Bruce M., and Stephanie M. Tharp. *Discursive Design: Critical, Speculative, and Alternative Things.* Cambridge, MA: MIT Press, 2018.

Tharp, Bruce M., and Stephanie M. Tharp. "The 4 Fields of Industrial Design: (No, Not Furniture, Trans, Consumer Electronics, & Toys)." *Core77*, January 5, 2009. https://www.core77.com

The Public Domain Review. "A 19th-Century Vision of the Year 2000," June 30, 2012. https://publicdomainreview.org

Twede, Diana. "Uneeda Biscuit: The First Consumer Package?" *Journal of Macromarketing* 17, no. 2 (1997): 82–88.

Twyman, Michael. *Printing 1770–1970: An Illustrated History of Its Development and Uses in England.* London: Eyre & Spottiswoode, 1970.

Tzeng, Ovid J. L. "Relationship between Orthographic Characteristics and Reading Behavior: A Final Technical Report, March 20, 1981 to March 19, 1983." Washington, DC: National Institute of Education, 1983.

Additional References

PEOPLE + PROJECTS

01kg.com
adamfarcus.com
aetherpoint.com
aldernewyork.com
aljoschahoehborn.de
amandinealessandra.com
ankrom.org
anushkatendolkar.com
arabiccalligrapher.com
aramhansifuentes.com
astoriasigns.com
barryspencerdesign.com.au
bauertypes.com
behance.net/adamlenzinger
behance.net/EliHorn
behance.net/hdelvaray
behance.net/olavodaguiar
behance.net/ranaabourjeily
behance.net/theboredkids
behance.net/UnikFrik
benblount.com
bethanyjoycollins.com
boamistura.com
bowyer.kr
broosstoffels.be
buck.co
burgess-studio.co.uk
candychang.com
captivatingcalligraphy.com
chantalgibson.com
chloebass.com
corbettfogue.com
daanlievense.tumblr.com
daku156.com
danimolyneux.com
dariorobleto.com
dasoljung.com
dirtybandits.com
doubletwo.net
edruscha.com
emalyssebowd.com
erickawalker.com
evan-roth.com
evelinkasikov.com
fadebiaye.com
finlandica.fi
freitag.ch/en
fromkeetra.com
genramirez.com
gordonyoung.info
hansje.net
helsinkitypestudio.com
hollyakkerman.com
hsinchienhuang.com
humanssince1982.com
idawoldemichael.com
invade.design
itaintokmama.com
jeffreygibson.net
jimflora.com

jk-keller.com
jomalinis.com
julietshen.com
kampanjat.hs.fi/climatefont
kayrosen.com
keepcalms.com
kesselskramer.com
kianahonarmand.com
kontrapunkt.com
laurentmareschal.com
laurieanderson.com
leoburnett.ca
lisataniguchi.com
lissongallery.com/artists/lawrence-weiner
louisefili.com
lukasverstraete.blogspot.com
marionguy.com
marycwillette.com
moniquegoossens.com
motiontypeproject.org
msandberg.nl
nancywudesign.com
nariwardstudio.com
nonty.net
overpasslightbrigade.org
portfolio.taekyeom.com
prettystrangedesign.com
pulpo.com.mx
rachellevasquez.com
radicalnorms.com
rain.works
remediosrapoport.com
sharleenchen.com
showusyourtype.com
simonandmoose.com
someguy.is
spaceparanoids.net
starshaped.com
subversivecrossstitch.com
swamp.nu
tirzabp.com
tulaliplushootseed.com/alphabet
tulaliptribes-nsn.gov
typearture.com
typesenses.com
uglygerry.com
vocaltype.co
waldenfont.com
wes-wilson.com
xubing.com
yandl.com
yeoahn.com/designandchange
ymathur.com
you-are-beautiful.com
yumijroth.com

ORGANIZATIONS, ARCHIVES, AND INSTITUTIONS

anothermother.org
americanhistory.si.edu
archive.org
digitalcollections.nypl.org
interrobang-mks.com
kavigupta.com
loc.gov
lubalincenter.cooper.edu
mirellabentivoglio.it
muralsdcproject.com
nativegov.org
nps.gov/gett
publicartstpaul.org
rijksmuseum.nl
st-artindia.org
tate.org.uk
thewalters.org
type63.carrd.co
vam.ac.uk
wartimeposters.co.uk
wellcomecollection.org

ONLINE TYPOGRAPHIC RESOURCES

fonts.adobe.com/
fontsinuse.com/
letterformarchive.org/
typenetwork.com/
typography.com/

INDEX

Page numbers in **bold** indicate figures.

Adebiaye, Frank **100**
Adobe Flash Player 133
Adobe Jenson 107, **108**
affiliation 96
AFRICOBRA 167, **169**
Ahn, Yeohyun **103**
Akkerman, Holly **11**
Alder New York, Breakout Control Kit **179**
Aldine Press 130, **130**
Alessandra, Amandine **123**
alliteration 55
alphabetic systems 190
Alternative Rule (Kenyon) **92**
Altmann, Andy **71**
American Wild West 154
ampersand 129
anachronism 153–4
analogies 11–14, 67–9
& GIVEN & REPLACED (Weiner) **90**
And Yet (Dixon and Keller) **68**
Anderson, Laurie **105**
Ankrom, Richard **35**
antica corsiva 130
antiquated 147
antique 147
Anzollitto, Andy **160**
Apollinaire, Guillaume 56

apparel 96
Apple Macintosh 132–3
appropriation 36
AR Optical Typography (Johnson) **104**
Archer typeface **6**
architectural materials 71–4
Arial Sarcastic typeface **195**
Aristotle 10
Art Nouveau 151–2
asemic writing 191, 194
"askew" Google search **106**
Astoria Design Studio 165–6
augmented reality 103–5
authenticity 67

Badia, Lisi **136**
Baldwin's Nervous Pills **156**
Barhad, Koby **196**
Baskerville typeface 5
Bass, Chloë **38**
Bazin, Hervé 195
Before I Die (Chang) **83**
Benguiat, Ed **155**
Bent, Jordan **80**
Bentivoglio, Mirella **57**
Berer, Josh **23**
Bickham Script (Lipton) **113**
BIX and TRAM album cover

(Flora) 54, **55**
BLACK IS (LeRoy) **81**
Black Lives Matter Mural, Washington DC **79**
blackletter 107
"blobject" 144
Blount, Ben **141**
Blow-Up (film) 1
BLURRED (Rosen) **90**
Blursday (Blount) **141**
Book about Food, A (Offaim) **18**
Book from the Sky (Xu Bing) **193**
bouba/kiki effect 51
bounce lettering 145
Bourdieu, Pierre 31–2
Boutros, Mourad 28
Bovril advertisement 190
Bowd, E. M. Alysse **125**
BOWYER **42**
branded products 32–3, 96
Break up Cough advertisement (Lubalin) **48**
Brusky, Joe **34**
BUCK **7**
bumper stickers **98**
Burgess Studio **59**
Burma-Shave advertising campaign 179–80, **180**

Calligrammes: Poems of Peace and War (1913–1916) (Apollinaire) **56**
calligraphy 21–4, 108–9, 112, 145
Captivating Calligraphy **110**
Carr, Paul Antony **80**
Cave, Jamar **119**
Chalkroom (Anderson and Huang) **105**
Chang, Candy **83**
Change is Constant (Taniguchi) **110**
Chaparral typeface **168**
Chen, Sharleen **67**
Cheng, Alicia Yin **176**
Chestnut, Loren **110**
Childline video **7**
"chop suey" typeface 176, **177**
"chopstick" typeface 176, **177**
chromolithography **134**
Church, Peregrine **184**
Cila, Nazli **12**
Clara typeface **197**
Climate Crisis Font **188**
clothing 96
Coastlines (Korkala and Coull) **188**
Collins, Bethany **119**
community participation 79–84
concrete poetry 55–9
conference swag 96
connotation 3
  social connotation 8–11
conspicuous consumption 32, 131
contemporary 146–7
context
  cultural context 14–22
  meaning and 1–14
  recontextualization 36–8, 155
  social context 62
contour bias 7–8
Cooper Black typeface 147, **147**
corporeality 122–6
Costantino, Nicola, lecture poster (Chen and Jung) **67**
Côte, Jean-Marc **144**
Coull, Daniel **188**
counterculture 18
Crayola 8, **9**

cultural appropriation 36, 38
cultural capital 31–2
cultural context 14–22
cultural stereotypes 176
current events 137
cute typeface 8
Cyberotica typeface 144, **144**

Daam-Rossi, Daniel **196**
Dadaists 55–6
D'Aguiar, Olavo **50**
Daku **183**
Dancy, Andrew **148**
Dead-Alive (Mathur) **49**
death metal logos 8–9
Deck, Barry 144, **144**
Defiant Gardens (Robleto) **66**
Delft Salad Oil advertisement 150, **151**
Delvaray, Homa **24**, **25**
denotation 3
digit **120**
digital methods 101–3
digital type foundries 133
Disarm Hate Subbrand (Woldemichael) **98**
discursive design 188
Dixon, Keetra Dean **68**
DNR (No Code) (Fogue) **70**
Doessel, Ben **139**
Donaldson, Jeff **169**
dry type transfer sheets 101
Dunne, Anthony **195**
Dysart, Aaron 85–8

Eames, Charles and Ray 166–7
Edie typeface **197**
Ehrnberger, Karin **178**
Ekman, Paul **120**
Elizabeth typeface **168**
em dashes 53
Emigre 133
emojis 121
emoticons 121
en dashes 53
Enoki Solutions logo (Wu) **43**
environmental graphic design 71

ethos 10
Every Pair of Eyes (Taniguchi) **110**
Everytown for Gun Safety, *Disarm Hate* campaign **98**
Exist/Exit (Willette) **39**
Expanse, The, title sequence **47**
expectation 5
expression 120–1
expressive typography 47–9
Eye Snellen Chart (Malinis) **174**

Fabel typeface **13**
Facetype (Lenzinger) **122**
Fahlman, Scott E. 121
Fancy Fuck (Jackson) **39**
Farcus, Adam **63**
Farrell, Jennifer **156**
fART (Akkerman) **11**
fat faces 72–3
Felicidad Bakery (invade design) **121**
figure-ground 41
Filete Porteño **162**
Fili, Louise **160**
Finlandica (Helsinki Type Studio) **21**
First Step animation **7**
First World War propaganda poster **157**
Fischer, Xack **184**
fist **120**
Flash 133
Flora, Jim 54, **55**
Fogue, Corbett **70**
form, relative to language 189–94
FREITAG bag **97**
Friedländer, Elizabeth 167, **168**
future typography 188–95

Galerie Block C posters **46**
galleries 89
Gap, The, logo 3–4
gender identity 178–9
generative typographic selfies **103**
gerrymandering **139**
Gestalt principles 41–2

gesture
    expression and 120–1
    gestural space 105–13
    gesture in and of letterforms
        108–13
    gesture of mark 118
Gettysburg National Military Park
    73–4
ghost signs 187
Gibson, Chantal **58**
Gibson, Jeffrey **64**
gifs 121, **136**
glyph 190
Goertek typeface **51**
Goffman, Erving 95
"good taste" 31–2
Goossens, Monique **65**
Gothic script 107
graffiti 93–5
grapheme 190
graphic tee 96
gravestones 72–4
Greiman, April 133
Griffo, Francesco 130
Grinning Face Coconut Milk
    packaging **50**
Grondal, Amanda **80**
Guasch, Ana **136**
Guerilla Public Service (Ankrom)
    35
Guy, Marion **118**

Hall, Lane **34**
hand/handwriting 106–9, 112
handling text 106
Handprinted Alphabet (Kasikov) **69**
Handy Heart Neo typeface 8, **9**
Heather, Jarrett **181**
Hell is Other People (Jackson) **39**
Help, 1982 (Collins) **119**
Helsinki Type Studio **21**
Hess, Thomas 17
Hilbert, Vi 17
history
    historical type in contemporary
        use 146–58

history-inspired type 158
    material meaning 65–7
    time and 129–46
History of Monument (Bentivoglio)
    57
Ho, Ting-An **45**
Hoefler&Co **6**
Hoffman, Matthew **82**
Holt, Steven Skov 144
Holzer, Jenny 76
Honarmand, Kiana **182**
Honobono Pop typeface 8, **9**
Hook (Malinis) **174**
Horn, Eli **80**
Hôtel de Paris, Monte-Carlo 9, **10**
Hotel Tango Distillery, identity **163**
Hourani, Cecil 28
Huang, Hsin-Chien **105**
humanistic scripts 107, 130
Humans since 1982 **186**
Hume, David 31
100 years (Black Wall Street) (Blount)
    141
hyphens 53

I amsterdam sculpture 76–7
icons 2
identity 175–9
idioms 14, 153
Ilstedt, Sara **178**
I'm a Piece of Garbage (Lydenberg)
    111
Impact typeface **99**
index 120
indexical sign 2
Industrial Revolution 131
intercultural context 17–19
interrobang 195
intracultural context 17–19
invade design 121
Iran Silk Screen School poster
    (Delvaray) **24**, **25**
Islam 22
It Ain't Okay Mama (Selman) **189**
italics 130–1
ITC Benguiat typeface **155**

Jackson, Julie **39**
Japan
    cuteness concept 8
    future concept 144
Jarrell, Jae **169**
Jarrell, Wadsworth **169**
jazz typography 54, **55**
Jazzy (Remírez) **42**
Jenson typeface 107
Johnson, Andrew **104**
Johnson, Lecter 9, **10**
Jones-Hogu, Barbara **169**
Jung, Dasol **67**

Kant, Immanuel 31
Kasikov, Evelin **69**
Kawaii 8
Keep Calm and Carry On poster
    148–9
Keep Calm-o-Matic website 148–9
Keller, J. K. **68**
Kenyon, Matt **92**
Keren & Golan Graphic Design
    Studio **18**
KesselsKramer 76
Khasanov, Ruslan **185**
Khattar, Nasri 28
kinetic typography 43–7
Kontrapunkt **51**
Korkala, Eino **188**

Ladies! Triptych (Farrell) **156**
language
    culture and type 15–17
    form and meaning 189–94
    product language 178
leading 105
Lee, Geoffrey **99**
Lee, James **139**
Lee, Taekyeom **135**
Lenzinger, Adam **122**
Leo Burnett Toronto **50**
LeRoy, Ciara **81**
Letterform for Ephemeral Messages
    (Alessandra) **123**
lettering 108–9

Level the Playing Field (Wilder) **111**
Licko, Zuzana 133
Lievense, Daan **37**
ligatures 112, 116
Lightfoot, Gordon 158
line length 55
Linear A **191**
linguistic meaning 190
Lining Wide Latin typeface 54, **55**
Lipton, Richard **113**, 144, **144**
Liquid Calligraphy (Khasanov) **185**
lithography **134**
Loewy, Raymond 3
logographic systems 190
logos 11
Long, Natalie **136**
long "s" **192**
Loose Lips Sinks Ships poster 148
Lopez, Sabrina **114**, 115–17
lowercase letters 105, 107
Lubalin, Herb **48**
Lushootseed language and typeface 15–17
luxurious-feel typeface 9–10
Lydenberg, Annica **111**

Malinis, Jo **170**, 171–5
manicule **120**
Manifest (Chestnut) **110**
Manofim Jerusalem Contemporary Art Festival catalog **19**
Manutius, Aldus 130, **130**
Mareschal, Laurent **124**
Marinetti, F.T. 55
mark-making 108, 118
Marseille typeface **160**
Martin typeface **159**
material
  meaning 60–2, 65–7
  metaphors and analogies 67–9
Mathur, Yash **49**
MAYA 3
McAnally, Glenn **195**
meaning
  context and 1–14
  historical meaning 65–7

material meaning 60–2, 65–7
  place-based meaning 75–6
  relative to language 189–94
  social meaning 6–11
memes **99**
memorials 72–4
mesostic (poem) **59**
metaphors 11–14, 67–9
metonym 62
mid-century modern scripts 142, **143**
Middle Eastern calligraphy 21–4
mihrab **22**
million Times, A (Humans since 1982) **186**
Mirsaal typeface **26**, 27–31
Misani, Nick **160**
Mistura, Boa **78**
mixed reality 103–5
modern calligraphy 145
modernism 36
Moline, Lisa **34**
Molyneux, Dani **49**
Monograms (Guy) **118**
Monsters Inc. title sequence 54
monuments 72–4
Moonrise album design (Delvaray) **24**
morphemes 190
Morris, Errol 5
mosques 22
Mother & Child logo (Lubalin) **48**
Motion Type Project (Ho) **45**
museums 89
Muybridge, Eadweard 43, **44**

narrative pacing 180–1
Neighbor (Walker) **157**
Next (D'Aguiar) **50**
Nextbus logo (Wu) **43**
Niccoli, Niccolò 130
Non Fungible Type (Adebiaye) **100**
nostalgia 154

objective approach 2
On Edge (Honarmand) **182**

One More Wall Well Done (Sandberg) **72**
One Small Moment (Lievense) **37**
Onomatopee (Stoffels and Verstraete) **52–3**
Open Up and See (Wilson) 151, **153**
OpenType files (otfs) 112
outdated 147
Overpass Light Brigade **34**

pangrams 15
Party Cannon 9, **10**
passé 147
paste-up 101
pathos 11
Pay Nothing Until April (Ruscha) **91**
Peace is Possible (Rapoport) **162**
Pennsylvania Memorial, Gettysburg National Military Park **74**
PENSAR/SENTIR (Mistura) **78**
performance 122–6
personal space 95–9
persuasion 10–11
physical space 59–74
pictographic systems 190
place-based meaning 75–6
Planting Poetry (Burgess Studio) **59**
poetry
  concrete and visual 55–9
  sidewalk **84**, 85–8
politics 97–8
Populists are not my people (Lievense) **37**
Porat, Tirza Ben **19**
postmodernism 36
power structures 31–5
prayer niche **22**
prejudice 176
Primer (Schneider) 137–9
printer's fist **120**
private space 89–95
product language 178
promotional giveaways 96
Protest Banner Lending Library (Sifuentes) **140**
psychedelic design 151–2

public art 94
Public Art Saint Paul **84**, 85–8
public space 75–80
public type 79–84
Puck magazine **121**
punctuation 55

Qur'an 22

Raby, Fiona 195
Radical Norms **196**
rainwork (Rainworks Typography) **184**
Rapoport, Remedios **162**
Räsänen, Minna **178**
Real-Fake (Mathur) **49**
reciprocal pronouns (Gibson) **58**
recontextualization 36–8, 155
references 150–4
Regard Each Other as Brothers (Berer) **23**
Remírez, Gen **42**
resurgences **155**
retro 147
revivals 150–4
Revolutionary (Jarrell) **169**
Rjeily, Rana Abou **26**, 27–31
road markings/signage 35, **60**
Robleto, Dario **66**
Roller, Alfred 151
roman typeface 107
Roosma, Femke 77
Rosen, Kay **90**
Roth, Evan **93**
Roth, Yumi Janairo **127**
Ruscha, Ed **91**

Salbabida Sans V2 typeface **170**
Sandberg, Martijn **72**
Sanvito, Bartolomeo **108**
Schneider, Lorraine Art 137–9
Science (Weber) **164**
Seals, Tré **159**
Secret Eater, The (Bowd) **125**
Seeschaaf-Veres, Angelika **196**
self-presentation theory 95

selfies **103**
Selman, Johnny **189**
semantics 2
Semataphore (Mareschal) **124**
semiotics 2
Senefelder, Alois **134**
setting type 105
shape 51–4
Shaw, Paul 176
Shen, Juliet 17
Shimano typeface 144, **144**
"Shop Vac" (Heather) **181**
shopping bags 96
ShowUsYourType **136**
sidewalk poetry **84**, 85–8
Sifuentes, Aram Han **140**
sign (signifier, signified) 2–3
sign-painting 165–6
Signs (Farcus) **63**
Signs of Change (Radical Norms) **196**
Silence Please Science Please (Sandberg) **72**
Singer, Brian **12**
site-specific works 76
Skarsgard, Susan **194**
Slimbach, Robert 107, **108**
social connotations 8–11
social constructs 61
social context 62
social meaning 6–11
sound 51–4
space
   feeling of luxury 9–10
   gestural space 105–13
   personal space 95–9
   physical space 59–74
   private space 89–95
   public space 75–80
   virtual space 99–105
   visual space 41–59
Speckter, Martin K. 195
speculative typography 195, **197**
speech 51–4
Spencer, Barry **197**
Spin (Roth) **127**

steam press 131
Stephenson Blake & Company, Ltd 54, **55**
stereotypes 176–9
stippling **118**
Stoffels, Broos **52–3**
Storia Del Monumento (Bentivoglio) **57**
street art 94
subculture 18
subjective approach 2
Subjective letters (Adebiaye) **100**
Subversive Cross Stitch **39**
supermarket branded products 32–3
Superme counterfeit bag **32**

tagging 94
Take Up More Space (Molyneux) **49**
Taniguchi, Lisa **110**
"taste", concept of 31–2
tattoos 36, 97–8, **99**
technology, society and 131–3
Tendolkar, Anushka **102**
Tharp, Bruce and Stephanie 188
These Truths (Singer) **12**
36 Days of Type (Malinis) **174**
36 Days of Type 2020 (Tendolkar) **102**
This Time Just the Girls (Vasquez) **70**
3D-printing **135**
time
   future typography 188–95
   history and 129–46
   as medium 179–87
   recontextualizations 155
Time Changes Everything (Daku) **183**
Tobias, Naama **19**
Toorop, Jan 150, **151**
trends in typography 141–6
TrueType files 112
trustworthiness 5
TSA Communication (Roth) **93**
«TTANZIT» (BOWYER) **42**
26 of 26: An Edition of Twenty-Six Alphabets (Skarsgard) **194**

Twombly, Carol 167, **168**
type foundry 106
TYPE Portraits (Ahn) **103**
Typearture **13**
Typesenses **114**, 115–17
Type63 171–5
Typographical Art (*Puck* magazine) **121**

Ugly Gerry typeface **139**
uppercase letters 105, 107

van Halem, Hansje **46**
VanderLans, Rudy 133
Vasquez, Rachelle **70**
Veblen, Thorstein 32
Venetian typeface 107
Verstraete, Lukas **52–3**
Victorian type 131–2
Vienna Secession 150–1, **152**
vintage 147
virtual reality 103–5
virtual space 99–105
visual inflection 4–6
visual metaphors and analogies 11–14

visual poetry 55–9
visual references 150–4
visual rhetoric 2
visual space 41–59
voices in design 166–8

Wake Up And Live (Cave) **119**
Walden Type Co. **161**
Walk of Art 2 (Young) **71**
Walker, Ericka **157**
Ward, Nari **91**
Washington, George 97
Waste Typography (Goossens) **65**
We The People (Ward) **91**
We walk the world two by two (Jerry) (Bass) **38**
wealth 32–3
Weber, Anna **164**, 165–6
Weiner, Lawrence **90**
Weiss, Oliver **161**
Where (Walker) **157**
Whispers Project **80**
Wide Latin typeface 54, **55**
Wilder, Cymone **111**
Willette, Mary **39**

Williams, Gerald **169**
Wilson, Wes 151, **153**
Woldemichael, Ida **98**
Wong, Man Wai **50**
"wonton" typeface 176, **177**
World War I propaganda poster **157**
Wreck of the Edmund Fitzgerald, The (ballad) 158
Wu, Nancy **43**
WUAG "In Print" zine **20**

Xu Bing **193**
XXII Morduk typeface 9, **10**

Y2K typography 143–4
You Are Beautiful (Hoffman) **82**
YOU'LL BE GIVEN LOVE (Gibson) **64**
Young, Crawford **157**
Young, Gordon **71**
Young, Marcus **84**, 85
Young & Laramore **163**

zines 18, **20**